Ecology Is Permanent Economy

Ecology Is Permanent Economy

The Activism and Environmental Philosophy of Sunderlal Bahuguna

George Alfred James

Cover image: "On the Pilgrimage Route between Gangotri and Gaumukh, June 1998."

Published by State University of New York Press, Albany

For information, contact State University of New York Press, Albany, NY
www.sunypress.edu

Production by Diane Ganeles
Marketing by Anne M. Valentine

Library of Congress Cataloging-in-Publication Data

James, George Alfred.
   Ecology is permanent economy : the activism and environmental philosophy of Sunderlal Bahuguna / George A. James.
      pages cm
   Includes bibliographical references and index.
   ISBN 978-1-4384-4673-8 (hc : alk. paper)—978-1-4384-4672-1 (pb : alk. paper)
      1. Bahuguna, Sunderlal, 1927–   2. Environmentalists—India—Biography.
3. Environmentalism—India—Philosophy.   4. Chipko movement.   5. Tehri Dam (India)   I. Title.

   GE56.B34J36 2013
   333.72092—dc23
   [B]   2012026097

10 9 8 7 6 5 4 3 2 1

To Gladys and Alfred James.
Let light perpetual shine upon them.

Contents

Illustrations

Acknowledgments

It would be more than arrogant to give the impression that this book is the result of the work of the author alone. There are many persons I must thank for their help. First among them are Sunderlal and Vimla Bahuguna for their many hours of attention to my persistent questions and for accommodating me to their often very hectic schedule of appointments and obligations. In addition, I thank Pandurang Hegde whose present work with the Appiko movement of South India is perhaps the most explicit and effective extension of the *chipko* vision. I thank him for his constant encouragement and his help in making contact with Sunderlal and Vimla Bahuguna when the usual channels of communication had failed. For extensive information and documentation concerning the Tehri Dam I thank Shekhar Singh. For additional information and documentation on the life of Sunderlal and Vimla Bahuguna I thank Bharat Dogra, and Jayanta Bandyopadhyay. For his assistance in helping me understand the importance of the life and activism of Sarala Behn I thank Anupam Mishra. For his help in tracing the route of Bahuguna's famous foot march from Srinagar to Kohima I express my thanks to Anil Joshi, founder of the Himalayan Environmental Studies and Conservation Organization (HESCO). I also acknowledge with thanks the help of Shannon Mooney for rendering into a map the route of Bahuguna and his colleagues from Srinagar to Kohima. I wish to thank Bidisha Kumar for creating an accurate, detailed, and readable map of Uttarakhand indicating the principal sites of chipko activism. For their excellent scholarship on the Chipko Movement of which I made extensive use, I thank Thomas Weber and Ramachandra Guha. I also express my thanks to the University of North Texas for a succession of Faculty Research Grants, a Faculty Development Leave and a grant from the Charn Uswachoke International Development Fund, and to the Fulbright Foundation for a fellowship that made possible the research on which this book is based. I wish also to thank Bidisha Kumar for reading through the entire manuscript at an early stage in its development and for her many and helpful corrections and suggestions. For their thorough reading of the entire manuscript and for many helpful suggestions I express my heartfelt thanks to Mary Evelyn Tucker, Chris Chapple, and Thomas Weber. For a thorough proofreading of the manuscript I thank Richard Watson, and for his help in the final preparation of the manuscript I thank Matt Story. There are many others too numerous to mention without whose assistance this work could not have been completed. Among them I must include Nancy Ellegate and the editorial staff at the State University of New York Press. For any inaccuracies or omission of important details I take full responsibility.

Introduction

The person about whom this book is written is by no means a household name in the West. Even the pronunciation of his name presents a challenge to native readers of English. Yet the issues with which his life has been engaged are familiar. Today, in the West, the condition of the environment is drawing increasing public attention. Environmental issues are also widely recognized as global in scope. What remains largely unknown in the West is the struggle for the environment in non-Western countries, sometimes in areas of those countries little known to their urban dwellers. This book is the story of the activism and the environmental philosophy of a man whose work has focused on the Western Himalayas of India. Yet the concerns for which he has fought transcend the location in which he first expressed them. They include the depletion of the planet's forests cover, the just distribution of water, and the rights of the poor and disenfranchised to an equitable share of the earth's resources. The environmental philosophy that developed in the crucible of the struggles for which he is known represents the vision of a sustainable relationship between human beings and the natural world that is globally significant. The title I chose for this book is the quotation and slogan for which he is perhaps best known. That ecology is permanent economy is his reply to those of all countries who believe that environmental concerns have to be weighed against the demands of our economic well-being. Both words have the same root which refers to the *oikos* or the home in which we all live. It expresses in capsule form the heart of his environmental philosophy. This story, though it is set in the Western Himalayas of India, is relevant to an understanding of environmental struggles everywhere.

Born in 1927 in the practically unknown village of Marora, in what was then the United Provinces of British India, his parents named him Sunderlal. In Hindi, "Sundar" means beautiful, and "Lal" means child (particularly boy child). The equivalent of his names in English might be something like "Fairchild." At the age of thirteen under the guidance of a prominent Gandhian activist, Sunderlal Bahuguna (pronounced Ba-hoo-gun-a) joined the struggle for India's self-rule. For his involvement with this movement he was jailed for the first time at the age of seventeen. After India achieved independence Bahuguna became involved in Gandhi's program for the development of independent and self-reliant villages. His concern for the villages of the hills drew his attention to the degradation of the environmental upon which they relied. Bahuguna's environmental activism became internationally visible in his role in the famous Chipko Movement in the 1970's. Chipko (to hug) was a grassroots movement committed to saving the Himalayan forests by hugging the trees to shield them from the axe. Bahuguna supported and underlined the non-violent principles of this movement with foot marches, fasts, and speeches to village people concerning the economic, social, ecological, and religious significance of the forests. The success of the Chipko Movement engendered movements of a similar nature in the south of India, in Sri Lanka, and elsewhere. Bahuguna has lent much support to these movements. In 1981, Bahuguna began a foot march of 4870 kilometers (3026 miles) through the foothills of the Himalayas raising awareness of the exploitation to which their forests and their people were exposed. Today, at age eighty-six, his career in public life has spanned almost seven decades, in which he has been and remains a strong advocate for the environment, and especially for an integrated government policy concerning the Himalayas. His environmental philosophy is rooted in the soil of Indian philosophy, informed by the insights of contemporary ecology, and inspired by the vision of Gandhi.

This book is based largely upon interviews I conducted with Sunderlal Bahuguna over the course of several years. They began when I was undertaking a study of environmental movements in India at the Indian Institute of Advanced Study in 1998 and continued during the summer months through 2005, when, after a bout of dengue fever, I was advised to restrict my travels in India to the winter months. The first interviews were conducted at Tehri, a town in the Western Himalayas roughly 250 km (155 miles) North of Delhi. They were conducted at his *kuti* (hut) on the banks of the Bhagirathi River less than a hundred meters from the foot of the coffer dam of the Tehri Hydroelectric Project. When I arrived, he had been living there for ten years in protest against the construction of a dam he believed to be inappropriate, unsafe, and an unjust burden on the local people.

In the spring of 2001 he was evicted from this dwelling as the waters rising behind the dam covered his *kuti*. His protest, articulated in the cutting of his hair and beard, expressed the mourning appropriate for the death of his mother, the Ganges. He then moved to an abandoned house near the highest point of the town of Tehri where he continued to live in protest for another three years, and where I conducted the next two extended interviews. In 2004, after the monsoons covered the town, isolating his house from provisions of food and potable water, he and his wife, Vimla, were removed by boat to dwell in a house overlooking the lake created behind the dam, a dwelling he had been given because he had refused monetary compensation for his ancestral home. He lives there with his wife when he is not engaged in speaking tours or other activities.

This book is not precisely a biography. There are many details of his life that I have not so much as touched upon. It is rather a study of Bahuguna's activism, his emerging philosophy of life, and the influences on his life that shaped his philosophy of nature. We treat these influences and his activities roughly in the order in which they emerge in the course of his career. Through a discussion of some crucial events, the book develops the environmental philosophy that informs and supports some extraordinary acts of protest against the degradation and abuse of nature. The final chapter brings together the diverse elements of his activities and thought to demonstrate the inner consistency and the viability of his approach to nature. Written in common language, the book does not require any special expertise or specialized vocabulary. Its intended audience is people of all ages, but especially young people who will be inspired and motivated to further study the environment and to be involved in the struggle for the future of the planet. I situate the book in the context of the emerging field of religion and ecology. As such, the book will be useful to introductory university courses in environmental studies, and especially for environmental ethics. It will be relevant, to courses on global environmental issues, and to courses occupied with the environment and public policy. While the book contains much information of interest to graduate students and professionals, it is accessible to undergraduates and to the general public.

The question of the relevance of India's environmentalism to that of Western countries remains a contested issue in the field of environmental philosophy. Some Western scholars have tried to infer an Indian environmental ethic from their exploration of ancient Indian religious texts. Others have argued that the use of such texts is selective and misleading. By focusing upon the thought of a particular environmental thinker and the roots of his activism, this book will engender an understanding of

Indian environmentalism in practice. It will enable scholars and students to understand Bahuguna's environmental philosophy in terms of its principles and the application of these principles to specific environmental concerns. In this way the book will contribute to a better understanding of the significance of Indian environmental philosophy.

The activism of Sunderlal Bahuguna has often drawn the attention of the Indian media, sometimes in national newspapers and magazines. Yet even in feature articles the press has made little effort to articulate the principles of his thought. In discussing the movements with which he has been involved, historians, sociologists, and other experts have discussed his strategies and actions but have not made his environmental philosophy the focus of their research. The result is that the motivating ideals behind his activism have remained something of a mystery. Bahuguna himself has written a number of essays and pamphlets that discuss some important aspects of his thought. Many of these have been published by the Chipko Information Centre located at the ashram he founded in the small mountain town of Silyara. But these have had very limited circulation. Some of his essays along with essays about him and interviews with journalists have been collected in the short volume *Fire in the Heart, Firewood on the Back*, edited by Tenzin Rigzin and published by the All India Pingalwara Charitable Society in Amritsar (2005). The present work is the first book-length study of the thought and activism of one of the most influential environmental figures in India.

My procedure has been to study published accounts of Bahuguna's activism as well as essays he has written on a variety of environmental issues and to use these as points of departure for in-depth interviews. In the course of these interviews Bahuguna described his childhood, including the loss of his father when he was eight, and his mother when he was sixteen, his encounter with such persons as Sri Dev Suman who initiated him into the freedom movement and into Gandhi's vision for free and self-reliant villages, and his encounter with Mira Behn, Gandhi's English disciple who went to the hills to actualize Gandhi's vision for a free India. The interviews covered his first experiments in *satyagraha* (truth force) and the results he often encountered in ridicule, neglect, isolation, and insult. These interviews also disclosed his sometimes modest, sometimes significant victories, such as the legislation that imposed a ban on the felling of green trees for commercial purposes above the altitude of one thousand meters in what was then the State of Uttar Pradesh, and later extended to the State of Himachal Pradesh. With him, I have discussed specific historical events that occurred in the course of his public career, and the philosophical insights that have motivated him. I have supplemented this strategy with documentary research in the archives of a number of non-government organizations in New Delhi and in the records of newspapers, magazines, and journals. Bahuguna's philosophy has sustained him both in victory and in defeat as he has continued to crusade for the Indian and the global environment. My hope is that the story of his response to these challenges will prove an inspiration to persons of many countries concerned with the state of the environment.

Chapter 1

The Encounter

It was a cool but sunny day in Shimla, a picturesque town on the ridge of a mountain in the Indian state of Himachal Pradesh. At almost seven thousand feet, it was once the summer capital of the British. On a day in June 1998, a pleasant breeze was blowing, a nice escape from the torrid heat of Delhi. The songs of birds were intermittently drowned by the diesel engines of massive trucks that plied the narrow roads. "I want to make a call to Tehri," I said to the bearded man in the booth adjacent the telephone booth. He was wearing a shawl that covered most of his head.

"Do you have the number?" he called out to me over the din of a passing truck.

"Yes," I said and showed it to him.

"You please first dial zero, then this code, then the number." He was writing these numbers on the scrap of paper I had given him.

"OK," I said, "Kitna?" I was trying out my self-taught Hindi.

"What?" he said. Another truck passed. I sighed and raised my voice, "How much is the call?"

"Oh!" he said. "You please just make the call. Then you pay." It was the latest technological breakthrough, a telephone facility that records the length and destination of the call and calculates the charge. I closed the door behind me and picked up the receiver. Crackling sounds and static undermined my confidence. I pressed the numbers on the key pad and waited. Presently, I heard the reassuring sound of rings. They came in twos. I was used to that. Then just with the passing of another truck and the horn of a taxi following him I heard, "Hello." "Hello," I said. "Can you hear me?"

"Yes," the voice said in the distance.

I said, "I wish to speak with Sunderlal Bahuguna."

7

"This is Sunderlal speaking," he said. Really, I thought! I was elated. He answers his own phone! I had roughly planed out my introduction.

"My name is George James. I am a professor of philosophy from America. I am here in India researching environmental movements. I am very interested in your work . . . I have heard about your work in America. I mean . . . in America I heard about your work . . . to save the trees, to stop the Tehri Dam . . . " The sounds of more cars and jeeps on the road drowned his reply.

"Hello," he said.

"Hello, can you hear me?" I said.

"Yes, speak up," he said.

I continued, "If it is possible I would like to have an interview with you." This, I thought, is a long shot if ever there was one.

"Yes, yes," he said. "Where are you now?"

"I'm in Shimla," I said.

"Where?" he asked.

I said, "I'm in Shimla. I'm doing research on environmental movements in India. I'm at the Indian Institute of Advanced Studies."

He said, "Oh, Shimla! You will need to get a bus to Dehra Dun. From there you can get transport to Tehri. When will you come?"

I had been working in the library of the Indian Institute of Advanced Studies for the past two weeks. I was permitted to work there through the good will of the director. I had planned to spend another three weeks there and then set out on some field work. It was a sharp learning curve, and I was learning a lot, more than enough to recognize how little I understood about the background and motivations behind the movement that had so captivated the readers of environmental literature in the West. Another three weeks would enable me to digest a good part of the material in the library and render me passably conversant with the subject. It would qualify me, at least, to ask the right questions. "I am planning to be here for the next three weeks then come and visit you. Would that be okay?"

"Three weeks," he repeated. Then he continued, "In three weeks the rains will be coming. The roads will be bad. They may not be passable." The static on the line was now gone. Reception was clear. "Please come now!" The monsoon? I thought! The azure sky above me gave no hint of the weather in store. How did I not think of that, the rains of India that wash away roads and bridges and maroon whole villages? Come now, I thought, and risk an insult to the kindness of the director who was permitting me to work here!

Having spent a previous faculty development leave exploring a variety of environmental problems in India, my interest was now focused on Indian environmental movements. My expertise was in the history and philosophy of religion. By then I had been teaching for fifteen years in a Department of Philosophy and Religion studies that had recently begun to focus on environmental ethics or environmental philosophy as the center of its work. People with expertise in different areas of philosophy were exploring it from different perspectives. Having explored the range of the world's religions, I had been captivated by the relationship between humanity and nature that I found in the religious writings of India, and of Hinduism in particular. I had read much on the subject and had poured through debates as to whether Indian philosophy entailed an environmental ethic, supported environmental activism, or supported the neglect of nature. I had read much by Western specialists in environmental philosophy who seemed to know little about the traditions of India. They made their arguments anyway. With some book knowledge of the Hindu religious tradition, and having visited India before, I saw a space for some original research. It made no sense to debate about whether Hinduism or any variety of Hinduism might be a resource for environmental ethics. The question was whether the religious traditions of India had provided any support for the activism that was actually going on. This was the man to see. "Are you there?" he said.

"Yes, I am here." I said. "Yes, I see I must come soon."

"You *must* come soon!" he said.

"Can I call you tomorrow?" I asked.

"Yes," he said, "You can call me anytime! I will be here for the next two weeks."

"OK," I said. "I will call you tomorrow with my plans."

"OK," he said. "Thank you for calling. Bye bye!"

After months of planning for this trip, golden opportunities were falling into place before I was ready. I had read about the Chipko Movement and about the resistance to the Tehri Dam. The Chipko Movement was widely known as the most successful and influential of grassroots environmental movements. Back in America I had conversed with scholars who had actually met Bahuguna and had promised to give me contact information. But follow up e-mails had produced no replies. Now at India's Institute of Advanced Studies, a conversation about research interests had directed me to another scholar researching a similar topic. He knew Bahuguna and had his phone number. Without hesitation he told me, "You just call him! There is no need for an introduction. He is a very friendly man!"

It was time to close the books. Pensive and excited, I returned to the institute, and with apologies to the director and the promise that I would soon return, I quickly packed my bags. Within forty-eight hours, I was on a bus through winding mountain roads and down to the city of Dehra Dun. It was an arduous journey. When the bus arrived in Dehra Dun, the day was all but gone. I lodged at a hotel operated by the then Uttar Pradesh Tourist Development Corporation (UPTDC). I made inquiries about transport to Tehri. "There is no bus," the receptionist said. "You will have to take a jeep."

"Where will I find a jeep?" I asked. "You walk down this road. After two blocks, you turn left. After one block, you will see the stand. Jeeps will be there." It turned out I didn't need to hire a jeep but only purchase a ticket for a seat. After realizing they put three passengers in the front seat next to the driver, I decided to buy two tickets and made myself comfortable, my gear safely stashed on the roof of the jeep. It was eight in the morning when the jeep rolled out of town. With luck I would be there by noon. The route took me through some picturesque country, so beautiful I imposed on the driver to stop and let me take a photo. He was happy to do so. Bahuguna would eventually explain to me that the terraced paddy fields were not native to the area but had been introduced by the British to increase the agricultural productivity. The original economy of the area was animal husbandry with light farming and a strong reliance on the forests for food, fodder, fuel, fertilizer, and fiber. Eventually we crossed a narrow iron bridge and rounded a curve next to a sheer cliff on our right and entered the heart of the town. The jeep groaned to a stop at the side of the road where other jeeps were parked. Farther ahead was a bus stand, the smell of diesel fumes in the air, and dust. Along the road was a line of shops, and far up the hill to the left, the sign I had been told to watch for, Riverview Hotel. "You just come to the town and go to the Riverview Hotel," he had said.

"Will I need to make a reservation?" I had asked. "There is no need," he had said. "There is always room."

"And how will I find you once I arrive?"

"Just ask anyone," he said. "Everyone knows where I live." With a bag over my shoulder and another in hand, I started up the hill.

"Be sure to close the windows when you go out!" The young man who was helping me to my room was talking about the monkeys. "They will take anything they can," he said. "You need to be careful!" He gave me a bar of soap and a towel. "Is there anything else I can do for you?"

"Yes," I said, "Do you know the name Sunderlal Bahuguna?"

"Yes, of course I know him!" he said. "He's my uncle."

"Your uncle!" I exclaimed.

"Actually, he is not my uncle, but yes I know him very well. He's like an uncle to me and to many of the young people here. You see that iron bridge?" We were now standing in the breezeway outside the room. I looked down at the bridge over the Bhagirathi River, the one I had crossed in the jeep on my way into town. "He lives in a small hut just over that bridge to the left. You can't miss it. He's expecting you." I picked up my camera bag with my notebook and my tape recorder inside and started off to see him. I heard the voices of children practicing their cricket moves in an open area beside the bus stand near the market section of the town. They stopped momentarily to look at this stranger passing by and then carried on with their play. The iron bridge shook with the rumble of trucks as I walked along the narrow footpath beside the traffic over the bridge. To the left I could see a makeshift hut and a small temple. As I drew near the compound, a young man approached me. "Can I help you?" he said.

"Yes," I said, "my name is George James. I am from America. I am here to see Sunderlal Bahuguna."

"I am his assistant," he said. "He is busy now. Could you come back . . . " Just then I saw the man emerge from the hut. He looked at the two of us and waved.

"This is him, is it not?" I said. He turned to Bahuguna and then back to me. "Yes," he said, "please come." I hadn't taken the time to imagine what sort of a man to expect. He was a thin man, slight of build, and seemed to stand about five feet six. His long white hair and beard and his white homespun cotton clothing gave me the impression of a saint, but the most striking feature of his appearance was the light in his eyes. I knew about some of the fasts he had undertaken. One had almost taken his life. I wanted to know about the motivation that stood behind such extraordinary deeds. He shook my hand.

"Please come," he said. "Please sit." I sat down on the short white-washed wall surrounding the simple temple. "How was your journey?" he asked.

"It was good," I said. "I understand you are a busy man, so if I may, I shall get right to the point. It is my understanding that you have been an environmental activist for a long time and have undertaken fasts that have drawn a lot of media attention. I'm a professor of philosophy. I'm interested in the philosophy of life and the philosophy of nature that stands behind these activities. What motivates you? What is it that gives you the courage to take such extraordinary measures? These are questions I don't see addressed in the press." He nodded his head and then smiled.

"My entire philosophy," he said, "comes under three A's and five F's." Counting on the fingers of one hand, he went on. "The first A means austerity. We have a long-standing tradition of austerity, of treading lightly on the earth. The second A means alternatives: where you cannot find the answer with austerity then you have to find alternatives." His face broke into winkles as he laughed as though asking me whether I was getting his point."

"I understand," I said.

"The third," he said, "is afforestation, tree farming." He went on to say, "The five F's are about the trees we need for survival: trees are needed for food, fodder, fuel and timber, fertilizer, and fiber." He was now count- ing the five F's on the fingers of the other hand. I had the impression he had been over this material before, but I hadn't yet seen it in print. I understood that afforestation was what was known as reforestation in America. I needed to get this all on tape.

Fumbling through my camera bag, I asked him. "Would it be alright with you if I recorded our conversation on tape?" I held before him a simple micro cassette recorder.

"Yes, yes," he said. I turned it on, and with it began a conversa- tion that would be continued over the next several days and that would resume the following summer and over visits over the next years with the man who had been described as the first guru of India's environmental consciousness.

I had studied environmental philosophy in the West. I understood the roots of Western environmentalism in philosophical developments in the nineteenth century, in the thought of Ralph Waldo Emerson, Henry David Thoreau, John Muir, Aldo Leopold, and others. I understood that American consciousness about the state of the environment had been awakened in no small measure by a book by Rachael Carson largely about the environmental threat to the life of song birds and the specter of a springtime without the pleasure of their sounds. What about India, I thought? What did this environmentalism share with the environmen- talism of America? Years earlier I had read an influential essay that put the blame for the global environmental crisis on the religious traditions of the West. Lynn White Jr. had argued that Christianity was the most anthropocentric religion to emerge in the history of humankind. For this tradition, God had created human beings uniquely in his image and placed humans in charge of creation to use it as they pleased. I wasn't sure he was right, but it raised in my mind the question of other religious traditions, especially of Hinduism, that seemed to see divinity in nature. "For our tradition," Bahuguna said, "there is divinity in everything. Divinity is not just in the heavens, but in the birds, the beasts, the streams and rivers, in the mountains, and in the trees of the forests. In the biosphere there are many species. There are birds, animals, there are trees. There are plants, of many varieties. Rivers are flowing in a natural way. Now we live in a technosphere. There is technology all around. Now we have killed the rivers in order to build dams. And this is all in order to satisfy the never satisfying greed of human beings. And Gandhi in one sentence explained this: nature has enough to fulfill the needs of all, but nothing to satisfy the greed of one." Already I was beginning to see a pattern to his thought. There was the philosophical and religious understanding of nature embodied in the ancient traditions of India, there was a clear appreciation for the scientific insights of ecology, and there was the unmistakable influence of Gandhi. This would be a rich and fruitful journey.

Chapter 2

The Childhood of an Activist

Much of that first conversation centered upon the most recent events. I wanted to understand the motives of a man who, in protest against the construction of the Tehri Dam, undertook a fast in May 1995 that lasted forty-five days. That fast ended with the assurance of the then prime minister that the government would undertake a thorough review of all aspects of the project. I wanted to understand the inspiration of a man who less than a year later, in April 1996 when the promised review did not materialize, undertook a further fast, a *prayaschit vrata* (discipline of self-purification), lasting another seventy-four days, for letting down those people who had looked to his long fast as the act that would finally bring them justice and security. In an age when the motives of the most remarkable men and women are frequently reduced to more or less insidious manifestations of self-interest, I wanted to hear more than had been covered in the media or even in academic studies of peasant movements on the Himalayas. "If the dam goes forward," he said, "this hut will be the first human dwelling to be submerged." I looked and was taken back by the massive coffer dam looming above me. The hut was only about a hundred meters from its base. "I am living here in *satyagraha*." he said. "I am living here in nonviolent protest against the construction of this dam."

Bahuguna was then in his midseventies, and much of his public credibility had come from respect for his age and experience. In an effort to understand where his involvement with the environment began, I found myself asking questions about his very early life. Sunderlal Bahuguna was born on January 9 in 1927, the fifth surviving child of a forest officer in the Tehri Garhwal region. He told me that his love of the trees and of the Himalayan forests came from his father. Some of his earliest memories were of riding on horseback in his father's arms through the forests of the Garhwal state. In those days, he said, there was no awareness of the need to conserve forest resources. The magnitude of the forests seemed unlimited. From both his parents he derived his love of the Ganges, to which they were both devoted. But his father died when Sunderlal was only eight years old, and his early life was nourished and supported by his loving mother.

"How did your father die?" I asked.

"He had suffered from hemorrhoids and had gone for surgery to Dehra Dun. There was a very good doctor there, Dr. Bouchard." He had gone there on a dandy or sedan chair, a device on which a patient could be carried normally by four persons. He added, "So when he was coming back, he came to a place called "Dhanolti." There he told the carriers to put the dandy down. He wanted to see the cedar trees that he had planted. Then he came back, and after two days he passed away."

"Did you have any siblings?" I asked.

"I had two elder brothers and two elder sisters living at that time. I also had another brother, the eldest, but he died at age fifteen or so."

"How did he die?" I enquired.

"From cholera, I believe," he said. "I have only heard this because he died before I was born. I was the fifth. I was the youngest of all."

"So what age were you when you came to live in Tehri?" I asked.

"I came to Tehri at the age of eight, after passing my primary examination. So I joined class five in Tehri in 1935. And from 1935 to 1944, I was in Tehri until I appeared for intermediate school examinations and until I was arrested." (Intermediate school is equivalent to American grades 11 and 12).

When the conversation turned to his mother, Sunderlal produced an issue of a journal published in Hindi in which he had written an article about her. It was entitled: "Hill Woman My Mother: A Reminiscence." Reading through the text, he summarized the main points in English. "I could not remember," he said, "if ever I had risen in the morning before her." He recounted that when he did awake he would find his father smoking his hookah and his mother standing before her children with hot water to wash their hands and face. But before they had awakened, she had already given fodder to the cows and brought water from a spring about a quarter mile from the village. Before they had awakened, she would have lit the hearth and put on the kettle for tea. Before they had awakened, she would have milked the cows, cleaned the cow shed, and prepared tea for his elderly father. She would prepare breakfast before sunrise and would take her breakfast only after the children were fed.

He recalls that his mother would eat only coarse grains and preparations made from buttermilk and green vegetables. Even as a child he had the impression that she considered curried dahl and rice to be something to which she had no right. "After feeding us," he said, "she would either go to the fields to work or take a sickle in her hands to cut the grass in the forest. And . . . when she returned from field or forest she was never without a load on her head."

What stands out most vividly in Sunderlal's memory was his mother's forbearance and patience in the face of extraordinary hardship. The irrigated fields of the village were about a mile's walk below the family dwelling. One of his mother's chores was to carry fertilizer to the fields. He recalls that after working through the day in the field and after the steep climb home with a sack of rice or a bundle of grass on her head, the children would run to her and try to embrace her tired legs. Putting down the load from her head, she would heave a long sigh and then take her children on her lap and love them. "Those times," he said, "are the best memories of my life." But this pleasure was never to last very long because water had to be brought again for the children and for the cattle. In the evening, his mother would milk the cows and light the lamps, and she would tell the children to say their prayers. The first to be served dinner were always the children, and even when vegetables were served, there was often little left for her. After cleaning the pots and the kitchen, she would go with a lantern to the cattle shed. She would give fodder to the cattle, secure the latches on the sheds and the house, and go to take her rest. By that time, he said, his older brothers and sisters would be fast asleep. But he remained awake. Though she was tired from the work in the fields and the care of the cattle, Sunderlal would wait for his mother's attention. Before she retired, he always insisted that she tell him a story. And always before he went to sleep, she acquiesced to this demand. After telling a story to her little boy, he could hear her deeply sigh and would sometimes hear the words that came to be engraved on his memory: "Oh God, there is not even death for me." But lest the child should take account of those despairing words, she followed them always with the prayer, "Oh God, be kind to my son."

His mother was deeply pious. On the full moon she would put on a ceremonial dress, put a gold ring in her nose, and observe a fast. She would walk one kilometer down the steep slope to the Bhagirathi River and to the temple. Sunderlal recalls that when there was *arti*, the service of worship in which lamps were lit and prayer made to the deities, the children would get some sweets. He recalls that despite her fasts, there was never any reduction in her work. Even on the days when she was fasting, she would still bring fodder on her head. She also kept Tulsi plants in the house, and she tended them with water and prayers every day, and in the evening she would place a lamp close by them. He notes that when his father died, the frequency of her fasts did not decrease. On the contrary, they increased from one to two days a month. This included the full moon and the eleventh day of the moon, *ekadashi*. Sunderlal told me that when he was only fifteen, his mother departed from him forever. It was *ekadashi* in July. The monsoon had begun, and the river was high. His mother had gone down to the river to bathe, and she was swept away in the turbulence of the water, never to be seen again. His mother's life was strenuous, and the care and dedication of his mother and of all the women of the hills remained a central occupation of Sunderlal's adult career.

When Sunderlal was a boy in school, and when his mother was still with him, she always made sure that he had a few coins in his pocket to buy milk. On one occasion the coins in his pocket provided the opportunity for a profound encounter with the most crucial influence upon in his early life. In 1940, when Sunderlal was only thirteen, he met the man to whom he would always refer as his guru. By this time the nonviolent movement for the attainment of Indian self-rule was gaining ground. As a boy in school, Sunderlal's life had been carefree, and the tumultuous events on India's political scene had not yet touched him. He was playing with his friends after school when they saw a man whose dress marked him neither as a man employed by the offices of the princely state nor as a common laborer. He was new to their town. He wore sandals, a Gandhi cap, and a dhoti, and he carried a small bag and an oddly shaped wooden box. Fascinated, they began to follow him. They thought, perhaps, that he was a magician and might entertain them. Other strangers had done so. But the question that animated their eager minds was the question, what was in that box? Eventually he consented to stop and talk to the boys, and under the shade of a tree he opened and revealed the contents of this peculiar box. It was a portable *charkha*, a spinning wheel. The boys looked at one another dismayed. Then he proceeded to demonstrate its use. Fascinated, the boys eventually raised the question of how long it would take to make enough thread to make the dhoti he was wearing. He replied he wasn't sure. But he told them what he was sure of. He told them that if all of the villages should begin to spin their own yarn and produce their own handmade cloth, then India could be free.

India could be free, he thought. Until then, Sunderlal wasn't really aware that it was not. The man they had met was Shri Dev Suman. Born in 1916 he had from his youth been a member of the Indian National Congress and had played a critical role in the work of the All India States People's Conference. He was now the leader of the Praja Mandal or Citizens Forum, established in 1939, and had written articles and made speeches concerning both local and national struggles. After his release from a period of imprisonment in Agra jail, he had returned to the state of Tehri and had begun to tour villages and organize meetings.[1] Eventually the stranger opened his bag. And the boys were enthralled at a selection of booklets and pamphlets, each explaining conditions necessary for the achievement of national independence and motivating young people to participate. He told them that if they wanted to understand how the spinning wheel could make India free, then they needed to read some of these books. With his milk money Sunderlal purchased two titles that would have a decisive impact upon the direction of his life. The first was *An Appeal to the Young*, by a Russian author known as Prince Kropotkin (Peter Kropotkin). The other was a book by Mohandas K. Gandhi called *Hind Swaraj*.

"Kropotkin!" I said. "It's my understanding that Kropotkin was an anarchist."

"He was very critical of government," he said. "But in this booklet he addressed himself to young people. It was a challenge to the purpose of their lives. It was a strong influence on my life." I would have to find this booklet.

"Is the booklet still available," I asked? Do you still have a copy?"

"This pamphlet was a Hindi translation from the Russian," he said. "Perhaps you can also find it in English. I don't know." Later, after a search through the bookstores of Delhi, I turned to the Internet where I found a website devoted to anarchism, where with a host of other anarchist writings was an English translation of this very title.[2] Reading through it I could see its potential impact upon a young and inquiring mind. In his *Appeal to the Young*, Kropotkin departed from the most celebrated themes of his writings: the victimization of the poor at the hands of centralized governments, the incompetence of government bureaucracies, "armies of office holders sitting like spiders in their webs," or even his central idea that free communes were the necessary channels through which the revolution could reach its maximum development. While such ideas are implicit in his *Appeal to the Young*, Kropotkin here addresses his intended reader on a personal level: "It is to the young that I wish to address myself today. Let the old—I mean of course the old in heart and mind—lay the pamphlet down therefore without tiring their eyes in reading what will tell them nothing."[3] His intended readers are young people who have completed the first stage of their education and who are preparing for professional life. He believes, he says, that he is addressing young people whose minds are free of the superstition that their teachers have sought to force upon them, and that they are not among those who even at their early age have only an insatiable longing for pleasure. "I assume on the contrary," he says, "that you have a warm heart, and for this reason I talk to you." To a youth at the age of thirteen, the question he addresses in this pamphlet could hardly have been more engaging. To them he put the question: what are you going to be? In raising this question Kropotkin was not interested in laying before his readership the possibilities of future professions and the preparation they would inevitably require. Rather, considering a broad range of professional possibilities, he puts before his readership a fundamental ethical challenge: whether that profession will be the opportunity for personal prestige and power or the avenue through which he or she might address the disenfranchisement of those who grovel in misery and ignorance. A brief look into this pamphlet will demonstrate its importance for the formation of the basic values that began to shape his life.

Let us suppose, he suggests, that you have received a scientific education and intend to enter the medical profession, to become a doctor.

> Tomorrow a man in corduroys will come to fetch you to see a sick woman. He will lead you into one of those alleys where the opposite neighbors can almost shake hands over the heads of the passersby; you ascend into a foul atmosphere by the flickering light of a little ill trimmed lamp; you climb two, three, four, five flights of filthy stairs, and in a dark, cold room you find the sick woman, lying on a pallet covered with dirty rags. Pale, livid children, shivering under their scanty garments, gaze at you with their big eyes wide open. The husband has worked all this life twelve or thirteen hours a day at, no matter what; now he has been out of work for three months. To be out of employ is not rare in his trade; it happens every year, periodically. But, formerly, when he was out of work his wife went out as a charwoman—perhaps to wash your shirts—at the rate of fifteen pence a day; now she has been bedridden for two months, and misery glares upon the family in all its squalid hideousness.

What, he asks, will you prescribe for this sick woman: a better diet, less exhausting toil, a dry and well-ventilated dwelling? "What irony!" he says, "for if she could have afforded it this would have been long since done without your advice." He continues with the words the young doctor would then hear about the neighbors of the patient: "They will tell you that the woman on the other side of the partition, who coughs a cough which tears your heart, is a poor ironer; that a flight of stairs lower down all the children have the fever; that the washerwoman who occupies the ground floor will not live to see the spring; and that in the house next door things are still worse." What will you say, Kropotkin inquires, to all these sick people?[4]

Kropotkin develops this theme by pointing out that the following day another case comes to your attention: Your partner tells you that yesterday a footman had come to fetch him, this time in a carriage. "He was being fetched for a lady worn out with sleepless nights, a woman who devotes all her life to dressing, visits, balls, and squabbles with a stupid husband. Your friend has prescribed for her a less preposterous habit of life, a less heating diet, walks in the fresh air, an even temperament, and, in order to make up in some measure for the want of useful work, a little gymnastic exercise in her bedroom." Kropotkin's point is that the one patient is dying because she has never had enough food or enough rest in her whole life, while the other pines because she has never known the reality of work. Then to his young readers Kropotkin puts forth this challenge: "If you are one of those miserable natures who adapt themselves to anything, who at the sight of the most revolting spectacles console themselves with a gentle sigh and a glass of sherry, then you will gradually become used to these contrasts. . . . Your sole idea will be to lift yourself into the ranks of the pleasure-seekers, so that you may never again find yourself among the wretched. . . . But if you are a Man, if every sentiment is translated in your case into an action of the will; if, in you, the beast has not crushed the intelligent being, then you will return home one day saying to yourself, 'No, it is unjust; this must not go on any longer.'" He continues, "If altruism is not a word devoid of significance for you, then you will end by finding yourself in our ranks, and you will work as we work, to bring about the Social Revolution."[5]

After placing these books in Sunderlal's hands, Shri Dev Suman departed but only to return to Tehri many times. Sunderlal told me that in his absence he and his young friends would sit together under the trees and read these booklets to one another. Their consciousness was aroused.

"Did you think of your mother as you read those words of Kropotkin?" I
later inquired. He silently nodded his head. For Kropotkin, however, the
medical profession is but one to which contemporary conditions present
a similar challenge. He proceeds from the profession of the doctor to that
of the lawyer and develops a similar dilemma: a rich landowner demands
the eviction of a tenant who has not paid his rent. The landlord has
done nothing to improve his estate, yet its value has tripled in fifty years
owing to a rise in price of land due to the construction of a railway, to
the making of new highroads, to the draining of a marsh, to the enclo-
sure and cultivation of wastelands. But the tenant, who has contributed
largely toward this increase, has ruined himself. Fallen into the hands of
usurers, he is deeply in debt; he can no longer pay the rent. Kropotkin
observes that the law, always on the side of property, is quite clear: the
landlord is in the right. But to the young reader, whose feeling of justice
has not yet been stifled by legal fictions, he raises the question, "What
will you do? Will you contend that the farmer ought to be turned out
upon the high road—for that is what the law ordains—or will you urge
that the landlord should pay back to the farmer the whole of the increase
of value in his property which is due to the farmer's labor?—for that is
what equity decrees. Which side will you take? For the law and against
justice, or for justice and against the law?" After this and several further
examples Kropotkin makes the point:

> If you reason instead of repeating what is taught you; if you
> analyze the law and strip off those cloudy fictions with which
> it has been draped in order to conceal its real origin, which
> is the right of the stronger, and its substance, which has ever
> been the consecration of all the tyrannies handed down to
> mankind through its long and bloody history . . . You will
> understand that to remain the servant of the written law is
> to place yourself every day in opposition to the law of con-
> science, and to make a bargain on the wrong side; and, since
> this struggle cannot go on forever, you will either silence your
> conscience and become a scoundrel, or you will break with
> tradition, and you will work with us for the utter destruction
> of all this injustice, economic, social and political.

In a similar way he addresses himself to the aspiring industrialist,
the aspiring engineer, the teacher, the newspaper man, the sculptor, the
painter, the poet, the philosopher, the musician, always presenting another

facet of the same dilemma. What will you do? And he states that if his reader should go among the people he will hear the voice of the laborer as he stumbles under the weight of his burden. And to move his young reader even further he places the words of this laborer in capitals:

WHERE, THEN, ARE THESE YOUNG PEOPLE WHO HAVE BEEN TAUGHT AT OUR EXPENSE? THESE YOUTHS WHOM WE FED AND CLOTHED WHILE THEY STUDIED? WHERE ARE THOSE FOR WHOM, OUR BACKS BENT DOUBLE BENEATH OUR BURDENS AND OUR BELLIES EMPTY, WE HAVE BUILT THESE HOUSES, THESE COL-LEGES, THESE LECTURE-ROOMS, THESE MUSEUMS? WHERE ARE THE MEN FOR WHOSE BENEFIT WE, WITH OUR PALE, WORN FACES, HAVE PRINTED THESE FINE BOOKS, MOST OF WHICH WE CANNOT EVEN READ? WHERE ARE THEY, THESE PROFESSORS WHO CLAIM TO POSSESS THE SCIENCE OF MANKIND, AND FOR WHOM HUMANITY ITSELF IS NOT WORTH A RARE CATERPILLAR? WHERE ARE THE MEN WHO ARE EVER SPEAKING IN PRAISE OF LIBERTY, AND NEVER THINK TO CHAMPION OUR FREEDOM, TRAMPLED AS IT IS EACH DAY BENEATH THEIR FEET? WHERE ARE THEY, THESE WRITERS AND POETS, THESE PAINTERS AND SCULPTORS? WHERE, IN A WORD, IS THE WHOLE GANG OF HYPOCRITES WHO SPEAK OF THE PEOPLE WITH TEARS IN THEIR EYES, BUT WHO NEVER, BY ANY CHANCE, FIND THEMSELVES AMONG US, HELPING US IN OUR LABORIOUS WORK?[6]

Even today it is hard to read these words of Kropotkin without being moved. The impact this pamphlet had upon the thoughts of this small group of school boys was nothing short of profound. It opened their minds abruptly to the realities of the social and political world in which they lived. The other pamphlet was easier to track down. I had read it with interest years before. "I presume," I said, "that *Hind Swaraj* was a little more difficult for younger minds to grasp."

"It was not easy, but we read it to one another," he said, "and gradually we got the meaning." The style of the pamphlet presented as a dialogue between the writer and his imagined reader must have facilitated the reception of this influential tract. It is interesting that Gandhi here also talks about the profession of the lawyer and the doctor. In the view of Gandhi, both had contributed significantly to the enslavement of India. Sunderlal suggested three themes that the pamphlet covered that especially engaged his mind. The first was the idea of *swaraj* (self-rule). For Gandhi *swaraj* was not simply a matter of the expulsion of the British, but the recovery of India's own identity. True civilization, says Gandhi, "is that mode of conduct which points out to man the path of duty." He argued that the performance of duty and the observance of morality are one and the same. "To observe morality is to attain mastery over our mind and our passions." He suggests that the mind is like a restless bird: the more it gets the more it wants, and yet it remains unsatisfied. "The more we indulge our passions the more unbridled they become." Our ancestors saw, says Gandhi, "that happiness was largely a mental condition." They understood that human beings are not necessarily happy because they are rich, nor are they unhappy simply because they are poor. They understood that true happiness and health consisted in the proper use of our hands and feet. They set limitations on our indulgences, dissuading us from inordinate luxuries and pleasures. They reasoned that large cities were a snare to moral development and that it was village life that could best cultivate true civilization. In this forceful pamphlet Gandhi argues that in these respects India's civilization had nothing to learn from others.[7] For Gandhi, it is *swaraj* when we learn to rule ourselves. But such *swaraj*, he said, had to be experienced by each person for him- or herself.[8]

A second theme that touched the young Sunderlal was expressed in the claim of Gandhi that true *swaraj* could only be brought about by non-violent means: by peaceful demonstrations, by fasting, and by accepting the suffering that arises in consequence of disobedience to unreasonable, immoral, and unacceptable laws. To the claim that the English would have to be expelled from India by force of arms, Gandhi reminds his reader that it was the Indian adoption of English civilization that makes their presence in India possible. In the chapter "Why Was India Lost?" he makes the point that the English have not taken India, but the Indians have given it away.[9] He suggests that hatred against the English ought to be transferred from the English people to the English civilization.[10] As in many other places in his writings, Gandhi here articulates the view that to expel the British by brute force would only be counterproductive for India. He argues that such a viewpoint fails to see the connection between the means of achieving self-rule and the end. If the extremists should succeed in driving away the British by violent means, then by what means will they rule? In that case, says Gandhi, the tyranny of the British will simply be replaced by that of another, and the civilization of India will have been compromised to the ideology of brute force. For Gandhi, it is only fair means that can produce fair results. He acknowledges that petitions are useless without the backing of force. But there are two kinds of force that can back a petition. One is brute force: "We shall hurt you if you do not give us this." The other kind of force says: "If you do not concede our demand, we shall no longer be your petitioners. You can govern us only so long as we remain the governed." This, he says, is soul force, what is popularly but less accurately called "passive resistance." Soul force is a method of securing rights by means of personal suffering. If the government should pass a law that applies to me, and I do not like it, and by violence I force the government to repeal the law, then I am employing what Gandhi terms "brute force" or "body force." However, if I do not obey the law, and I accept the penalty for its breach, then, says Gandhi, I am using soul force. That force involves sacrifice of the self, which is acknowledged to be infinitely superior to the sacrifice of others. "The force of arms," he says, "is powerless when matched against the force of love or the soul."[11]

The third theme that impressed Sunderlal, and one that closed the circle on the idea of the spinning wheel, was the idea of self-reliance or *swadeshi*. *Swadeshi* was the refusal of goods from abroad and reliance upon what could be produced at home. For Gandhi, *swadeshi* was the necessary strategy to exert the force of truth and love. Gandhi argued that the textile mills of England had impoverished India. But he also argued that it was meaningless to blame this impoverishment on Manchester. Manchester produced its cloth because Indians were willing to wear it. It is for this reason that the cottage industries of making cloth in India had all but disappeared. "Indeed," says Gandhi, "even our gods [the statues of the Hindu gods] are made in Germany. What need, then, to speak of matches, pins and glassware? My answer can be only one. What did India do before these articles were introduced? Precisely the same should be done today. As long as we cannot make pins without machinery so long will we do without them. The tinsel splendour of glassware we will have nothing to do with, and we will make wicks, as of old, with home grown cotton and use handmade earthen saucers for lamps. So doing, we shall save our eyes and money and support Swadeshi and so shall we attain Home Rule."[12] Gandhi closes this pamphlet with four critical points: (1) real home rule is self-rule or self-control, (2) the way to self-rule is soul force or love force, (3) in order to exert this force *swadeshi* is necessary in every sense, and (4) what we want to do should be done not because we object to the English or from hope of retaliation against them, but because it is our duty.[13]

Sunderlal was quickly engaged with these ideas. In a sense Kropotkin's appeal to the young had challenged him to make something morally significant of his life. The booklet by Gandhi pointed the way to the activities with which he should be engaged. In the course of time Sunderlal and his young friends pooled their resources to purchase a Charka for themselves, and in the seclusion of a local Muslim cemetery, they learned together the skill of spinning while reading to one another under the trees the books they had purchased. For this they earned the approbation of their school teacher, who observed them reading to one another in the cemetery and commended them to their fellow students as young people who were serious about their studies. But as influential as the printed word can be, these books would not have had the same force on the life of Sunderlal without the influence of the man who had put them in his hands. Sri Dev Suman, then only twenty-four, was the exemplar of the Gandhian principle of *swaraj*. He was committed to Gandhi's philosophy and was working to implement the principles of *sarvodaya* in the hills. Normally translated as "universal uplift," the word *sarvodaya* comes from the word *sarvam*, meaning "wholeness" and *uday*, meaning "holistic emergence." According to Vimala Thakar the word implies "the wholistic growth and all round development of all the sections of global humanity."[14] The term came to be regarded as practically synonymous with the philosophy of Gandhi, especially as it pertained to his constructive program for the development of economically independent villages. Bereft of the guidance and counsel of his own father, Sri Dev Suman became a critical influence on Sunderlal's life. "What will you do when you grow up?" he once asked the young Sunderlal.

Reflecting the views of most young boys of the villages he replied with an eager smile, "I shall serve as an official." Like many other young people of the area he hoped to be trained as an official of the state, the princely state of Tehri Garhwal.

"Then who," he inquired, "will serve the poor people?"

Again with an optimistic smile he declared, "I shall do that too!"

With a penetrating look Suman then uttered the rejoinder, "But how can you serve two different masters at the same time?" and left the boy to ponder the implications of his question. The more he thought about it the more clearly he saw the implications of Suman's admonition. In the course of time he saw that the raja or king and the officials of the state were by no means occupied with the interests of the people. From that time he began thinking about making service to the people the focus of his life.[15]

Under the guidance of Sri Dev Suman, Sunderlal and some of his friends became interested in the freedom movement. When his mother heard about this interest, she was upset. To her traditional mind any activity in opposition to office of the raja must be morally wrong. Relatives were concerned as well, and tried to keep him under scrutiny in his village. But often he would find some excuse to leave the village to stay with Sri Dev Suman. By the age of fifteen Sunderlal had begun to spend his summer vacations with Sri Dev Suman in Mussoorie, the base of his work against the ruler of the princely state of Tehri Garhwal. There Sri Dev Suman had begun a night school program for laborers, and Sunderlal became a teacher. Suman had now departed from Mussoorie, leaving Sunderlal there to carry on the work by himself. Life was exciting. Immersed in the literature of the independence movement, Sunderlal was learning new and meaningful lessons about the state of the world around him, about the economic and political conditions in the state, and about social issues to be addressed. He had a found a meaningful venue for significant service under the guidance of a man whose vision and actions he believed in, a man who had put Gandhi's principles into action. But this meaningful setting was soon to be disturbed. It was during these days in Mussoorie that Sunderlal's elder brother arrived one day with the news that his mother had passed away, lost without a trace in the turbulent waters of the Bhagirathi River. Her body was never recovered. Grief stricken, he returned with his brother to Tehri to observe the rites for the dead. But his return to Tehri brought him further devastating news. Sri Dev Suman had been arrested. In a summary trial in the Tehri jail, he had been prosecuted and convicted of sedition. Now imprisoned in the Tehri jail, he was undergoing torture. It was hard to take it all in. Sunderlal suddenly began to see where the values and activism he was learning stood in the view of the government of the state. But Suman's arrest and imprisonment did not put an end to his activities. With Sunderlal's help he managed to get word of his arrest and his condition in the jail to the outside world. By smuggling the statement he made at his summary trial in the Tehri jail and sending it to the *Hindustan Times* in Delhi, Sunderlal was instrumental in bring the case of Sri Dev Suman to public attention. For this, at age seventeen, Sunderlal was himself eventually arrested. And with his arrest began a venture in nonviolent activism that has spanned over six decades and continues today.

Chapter 3

Going Underground

Sunderlal Bahuguna speaks to this day of Sri Dev Suman as his guru.[1] There is no precise equivalent to this term in the English language. The guru is certainly a teacher. In that sense the term can apply in modern Hindi to a teacher in a public or private school. But the Sanskrit term comes from two syllables: *gu,* (darkness) and *ru* (dispel). The connotation refers both to the subject matter that is taught and to the person who teaches. The subject matter is not mundane. It is knowledge that enlightens, that liberates. The guru is a person who represents that enlightenment and who exemplifies in his life the meaning of this teaching. Sri Dev Suman was a political activist who not only taught Mahatma Gandhi's doctrine of *swaraj,* but he also embodied it. Born in a Garhwali village, he was an organizer of opposition against the government of the princely state. When Sunderlal came to know him, Sri Dev Suman was perhaps the most famous freedom fighter in Garhwal. His work was centered in the Tehri Rajya Praja Mandal (the Tehri State Peoples' Forum), located in Dehra Dun. From there he traveled to various towns in the region to organize branches of the Praja Mandal (Citizens' Forum). His goal was to set up an organizational forum to mediate between the raja and the praja (the people). He wanted an agreement with the king and his officials under which the Praja Mandal could undertake constructive work with the support of the raja. It was in the context of travels through the towns and villages of Garhwal that he came to Tehri where he first encountered the young Sunderlal. Sri Dev Suman promoted *swadeshi* (self-reliance) by means of the development of economically independent villages. He was committed to Gandhi's constructive program.

Sri Dev Suman was arrested somewhere in Garhwal in 1942. Expelled from the state, he continued his work in British India and was later arrested and jailed in Agra, then under direct British rule. Eventually released from the Agra Central Jail, he made his way back to Tehri. After a period of productive work, he was again arrested and then incarcerated in the Tehri jail. When Sunderlal returned from Mussoorie, he found lodging in a quarter of the local hospital with the brother of his sister-in-law, a pharmacist in the hospital. This pharmacist was married to Sri Dev Suman's sister. Because of an amiable relationship with the warden of the jail Sunderlal was permitted to forward newspapers to Sri Dev Suman, and with the papers, correspondence. Among the correspondence that crossed between them, Suman gave Sunderlal a copy of the statement he had made at his summary trial in the Tehri jail, an explicit defense of Gandhi's doctrine of *swaraj* through self-reliance. Sunderlal explained to me that in those days all provisions for the hills—food, clothing, everything that was sold in the shops in Tehri—came on the backs of mules from Rishikesh. By a strategy of cunning and courage, Sunderlal managed to hide this statement under the saddle of one of the mules. He arranged for an accomplice in Rishikesh to retrieve it and forward it to friends in Delhi, where it eventually appeared in the Hindi language edition of the nationalist paper the *Hindustan Times*.

News of Suman's arrest and treatment in jail quickly turned public opinion against the princely state and its policy of repression of the local people. The local police were angered by the publicity. How did the word about the arrest of this opponent of the state make its way to a newspaper in Delhi? A search for the source of this information led them to one young man who had contact with him in prison. Sunderlal was immediately arrested. But they had no specific evidence against him, and the principal of the school he was then attending attested that he was a student in good standing and should be permitted to finish the school term and take his exams. Reluctantly, the authorities permitted him to return to school but stationed a police guard where Sunderlal was living. When the time came for the school exams, a police guard delivered Sunderlal to the principal at the examination hall. There he sat for his exams. When he was finished, the police guard returned him to his home. This routine continued through the duration of the examination period. But once his exams were over all special considerations for the studies of the young student came abruptly to an end. Because they didn't want both he and Suman to be quartered in the same place, they transferred Sunderlal to a jail facility in Narendranagar, about 40 kilometers to the South of Tehri. There he remained without trial for almost five months. He was not treated well. Often he would find small stones or kerosene mixed with his food. Conditions were unsanitary. He was made to go without a bath for as long as sixty-three days. Eventually boils began to appear on his neck and under his chin. He became very ill.

Back in the Tehri jail, Sri Dev Suman was bound in heavy shackles and underwent beatings. He eventually resolved to undertake an indefinite fast for the basic rights for the people of the princely state of Tehri Garhwal. His demands were threefold: First, he demanded that the state recognize the Praja Mandal and permit it to work in the area without hindrance. Second, he demanded that the case against him be heard by the raja himself, for whom he professed complete devotion. Finally, he demanded that he should be permitted contact with the outside world. As days of fasting turned to weeks and weeks to months, he received no response. His fast continued. Finally on July 25, 1944, after fasting for eighty-four days, he died in the Tehri jail.[2] Without recognition or ceremony, his body was stuffed into a sack and thrown into the Bhagirathi River. In his jail cell in the police station in Narendranagar, Sunderlal eventually heard about Suman's death. The news affected him deeply. He was shocked and grief stricken. In his own now sickly condition he saw that Sri Dev Suman was committed to a cause that carried a serious cost. At the tender age of seventeen, Suman's torch now seemed to be falling to him. In jail he was presented once a week to the chief officer of the police. There he was always asked the same question, "How is your mind now?" His reply was always the same, "It is as it was when I was taken to the lockup!" His physical condition worsened.

Eventually the chief officer of the police called for a doctor to see the young prisoner. After examining the patient, the doctor reported that the young man needed immediate medical attention. He also indicated that if he should try to operate on the patient in the unsanitary conditions of the jail, the prisoner would surely die. He needed to go to a hospital. The following day on orders from the chief officer, he was taken on stretcher to the hospital in Narendranagar. But his reception at the hospital was hardly one of welcome. Before the police officers entered the hospital with their sickly and emaciated patient, the medical supervisor shouted at them, "Take him back! Why are you bringing this dying prisoner here?" Not knowing what else to do, the police left him like a dead body on the stretcher outside the hospital and returned to the police chief for further instructions. His reply was that since the boy was dying, it would be better that they let him die where he was, where responsibility for his death would not fall on the police. The doctor, however, was a friend of Sunderlal's family, and the following day, he took the young prisoner to his own home, where on his veranda, he assembled implements for an operation. Eventually he confided to Sunderlal that the operation would be very simple and that a quick and full recovery was assured. His purpose was simply to get Sunderlal away from the police. After treating Sunderlal, the doctor sent word to the chief of police that his condition remained serious and that he would require two months of complete bed rest to recover. The chief of police then released Sunderlal to the doctor's care. A week later, barely well enough to travel, Sunderlal slipped away and traveled by train to join his elder brother, a student in Lahore.

Sunderlal arrived in Lahore with only twenty-five rupees in his possession. Squeezing into his brother's room in the college dorm, he soon secured an income of ten rupees a month as a tutor of children, a job to which he had to walk three miles every morning. With this income he managed to buy *chapatis* (Indian flat bread) and tea. Every day he would buy two paisa worth of milk for his tea, until the milk seller eventually refused to sell him milk in such miniscule quantities. "What do you want?" he said, "Are you buying milk to put in your eyes?" After that he took his tea without milk and focused on his work. The walk to his work and the lack of nutrition were a strain. Nevertheless, with strong motivation, he applied and gained admission to the B.A. program at Sanatan Dharma College, where his subjects would be english, history, and political science and where, despite his difficulties, he eventually stood first in history and political science in the half yearly exams. His academic performance soon attracted the attention of Professor Roshan Lal Varma, who had also been jailed during activities in the quit India movement. He was impressed not only with the young man's academic achievement but also with the fact that Sunderlal wore *khadi* or homespun clothes. Professor Varma also wore *khadi*, the visible symbol of his commitment to Gandhi's call for *swaraj*. He became interested in Sunderlal and persuaded him to take up an honors course in political science. The difficulty was that Sunderlal could not afford the textbooks. Nevertheless, he accepted the challenge and took his work seriously, spending most of his time in the library. In the following examination period, he again received high grades and eventually received a scholarship. In recognition of his achievement, the college presented him with a copy of Jawaharlal Nehru's *Discovery of India* at the annual college function.

Sunderlal was now well established in the college community. His professors had high hopes for his academic future. By then his brother had finished his studies toward an M.A. and had returned home. There was also a Praja Mandal branch in Lahore organized by people from Tehri State who had come to Lahore for employment. Sunderlal began attending their meetings. The days of adversity seemed to be coming to a close. But the police had not forgotten about his earlier activities in Tehri. On Sunday, June 19, 1945, after studying in the library and taking his meal in the college dining room, Sunderlal was returning to his lodging when he noticed the bicycles of policemen outside his room. As soon as his friends in the hall saw him at the gate, they whisked him away. One of his friends walked with him to the end of the street where he explained to him that police officers were after him. They were waiting for him, sitting in his room. His friends quickly arranged for him to stay in another college hostel, where a friend hid him in his room, allowing him to come out only at night. This went on for a week. After that his friends decided he should seek refuge at a place remote from Lahore, where he would not be recognized, where he would not even be known. These friends had a plan. Leaving aside his usual *khadi kurta* (tunic) and his pajama or drawstring pants, and dressed in a shirt and dress pants with glasses and a hat, he was taken by bicycle to the Sahdara Railway Station, where he was entrusted to Tufail Ahmed, the secretary of the local labor union. Together they boarded a train for Lyallpur, about two hundred kilometers away.

Lyallpur was a district in Punjab, where the culture of the region was informed by the religious tradition of the Sikhs. When he arrived in Lyallpur, Tofail Ahmed introduced him as a person from Ambala seeking employment. With the advice and help of Tofail Ahmed, he took the name S. Maan Singh and applied for a job in a cotton mill. But because he had no experience, he was quickly turned away. Then he heard about a job in the canteen washing dishes. He applied for the job and was told to return with a new application the following day. That evening in the office of the labor union, he met S. Basant Singh, the secretary of the District Communist Party. When Tufail Ahmed explained that Sunderlal would be joining the cotton mill as a dishwasher he insisted that he could find him a job as a teacher. The next day Sunderlal was taken to the home of S. Gurdyal Singh, a grain merchant, where arrangements were made for Sunderlal to go to his village. Before the visit ended, S. Ghula Singh appeared on the scene, and pointed out that he was from a village so remote that no teacher would go there. He suggested that Sunderlal go with him. The matter was discussed. Because such a remote village would keep him far from the police, Sunderlal eventually accepted the offer. The following morning, after a ride of three hours by horse-drawn carriage, they arrived in the village of Sikhanwala which would be Sunderlal's home for the following year.

Sikhanwala was the center of an economically productive area. Irrigated by the Jhang Canal, it brought prosperity to a region populated largely by veterans of the First World War. S. Ghula Singh was a prosperous farmer, a Murrabadar. He lived in a large house near Chak Jhumra. The house was walled like a fortress, and outside of it were the small huts of the laborers. He and his wife had three sons and four daughters. Two of his sons, the ones closest to Sunderlal's age, were delighted to have a new companion. Sunderlal looked forward to a pleasurable and productive time ahead. But it soon became clear that there were serious obstacles to overcome. To begin with, he discovered that that he did not understand the dialect of Lyallpur. In addition, although S. Basant Singh had recommended him as a teacher, it soon became clear that he could read neither Urdu nor Gurmukhi, the languages of the region. It appeared that he would be useless as a teacher of these boys. Sunderlal, however, was determined. He was given a separate room outside of the house, where he closed himself off from outside contact to try to study Urdu. Despite enormous effort he concluded that it was just too difficult a task. The farmer concurred. After a week the farmer decided it would only be reasonable to send the young teacher back to where he had come from. Sunderlal was disappointed and beset with anxiety at the possibility that the police might pursue him again. But the eldest son implored his father to retain the young Sunderlal as his companion, and the father finally agreed. His stay with this family was thus confirmed, and Sunderlal was relieved. He became not simply a tutor of the boys of the family but almost like the family's eldest son. Moreover, his pupils became his teachers. Eventually, he found that Gurmukhi, the script of the Punjabi language, was easier to master than Urdu. With their help, he was able to master that language, and eventually he mastered Urdu as well. From him, the children learned Hindi. As his reading ability increased, he began to study the Granth Sahib, the sacred scriptures of the Sikhs. While the children were in school, he would go to the local Gurudwara, the Sikh house of worship, and immerse himself in the sacred writings. Eventually, he was able to read and understand them. He found them both intriguing and profound. In the Granth Sahib, he found that the deepest spiritual insights and highest moral ideas were often expressed in language to which the common man could relate. This impressed him deeply.

During these days, he also read Nehru's famous book, *The Discovery of India*, which he had been awarded for his achievement at school. Here he found a new idea of the subject matter with which historians were occupied. He found that the writing of history need not be restricted to accounts of empires and kingdoms and their exploits and wars, but could also include the cultural history of the people. Recognizing his interest in books, the family provided a wealth of reading materials with which Sunderlal became engaged. S. Basant Singh would occasionally visit the village and would always bring books from the Peoples' Publishing House, often Punjabi translations of Russian books. Here he read *The Seven Colored Rainbow* (*Sat-Rangi-Peength*), the story of the sacrifice and patriotism of the common people of Russia during their conflict with the Germans. He also read the novels of the great Punjabi novelist S. Nanak Singh, the writings of S. Gurbaksh Singh, and the poems of Amrita Pritam. But the books that influenced him the most were those of Gandhi. In these days he made a thorough study of Gandhi's autobiography, which bore the subtitle *The Story of My Experiments with Truth*. With the life and martyrdom of Sri Dev Suman in the back of his mind, he was impressed not only with Gandhi's ideas of truth and nonviolence, but also with the application of these ideas to down-to-earth political and social conditions. Through the study of his constructive program, Sunderlal came to recognize that the heart of Gandhi's thought was the arduous task of reconstructing communities from the grass roots up. This entailed the establishment of national unity through respect for one's neighbor's religion, respect commensurate with the respect one has for one's own. But it also entailed such mundane issues as village sanitation, the neglect of which, according to Gandhi, had turned India's graceful hamlets into dung heaps. It entailed the recovery of village industries, not only of the ginning, carding, and spinning of *khadi* cloth but of those industries such as oil pressing, hand grinding of grains, the making of soap, paper, and matches that he called the handmaidens of *khadi*. It entailed the decentralization of the production and distribution of the necessities of life. Sunderlal was intrigued with the intricate details of this enterprise. Like Gandhi, he found in the Bhagavad Gita the ideas of service and devotion in which he found spiritual support for the program that Gandhi envisioned and practiced.

During his days in Lahore, Sunderlal had accommodated himself to poverty. Now, in Sikhanwala, completely separated from any of his own relatives, he was living within the embrace of a prosperous family. There were few luxuries that were not now available to him. For one thing, he was able to realize his childhood dream of riding a horse. His father was a great lover of horses, and when Sunderlal was a child, his father would take him for excursions on horseback. But since his father's death, when Sunderlal was eight, he never had the opportunity to ride a horse. Now in the evenings he was able to join his friends Niranjan and Karnail riding horses along the Jhang Canal. He enjoyed the luxury of rich food and a comfortable life. But his continued reading of Gandhi's writings challenged his accommodation to these conditions. He was especially moved by Gandhi's ideals of selfless service (*sewa*), the personal study of religious texts (*swadhyaya*), the practice of voluntary physical labor (*shram*) and self-discipline, through austerity and restraint. He began to apply these principles to his own life. He began to question his right to the rich food available to him. He tried to persuade the elders of the family to arrange simple meals for him. It was a hard sell. Finally, he found that the best way to practice Gandhi's ideal of restraint of the palate was to take only one meal a day. Later in life, he would find this discipline to have been a fitting preparation for the severe fasts he would eventually undergo. Second, recalling his first instructions from Sri Dev Suman, he turned again to the *charkha* (spinning wheel) and resumed his practice of spinning. Cotton was grown in the fields around Sikhanwala, and the spinning of cotton was common in every home. But it was regarded as women's work. When the children first saw Sunderlal working at the *charkha*, they thought it was something he was doing for fun. But when they saw him at it for several hours a day, he became the subject of curiosity and sometimes humorous remarks. To his new family it became especially embarrassing when he refused to wear even fine *khadi* clothes from the Khadi Bhandar or market and insisted on wearing the coarse clothes made from his own handspun yarn. Third, he noticed that the village surroundings were unsanitary, littered with human waste. Some of the scavengers whose work was to clean the streets had abandoned this work for employment as landless laborers. He decided to do something about it. Empowered by Gandhi's idea of selfless service, Sunderlal became a scavenger among the scavengers. He would cover the waste with ash or soil, collect it in a bucket, and deposit in a garden. This behavior eventually became an annoyance to his family. It was against their prestige that their eldest son should do the work of a scavenger. But they believed in Sunderlal and were committed to him. Thus, rather than rejecting Sunderlal, they cursed those who spoiled the streets with waste. For Sunderlal, it was important that the village should be clean, and it was important that he should practice physical labor for the welfare of the community. In his own practice, he found it to be honorable work, a useful tool to put an end to his ego, which for the Sikh tradition is the principal obstacle to communion with God. Many years later, he recognized the full importance of this activity, when the veteran Gandhian social worker Baba Raghav Das gave him the Servant's Prayer, a prayer composed by Gandhi himself at the request of his English disciple Mira Behn. Bahuguna quoted for me some of the words of this prayer rendering them into English translation:

> Oh! The Emperor of humility,
> Who resides in the tattered hut of the poorest scavenger,
> Help us find you in this country,
> Nourished by the waters of the Ganges, Yamuna, and
>   Brahmaputra.
> Give us inquisitive and open hearts.
> Give us strength and eagerness to be one with the common
>   people of India.

For Gandhi, God was not the dweller of costly temples or golden images. God was among the poorest of the poor. While collecting night soil, Sunderlal realized the agony of all the scavengers who had to carry night soil from the dry latrines. He came to identify with those most oppressed by society, those whom Gandhi identified as the people of God.

Along with his work of spinning and sanitation, Sunderlal continued to be an effective teacher to the children of the family. But the simple life he lived impressed the children even more than the academic subjects he taught them. Following Sunderlal's example, the boys of the family began to refuse meat and to express opposition to the serving of wine to the guests. This created a storm in the household. The mother of the family came to Sunderlal and asked, "What have you been teaching these boys? They have to move in society. If they behave in the way you are teaching, people will not believe they are the sons of a respectable family." Sunderlal explained that in those days, just as it is today, the consumption of alcoholic beverages and meat was a symbol of status in the society. The family was unsettled. Yet, while his behavior and his own emerging principles of life presented a challenge to the elders of the family, his moral influence upon their children continued to endear him to them, and their affection for him continued to deepen. S. Ghula Singh, the father of the family, felt a strong sense of pride in introducing him to his distinguished guests. He would always point out that Sunderlal spoke English and was the tutor of his children. On one occasion the visitor was an officer of the police station in Chak Jhumra, the nearest law enforcement outpost to their village. He had come, as was his custom, after the harvest season to receive his share for not taking cognizance of any minor crime in the village. Against the possibility that the officer might know about him and recognize him, Sunderlal hid himself in the garden and came out only after the officer had departed. But he soon saw that the possibility of recognition was remote. He had taken a Sikh name, dressed according to Sikh tradition, and was accommodated in a prestigious Sikh family in a predominantly Sikh community. His only difficulty was that he was never able to tie the turban. While in Sikhanwala, he always had the help of the boys of the family. On one occasion, he visited Khalsa College in Lyallpur and stayed the night in the college hostel, where he had to remove the turban with great care and replace it with equal care the following morning. In those days, to all appearances, Sunderlal had become a Sikh.

In May 1946 Sunderlal wrote a letter to his former professor, Roshan Lal Varma of Sanatan Dharma College, with whom he had begun his studies the year before. He was now nineteen. He told the professor where he was residing and the activities that were occupying his time. Professor Varma immediately wrote back and assured him that the police had lost all interest his case and that there was no longer any threat of arrest. Besides that, word of national independence was in the air. He requested that Sunderlal come to Lahore and complete his degree. Sunderlal quickly made plans to visit Varma and made the journey. By that time he had so appropriated the appearance and manners of a Sikh that even his friends in Lahore were unable recognize him. On the morning of his arrival, he appeared at the door of his former teacher. Professor Varma, who had known him very well, did not know who he was. But when he spoke, his first utterance gave him instant recognition. The result was a very happy reunion. Arrangements were quickly made for Sunderlal to return to Lahore to resume his studies. He went back to Sikhanwala to bid farewell to the family who had given him a home, a refuge, and the space to clarify the priorities of his life. It was a tearful parting; all the children wept to see him go, but he promised to return for the holidays at Diwali. He then returned to Lahore and to Sanatan Dharma College. No longer was he S. Maan Singh; now he was Sunderlal Bahuguna, the college student again, but a college student with a new perspective on life.

When he returned to academic life, Sunderlal took his studies seriously. But he gradually came to the conclusion that the study of political theories and historical events had little to do with the realities of life on the ground. For this he had found more relevant insight from the constructive work of Gandhi, from the Bhagavad Gita, and from the Granth Sahib. He became involved with the activities of the local Praja Mandal. In the spring of 1947 Sunderlal took his exams for the B.A. in english, history, and political science. He was awarded the degree just at the culmination of the Indian independence struggle, with the birth of the nation occurring on August 15. But with the end of that struggle came the partition of India, when Punjab was torn apart. After he completed his final exams and received his degree, he departed again for Tehri never to see Lahore or Sikhanwala again.

Chapter 4

The Short Career of an Activist Politician

From his sojourn in Lahore and Sikhanwala, Sunderlal returned to the Garhwal region in June 1947.[1] Arriving in Dehra Dun, he quickly became involved with the Praja Mandal there and began to be engaged in aid work with refugees displaced by the partition of the country. In a short time he was appointed publicity secretary for the Praja Mandal, a responsibility that frequently took him to Delhi and put him in contact with officials of the emerging national government and with a number of major newspapers. While independence came to India in August of that year, the Tehri Garhwal region remained under the rule of the princely state of Tehri. When Sunderlal arrived there, the movement against the colonial rule of the princely state was at its peak. Sunderlal wanted to return to his hometown of Tehri to participate in the freedom struggle there. His arrival in Tehri became the occasion for his first experiment in *satyagraha*. At the principal entrance to the town of Tehri was an iron bridge over the Bhagirathi River. The policemen of the princely state still guarded the iron bridge, and they had not forgotten the young man who years before had vanished from their sight. They refused to permit him to enter the town. In response, Sunderlal undertook a fast. Taking Gandhi's recommended strategy to heart, he sat in silent nonviolent protest, an act of *satyagraha* (truth power), near the bridge for nearly a week. During that time many people from the town and neighboring villages came to meet with him to support him and to convey the news about what had been happening in Tehri during his absence. Resistance to the repressive rule of the princely state had been growing. A strong people's movement had emerged in the area of Saklana. Within Tehri youths such as Virendra Dutt Saklani were organizing people against the ruler of the state. Sunderlal and Virendra Dutt Saklani became comrades in the struggle. After a week, the police assumed that the young man had grown too weak and lethargic to undertake any further resistance. As a result he completely escaped their attention as he walked triumphantly into the town to take his place in the struggle against the ruler of the state. The success of this first experiment in *satyagraha* fortified his resolve for future acts of non-violent protest. Working with others in the freedom struggle, Sunderlal was active in a massive protest in Tehri that occurred in January 1948, a protest that eventually brought an end to the political authority of the ruler of the princely state, and led in August of the following year to the integration of Tehri Garhwal within the governance of an independent India in the state of Uttar Pradesh, formerly the United Provinces.

With the liberation of the princely state, his colleagues in the freedom struggle decided that Sunderlal should be the general secretary of the state Praja Mandal. His work in this capacity proved to be the opportunity to address some critical social issues in the community. The offices of the Praja Mandal in Tehri were located close to the colony of what had been called the untouchables. Gandhi had stood firm against the idea that any human being should be considered untouchable. He renamed them the Harijan, the people of God. In Tehri these people were employed as the scavengers. They cleaned the latrines of the town. Sunderlal observed that every day in the evenings, the men of this colony would drink and would fight. Having done the work of a scavenger, Sunderlal sympathized with their fatigue. He understood that they drank in the evenings to forget the dirty and strenuous work of the day. But he saw that after drinking they would fight amongst themselves, neighbor against neighbor. Many times he saw them injure one another, breaking bottles over one another's heads. This disturbed him deeply, and he sought a way to address the issue. On one occasion, on the celebration of the birthday of Mahatma Gandhi, the state government had sent him one hundred rupees. In his capacity as secretary of the Praja Mandal, he was to distribute sweets among the scavengers. As Sunderlal puts it, "It was the government's way to honor Gandhi!" So he went to their colony, met the people, and sat with them to visit. He used fifty rupees to buy sweets to distribute among them, but with the remaining fifty rupees he bought a lamp and a ground cover for them to sit on. With those simple provisions, he began to have meetings with the Harijans in the evenings. These meetings began as services of prayer. But before long the meetings expanded to services of prayer with talks and devotional songs. Gradually the number of participants increased, and the meetings became popular, the center of the devotional life of the colony. The popularity of these devotional sessions, however, was not shared by all the members of the larger community. Some of the people of high caste were angry with Sunderlal that he was sitting and engaged in conversations with the Harijans. They began throwing stones and other objects at Sunderlal during the services of prayer. Strong in will, Sunderlal persisted, and the meetings continued. And as the size of the gatherings grew, the people of other castes began to join them, and the opposition began to diminish. Eventually these meetings became a gathering point of the larger community. In the course of time, the site of these meetings became the venue of a night school for the Harijan community.

In the town of Tehri there was an intermediate College, what Americans know as a high school or secondary school. The school was normally open only to students of high caste, but a tailor employed in the court of the raja had managed to have his son admitted to that institution. He was from Narandranagar, where there was a school providing education only as far as the eighth grade. For higher studies he had to go to Tehri. There he was admitted to the school, and was residing in the school hostel. But owing to customs of caste he was not allowed to sit with the other students at meal times. For this reason he was not permitted to take his meals in the dining hall of the hostel. Instead at about noon each school day, he was required to take his food outside the hostel. Bahuguna explains that in the Tehri region caste discrimination applied not only to scavengers and cobblers, but to people like tailors and carpenters as well. It was all part of a strategy to keep certain people in a servile relationship to persons of high caste. They were regarded as lower caste; and although they could be touched, they were not permitted to take their meals in the company of high caste people. There were two high caste (Brahmin) boys who were students living in the same hostel. The name of the elder boy was Kameswar, and the younger boy was Vidyasagar. They had taken part in the independence struggle and were aware of the principles of the independence movement, and especially of Gandhi's repudiation of untouchability. They came to Sunderlal in the office of the Praja Mandal and told him that his rhetoric about the equality of all people in *swaraj* or self-rule was useless because here in their school was a boy who was being discriminated against on grounds of caste. He was not allowed to take his meals with the other students. They also told him what they planned to do about it. They intended to take the tailor's son into the dining room with them. Word of this idea had already been rumored within the hostel, and the school and already students of high caste were threatening violence if they tried to do this. The high caste cook in the kitchen of the hostel told the students that if they proceed in this way, he would break his sacred thread, provoking further violence. Tensions were high!

Sunderlal's response was that as a minority of two and by a single act of protest, they were not likely to change the sentiment of the community. He explained that Gandhi's principle was not simply to provoke hostility but to win the hearts of the people. He suggested that by winning their hearts, these young people could enable other students to realize the injustice that for so long they had done to the people of low caste. He suggested that the two brothers should also take their meals outside the hostel. Thus for several days these progressive students took their meals in protest outside the hostel with the tailor's son. In the course of two or three days, they found it was difficult and uncomfortable to take their meals in the scorching heat. Bahuguna explained that what they were experiencing was precisely the kind of discomfort that the people of low caste had suffered for countless generations. Then he invited the protestors and the tailor's son to come and stay with him in what was now the office of the Congress Party. So the three students came to stay with Bahuguna. Later he managed to secure the use of a larger house for these students in which they were comfortably accommodated and where they were joined by other students from scheduled castes who came to study in Tehri. Before long they recognized that they were now living in a hostel for students for all communities. They named it Harijan Chhatravas, the *chhatravas* (hostel) for Harijans, the people of God.

As secretary of the Praja Mandal, and later of the District Congress Committee, Bahuguna eventually managed to obtain a small grant of land in the section of town where the schools and colleges were located, and where he himself was living. There they began construction on a new hostel building. Sunderlal employed laborers to work on the building and worked along with the laborers on the project. When people came to him for work, he found a place for them in the project. In the course of time, highly placed people in the community also began to contribute their labor to the project. Some would help by bringing just one stone to add to the building material. Sunderlal would spend his whole day working with the laborers on the construction of the building and conducted the work of the congress party in the office in the evenings. On Sundays, which would normally have been a holiday for him, he went about the community to collect donations to pay the laborers. The hostel was constructed under the influence of Gandhi's principle of *sharir shram* (bodily labor) and financed by means of donations from the people. To Sunderlal this was the more creative and effective way to address the issue of caste in the educational setting. In 1950, the building was completed and opened to the students. Sunderlal, then twenty-three years of age, named it Thakkar Bapa Chattravas or the Thakker Bapa Hostel, after Thakkar Bapa, the associate of Mahatma Gandhi who had taken up the work of eradicating the institution of untouchability and who had worked tirelessly toward the uplift of the Adivasis or Tribal People and of all the downtrodden people of India.

In the course of time, Thakkar Bapa Hostel became Sunderlal's headquarters for further work towards the uplift of all people and the implementation of other aspects of Gandhi's constructive program. From there, during school vacations, he would take students to the villages where they were engaged in programs of education for the people of the villages. Even with the influence of Gandhi, issues of caste discrimination and untouchability had by no means disappeared from the traditions of villages and temples. The headwaters of two of the most important rivers of India, the Ganges and the Yamuna, are located in the region of Uttarakhand. Here at Gangotri and Yamunotri were temples that were places of pilgrimage of national importance. Tehri was on the route to these places from which emerge the holy rivers of India. Bahuguna explained that Gangotri, Yamunotri, Badrinath, and Kedarnath are regarded as especially sacred. Traditionally Harijans were not allowed to enter these places.

To address this expression of caste prejudice, Bahuguna decided to take some students from the Thakkar Bapa Chattravas in Tehri to the temple at Yamunotri and to the temple at Gangotri. The group included some Harijan students from the Tehri region and some students from Harijan Udhyogshala, a vocational school in Delhi. Their experience at both places was positive, and their entry into those two temples occurred without violence or obstruction. With confidence from this experience, Bahuguna then took people of the *shilpkar* or artisan caste into the temple at Budhakedar near Tehri. But here the people of caste, both the priests and the visitors to the temple, were infuriated. As was the custom, Sunderlal and his group had entered the temple leaving their shoes outside. The gathering crowd wanted to prevent their entry into the temple. But the crowd was outside the temple gate, and Sunderlal and his colleagues were now inside. As Sunderlal saw the crowd approaching, he stood at the gate of the temple to prevent them entering to assault him. As he stood at the gate the crowd was shouting jeers and death threats against him. As a colossal expression of insult, the crowd then began beating Sunderlal with his and his colleagues' shoes. Strong in spirit, Sunderlal refused to yield and endured the beatings and insults until their assailants finally gave up, and the crowd dispersed. Sunderlal's colleague Virendra Saklani, the advocate and freedom fighter, stated that a case could be taken against his assailants in court, but Sunderlal chose not to pursue the case. He states that the confrontation was productive because it demonstrated the depth of animosity that lay beneath the surface of an apparently civil social order. This animosity had now come into the open. He pointed out that the people of caste were unwilling to extend equal rights to people of lower caste because the lower caste people did work for them on their farms. They were convinced that if the lower caste people were given equal rights, they could never expect any work from them at all. Sunderlal states that bringing about changes in social attitudes is more difficult than other changes because they are supported by traditions that have held sway for many generations. Committed to Gandhi's program of village uplift, Sunderlal was also committed to Gandhi's program of social reform. For him, as for Gandhi, this meant that the poorest of the poor were entitled to the same sense of dignity with which the most privileged were endowed.

Chapter 5

Meeting Mira Behn

It was in his work as general secretary of the Praja Mandal beginning in 1948 that Sunderlal came to know and to work with one of Gandhi's famous European disciples known as Mira Behn and to cultivate a strong and meaningful association with her that significantly influenced his life. To fully appreciate the significance of this association, it will be illuminating to understand some of the details of the life of Mira Behn that took her to India and to her work with Gandhi and that motivated her, after her arrest and imprisonment with Gandhi, his wife, Kasturba, and others, to move to the hills of what is now the state of Uttarakhand. It was after her extended association with Gandhi and during her efforts to settle in the hills that she first came to meet Bahuguna. In a sense the story of her life can be seen as the development of an environmentalist inspired and informed by Gandhi's vision for the establishment of independent and self-reliant village economies.

Born in London in 1892, the person known to India as Mira Behn was Madeleine Slade, the daughter of a British naval officer, Sir Edmond Slade, later Admiral Slade the commander in chief of the British naval fleet in the East Indies. Her venture from a privileged life in England, to her discipleship to Gandhi, her love for the Himalayan landscapes, and her commitment to Gandhi's constructive program seems almost to have been foreshadowed in her early life in England. In her autobiography, written in India in the late 1950s, she states that as early as the age of five or six there was something that every now and then, as she puts it "wafted me far away." Always provoked by the voice of nature, the song of a bird, or the sound of the wind in the trees, the experience engendered "an infinite joy." She states that at this stage in her life her mind began to search in what she calls the region of "the unknowable."[1] During her father's long absences from home, she found a feeling of fellowship with the trees, plants, and animals in the twenty acres of her grandfather's country home. She states that there were some trees for which she had a special affection, but that for her, all of them were personalities. She states, "I can remember throwing my arms around trees and embracing them." Writing those words in her sixties, she states that "to this day that feeling remains."[2]

Sunderlal explains that her response to nature was supported by an intense devotion to music. In fact it was her love of music that led her, through a circuitous route, to Gandhi. She states that at the age of fifteen, when she encountered it for the first time, the music of Beethoven illuminated her spirit. Exploring the life of Beethoven, she found that nature had been the inspiration for much of his music. She also learned that Beethoven had copied long passages from German translations of Sanskrit literature and that those texts had touched him profoundly.[3] Sunderlal states that her pursuit of the music of Beethoven led her at the age of thirty to Switzerland and to an interview with his biographer, the Nobel Laureate, Romain Rolland. On meeting him she found that Rolland was also intensely interested in contemporary events in India and in the ideas and activities of Gandhi. He had just then completed the writing of *Mahatma Gandhi* and indicated to her that the book was in press. He asked her whether she had ever heard of Gandhi. When she replied that she had not, he talked at length about him, comparing his character to that of Christ.[4] His words made such an impression that the conversation remained on her mind through her travels to Egypt. On her return to Paris, Madeleine bought the book and read it in a single day. She then immersed herself in the writings of Gandhi, wherein she felt she had found the meaning of her life. Before going home to England, she was convinced that she was called to go to India and to stand with Gandhi in his commitment to truth and nonviolence in the cause of India's freedom. That cause, in her view, though focused on India, was a cause that pertained to the whole of humanity.

After corresponding with Gandhi and a period of disciplined preparation, Madeleine sailed for Bombay on October 25, 1925, arriving on November 6. Colleagues of Gandhi were there to receive her. Without delay she boarded an overnight train to Ahmedabad, and from there she traveled by car to the Sabarmati Ashram where her eyes finally fell upon the man whose ideals she had made her own. She reports that she was conscious of nothing but a sense of light. She fell to her knees. Raising her up with gentle hands, Gandhi's first words to her were that she would be his daughter.[5] Bahuguna states that shortly after that Gandhi gave her the name Mira Behn. He had named her Mira after Mirabai, the medieval saint of Rajasthan, renowned for her devotion to Krishna. Bahuguna explains that in Gandhi's movement, the male participants were known as Bhai (brother), and the women were addressed as Behn (sister). In this way Gandhi introduced a human element, an aspect of family life, among his followers. In that context Gandhi himself was known as Bapu (father). Hence the name by which Madeline Slade was known in her Gandhian family and to almost all who knew her thereafter was Mira Behn or sister Mira, often rendered Mirabehn.

Following their initial meeting, Mira quickly became an active participant in the life of the Sabarmati Ashram and was dedicated to its rules. Shedding the habits of her privileged life, she arose at 4:00 a.m. to attend morning prayers at 4:30 a.m. With others she took part in the sweeping and cleaning of the ashram and the cleaning of the latrines and urinals. Having already taken up spinning in her preparation to be with Gandhi, she now learned the art of carding cotton and other activities related to the cottage industry of making homemade cloth. She took her turn in the kitchen where rotis, dahl, and vegetables were prepared daily for around two hundred people.[6] Bahuguna states that in a short time she became an Indian both in her food habits and in her manner of dress. It was in this period and after a long discussion with Gandhi that she chose to shave her hair and take the vow of celibacy. In order to learn Hindi, she journeyed first to Delhi and then to Haridwar. Then after further training at an ashram founded by Gandhi's disciple Vinoba Bhave, where she learned carding, spinning, and weaving, Mira Behn began to accompany Gandhi on his khadi tours, in which he instilled among the people of the villages the importance of independence through the revival of village industries, village government, village sanitation, and village education, which included the education of women. With Gandhi's advice, she traveled to Bihar, where with her knowledge of Hindi, she was able to support the khadi workers by introducing improved methods of carding and spinning. In 1929 she accompanied Gandhi on a khadi tour to the mountain town of Kausani, where her love of nature was fulfilled in her first sight of the eternal snows of the Himalayas.[7]

In the course of time, Mira Behn came to be known as one of Gandhi's closest associates, a distinction that took her to prison. In 1931, during his visit to the Round Table conference in London, she served as Gandhi's personal assistant. In 1932, with the resumption of the civil disobedience movement, Gandhi was arrested. From Bombay, Mira Behn collected information about the freedom struggle from all over the country and sent it to colleagues abroad to be published there. For this she was arrested and sentenced to three months' imprisonment in the Arthur Road prison in Bombay. On her release she was served with orders not to return to Bombay. She violated these orders and was arrested again and was sent to jail for another year. Her time in jail, however, provided the opportunity for some serious reading and study that deepened her understanding of Indian religious traditions and fortified her commitment to Gandhi's program of *sarvodaya* (universal uplift). In her first letter to Gandhi from jail she consulted him about books to read. He recommended first the Mahabharata and the Ramayana, the two great epics of the Hindu religious tradition. Later he recommended readings from the eleven principal Upanishads. She writes that their effect upon her was profound. "Here," she says, "I discovered things that seemed to be part of my inmost self, part of something I had known long before and since lost." "Here," she says, "there was no nightmare of the unanswerable, but instead a vast illumination of the Unknown making its contemplation not a horror, but an infinite inspiration."[8] During her second imprisonment, Gandhi added the recommendation of readings from the Vedas. In one of his many letters to her in prison he stated: "This course will certainly give you an insight into Hindu thought that would be valuable." And he adds, "I would balance this reading by a reading of the *Koran* and Amir Ali's *Spirit of Islam*."[9] As she read the Koran she wrote her impressions to Gandhi and received his reply: "You will find many more gems in the Koran."[10] In the Ramayana and the tale of Nala and Damayanti in the Mahabharata she was deeply moved by the conception of a woman's devotion to her beloved. "My idea of marriage," she says, "had always been something very sacred which I had silently cherished in my heart, an ideal of utter dedication, and self-expression through oneness with the beloved. And now in Sita and Damayanti I found wonderful pictures of that very ideal." Reading from the Upanishads and the Vedas, she says, "I heard the same note as in the music of Beethoven, and my heart stirred and then hushed again as if waiting for a later time."[11]

After her release from prison she went to Wardha, near Nagpur, where Gandhi lived. After consulting with Gandhi she undertook a speaking tour to England and America to present a true picture of happenings in the freedom struggle in India. Mira Behn was also instrumental in the founding of Sevagram Ashram that in the following years became the headquarters of Gandhi's constructive work and the independence struggle.[12] When the All India Congress Committee met in Allahabad in April 1942, Gandhi sent a draft resolution to this meeting with Mira Behn.

When it met again in Bombay on August 8 the Congress Committee adopted the famous quit India resolution. The following day Mira Behn was arrested along with Mahadev Desai, Gandhi's right hand man. Within days, Gandhi and his wife, Kasturba, a number of his associates, and the entire congress working committee were jailed. During her imprisonment in the Aga Khan Palace in Poona, Mira Behn witnessed the death of both Kasturba Gandhi and Mahadev Desai. She was finally released on May 6, 1944, with Gandhi and other associates.

After this imprisonment Mira Behn began to work more independently of Gandhi. It is evident from her writings that she began to recover the sense of communion with nature that had been so important in her youth and that had perhaps been neglected during the strenuous years of working with Gandhi in the struggle for political independence. The environmentalism that now emerges in her thought was expressed in a strong personal sense of devotion to nature, in a succession of efforts she undertook to establish communities in which human beings could live in communion with nature, and in a great many writings in support of nature and against its exploitation and abuse. Propagating Gandhi's program of constructive work, she set up Kisan (farmer) Ashram, between Roorkee and Haridwar. While this ashram was a success, she had other ambitions, especially in the area of cattle development. In 1946, acknowledging her expertise in agriculture, animal husbandry, and related subjects, the government of the state of Uttar Pradesh, known then as the United Provinces, appointed her as honorary special advisor for its newly established Grow More Food campaign. She says this introduced to her to "the absolutely new world" of government administration, a world with which she was not altogether comfortable.[13] Her ambition was to develop a center where human beings could work in harmony with nature to promote human development according to Gandhi's ideals.[14] To this end in 1947 she established Pashulok (animal world) Ashram, near Rishikesh, where she began research to improve cattle breeds for the hills. In one of his many letters, Gandhi expressed his approval of the concept and the name. The recovery of her sense of the wonder of nature is evident in her reflection on the setting she chose for the place. "The wild beauty of those great forests, and their wealth of animals and birds, stirred in me new strength. There is a vast vitality in untrammeled Nature which communicated itself to those who live with her." This, she says, was the first time she had come to live in a real jungle.[15]

It was there in the evening of January 30, 1948, that Mira Behn received the news of Gandhi's assassination. She was struck with grief.

Friends came to her in Rishikesh to make arrangements for her to go to Delhi. Her response was a reflection of her devotion to nature and to her understanding of Gandhi and his ambition for her. Hearing the news of his passing, she remembered his words to her that the spirit she loved was always with her. Remembering his admonition to "trust God and be where you are," she decided not to go. She made a visit to Delhi only after the rituals and observances of his passing were concluded. At that time she visited the site of his assassination and the cremation ground at Rajghat, but she found there no solace for her grief, and cried to herself: "Let me go back to the life and light of the fields and forests, where nature knows no such thing as mourning for the dead, because in her there is no death. For me Bapu is there, not here." With these reflections, she hastened back to Pashulok.[16] When she declined to be present at the immersion of Gandhi's ashes at the confluence of the Ganges and Yamuna rivers in Allahabad, his friends sent her a portion of his ashes for her to immerse in the Ganges at Rishikesh. She states that as she walked to the ghat with the little urn of his ashes in her hand, she lost any feeling of her body and did not so much as sense the ground beneath her naked feet. She writes: "Ganga's pure and sparkling water was swirling by the wooden platform that had been built out over the stream. As I cast the ashes into the swift blue current I felt, as never before, the glory of Nature who takes our earthly remains back to her bosom in all-embracing love."[17]

The Pashulok Ashram was not an unmitigated success. While government help was now available for many of its projects, Mira Behn found that bureaucracy often stood in the way of her purpose. Finally she was convinced that her work would be better done through a voluntary organization. She decided to put an end to the plans she had made for Pashulok and participate in the development of a registered organization called the Pashulok Seva Mandal. Its purpose as she conceived of it was "[t]o develop an area or areas where men and animals combine with Nature in the formation of a decentralized society demonstrative of Bapu's ideals for World Peace, where man in his own village will, along with his cattle, be self-sufficient, healthy and happy."[18] But this was not successful. Financial support for the endeavor gradually waned. Finally she decided to return the land of Pashulok to the government of Uttar Pradesh and began to look elsewhere for a place in which to realize her ideals.[19]

As stated above, Sunderlal's first encounter with Mira Behn was when he was general secretary of the Praja Mandal. In 1949, residing then at Pashulok near Rishikesh she was traveling by horse into the hills to find a venue for the ashram that was taking shape in her mind. In her travels she had come to Tehri. Having heard of her work, knowing of her close association with Gandhi, and knowing that she was committed to Gandhi's ideals, Sunderlal went to see her. He explained that because she was a woman of the ruling class she was accommodated in a large bungalow provided for guests of the state. But when he reached the room in which she was staying, he found her sitting on the floor and spinning at a portable *charkha*. Between them there was an instant rapport. Sunderlal explains that among Gandhian workers, there is no difference between philosophy and action, no distinction between the inside and the outside of the person. Gandhians are always eager to encourage younger workers. In the Gandhian movement, he says, there is no sense of competition. Politics, he says, makes little room for new workers. But the Gandhians are always eager to train new workers and to provide them with knowledge and opportunity for service. Sunderlal was then twenty-two. Mira Behn was fifty-six. She took a strong interest in Sunderlal because, as he put it, he was a youngster. To Sunderlal she was the embodiment of Gandhian principles. She had appropriated and assimilated the essence of Indian life as expressed in its philosophy and its religion. Our religion, he says, teaches us respect for all forms of life. That is why we worship the trees, the cow, and even the snake. The essence is that there should be reverence for all life on this earth. Although she was an English woman, Sunderlal found her to be more Indian than the Indians. Following their initial conversation, Mira Behn invited Sunderlal to her ashram near Rishikesh, which he visited from time to time.

Mira Behn eventually found what she believed was the place she was looking for, a scenic region replete with thick pine forests and a clear view of several glaciers. It was near the village of Geonli just twenty-six miles (forty-two kilometers) from Tehri, where Sunderlal was working. The forest department leased her two acres of land, which she called Gopal Ashram, taking the name from Lord Krishna in his role as cowherd.[20] In a volume celebrating the centenary of her birth, one of her associates, Krishna Murti Gupta, states that during her time in the Gopal Ashram he made frequent visits on foot to see her. He points out that on these journeys from Tehri, he sometimes had the company of Shri Sunderlal Bahuguna.[21] With independence and a new national government, Mira Behn found that development had become a national priority. But she questioned whether the development schemes that were then underway were sufficiently far sighted and whether they would benefit the people. She observed that "[h]uge industrial and other projects were being planned, for which gigantic sums of money had to be borrowed, or accepted as gifts from other countries. This was all so different to what one had pictured for free India."[22] In response she began the monthly publication *Bapu Raj Patrika*. The journal was produced in English and Hindi as well as Gujarati, Tamil, and Telugu. It was addressed in very simple language to the peasantry of India. Her objective "was to try to explain to the villagers the kind of self-reliant economy that Bapu had visualized for them, and to urge them to get together in a common demand for a simple decentralized society."[23]

Sunderlal came quickly to understand and support the ideals and objectives that Mira Behn developed. From her he derived much support for the development of his own environmental ideas and the purpose of his life. It was from her, he said to me, that he got his start in ecology. He also gave Mira Behn his help and support in the work of the journal in which these ideas were expressed. During these days he took weekly walks over the twenty-six miles (forty-two kilometers) from Tehri to Gopal Ashram to assist in the production of the Hindi translation of this publication. The journal was intended to propagate a number of principles that Mira Behn derived from Gandhi's thought:

1. There will be strong and healthy villages that will be self-sufficient in the manner of basic human needs like food, clothing and housing.

2. There will be a straightforward government in which there will be none to live in palaces or to consume petrol worth thousands of rupees; the administration will be mainly carried on by the Panchayats. The Panchayats will serve the villages and provide them proper guidance.

3. Laws will be simple without blood-sucking lawyers and people would not be required to run to the courts in big cities.

4. Police will function effectively and honestly and will serve the people by giving them due protection. The armed forces costing millions of rupees will be dismantled. Aircrafts would be dispensed with.

5. There will be no capitalists with their factories that destroy our own industries and there will be no landlords owning vast landed estates.

6. There will be good schools that will train our children to be honest and industrious.

7. All people will be required to put in physical labor, and nourishing and healthy food will be available to all.

8. We shall not resort to borrowing from any outside country. Our India will live simply, depending on its own strength, because dependence on others means becoming slaves.[24]

While publishing the journal, Mira Behn would travel by horse from one village to another, meeting with groups of farmers and addressing local communities. Yet her days at Gopal Ashram were also full of activity. Sunderlal explains that Mira Behn loved all aspects of nature but was especially committed to the care of cows. J. P. Uniyal, who worked as her secretary during these days, reports that after her morning session of letter writing and going through the newspapers of the previous day, she would immediately go to be among the animals, first of all to the cows. Uniyal states that Mira Behn was an ardent votary of ecological balance, organic farming, shallow plowing, and the use of compost and earthworms for preserving humus and that she carried on a sustained correspondence on these subjects with kindred spirits in the West, then chiefly among the Quakers.[25] Sunderlal points out that her love of animals even extended to the rats of the fields and on one occasion to a leopard. Sunderlal states that when he visited the ashram, he not only worked on the publication of *Bapu Raj Patrika* but also took an interest in the cows and worked in the vegetable garden. He relates that once while working with others in a maize field, they saw a rat emerging from a hole and went to find a cat to kill it. When they returned with the cat, they found Mira Behn feeding roasted maize to the rat, while birds were congregating to feed on raisins. He relates that another time a leopard was haunting the area. The villagers told her that the leopard was killing their cows and had to be trapped and killed. In accordance with the strategy of the hill people, they fashioned a trap with a live goat inside as bait. In the morning they were pleased to find that the trap was shut, but were disappointed to find only the goat inside. They were bewildered. Their curiosity was finally relieved as Mira Behn explained what had happened. She told the people that she was unable to sleep knowing that they we were intending to catch the leopard with such a trick. She told them that she had gotten up in the night and shut the trap herself. Reflecting further on the incident, Sunderlal explains that the leopard, apparently frustrated, departed from the village and was not seen again.

Throughout her career in India, Mira Behn wrote extensively for publications such as *Young India* and *Harijan*, publications that Gandhi founded during the freedom struggle. By the time Sunderlal came to know her, she was also writing for newspapers such as the *Hindustan Times* and the *Statesman*. Sunderlal states that Gandhi's son Devadas Gandhi was then the editor of the *Hindustan Times* and welcomed her contributions. While the importance of nature was a constant theme in her writings, the ecology of the hills became increasingly important after she moved there. Says Bahuguna, "When she first came to the Himalayan region during 1946–47, she sensed the dangers of deforestation for commercial forestry. Right then she had struck a warning against the grave danger of destruction of the Oak trees . . . She suggested a belt of broad leafed vegetation between cultivated land and reserved forest area."[26] Through these writings, according to Sunderlal, she was the very first to bring the environmental crisis of the Himalayas to public attention.

Her personal response to the disjunction between city life and rural life was a striking theme in these writings. In an article called "Paradise Lost," in 1946, she compares her brief stay in Delhi and a shopping visit to Chandni Chowk, to her arrival the next morning at Dehra Dun at the foot of the hills. Concerning Chandhi Chowk she says, "From all sides every sense was wounded. The din of traffic and shouting of harsh voices beat upon the ears, ugly sights of dirt and tawdriness hurt the eyes, and nasty smells invaded the nose." Approaching Dehra Dun at dawn, and looking out the train carriage window, she felt as if paradise were spread before her eyes. "The air was so clear and fresh, the forest rich in its autumn verdure—and now came a brook of crystal water dancing and sparkling over its rocky bed with flowering bushes and tall, feathery grasses on its banks." Continuing, she observes, "The forest opened out into a broad glen, the sun had risen over the mountains to the east, and a glimmer of golden light in the opening of the forest, showed Gangaji winding her sacred way towards Haridwar. My heart sang with the birds of the forest in thanksgiving to God." In the midst of this beauty she finds herself thinking of the people of the city, and questions in her mind, "Have they come to such a pass that they prefer that to this? Have their eyes lost the power to see God in nature?" She concludes that modern man has fallen victim to a cruel disease, "and glories in that sickness, calling it progress, enlightenment, knowledge!"[27]

But while she could rhapsodize about their richness and diversity, she recognized that all was not well in the hills. During her travels in the search of a site for Gopal Ashram she made many observations concerning environmental conditions which she published in seven installments in *Harijan* beginning in January of 1951. She called them "Himalayan

Lessons."[28] One observation concerned the shortage of water and fuel. "One hears of the shortage of wood and water in many Himalayas villages, but to realize what it means one has got to experience it. This long mountain ridge running from above Chamba Khal to Tehri, has been practically denuded of Banj [Himalayan oak], which in turn has resulted in the drying up of many of the springs; and the pine trees, though fairly numerous, have all had their lower boughs lopped off. The consequence is that fire-wood is almost non-existent." She notes that the peasants walk for miles to collect fuel for their domestic needs. Such observations brought her to the realization "that fuel is as important as food itself, for without it no *rotis* [breads] can be made or anything else cooked." She notes that in the place where she was staying there was a little inferior water available during the rainy season, but that drinking water had to be fetched from a spring a quarter mile down a precipitous path. She notes further that by the end of October the nearby water would be completely dried up. By that time people had to go down to a lower spring that got weaker with the advance of the dry season. These were conditions of the common people to which the privileged could have little understanding. "Town people living in houses with water laid on, and even country folk with wells nearby," she said, "can have no idea what such permanent water shortage means. It is such experiences that bring home to one the real needs of vast masses of our people."[29]

Mira Behn believed that the greatest material asset of the hills was in the forests. She notes that the government receives huge sums of money from its timber, but gives little to the villagers. "Water channels and tanks, better mule-paths, and better and more bridges are a crying need." While she recognized that some such measures were then being undertaken, she argues that they should be carried out on a more ambitious scale and agues that such efforts would profit the country. She argues that every rupee the government spends on water facilities would increase the food production of the country. "My impression" she writes, "is that there must be hundreds and thousands of untapped little springs and streams which if harnessed and canalized, could be brought to the fields." These would each be small undertakings, capable of giving immediate results, and of being kept in repair by the villagers themselves. She argues that with a little encouragement the villagers could learn and apply the practice of compost making and undertake better bunding of their terraced fields. "If these things could be achieved," she said, "the face of the countryside would be changed."[30]

At the time he met her, Sunderlal had already been involved in Gandhian activities. He had practiced spinning, addressed caste issues and the problem of untouchability, and he had suffered for his commitments. Yet his understanding of development was not yet fully formed. He explained to me that for him the idea of development meant that there should be motor roads, that there should be cities and all the facilities and conveniences associated with them. To him British education seemed a reasonable means to that end. He states that in his association with Mira Behn, he came to understand that Gandhi saw things from their roots. In this way, he says, Gandhi's way of seeing things was quite different from what he had known. Gandhi wanted to bring about a basic change. He wanted to change not only the lives of the people, but the whole economic system. For Gandhi, as for Mira Behn, the cities were the centers of exploitation. India, says Sunderlal, had been a country of villages. But British rule had changed this system and impoverished the villages. For Mira Behn the fundamental need was to regenerate the villages. But she also recognized that the regeneration of the villages of the hills depended upon nature and that the colonial economic system had altered the balance of nature in the hills. For Mira Behn the basic issue that touched the lives of the people of the hills was the use to which the land was put. Sunderlal explains that Mira Behn was against the proliferation of motor roads, because they bring no benefit to the local people and they damage their terraced fields. She argued that improved mule paths would be a better investment for the people.

Mira Behn was disappointed with many of the development schemes that the government had been supporting. In an article in *Harijan* in 1949, "Development or Destruction" and the follow-up article "Startling Facts," she points out that much of what has been called development has come at the cost of grasslands that had once been grazing land for cattle. She argues that the true development of such lands would have included the introduction of more appropriate species of grasses and the cultivation of fodder crops. "We can enormously increase our output of grain by better nourishment of the present fields with well-composted farmyard manure. This is the safe and sound method. Unfortunately it is not so easy or quick in immediate spectacular results as ploughing up of grasslands."[31] She saw another danger in the proliferation of large irrigation systems that have led to water-logging and soil alkalinity and have resulted in thousands of acres of once rich lands going out of cultivation. She points out the consensus among scientists that crops nourished with artificial fertilizers are inferior in quality to those nourished with compost and notes reports that vegetables and fodder grown with artificial fertilizers are actually harmful to men and beasts and that soil fed with artificial fertilizers, though it gives an impressive harvest for the first few years, eventually loses its strength, while soil fed with compost becomes richer in strength and texture over the course of time. Another of her concerns was the development of sugar cane, which "occupies the land on which it is grown for a period long enough for growing two to three grain crops." She states that the farmer gives his best land and most of the available water and manure to sugar cane. In this way the growing of sugar cane "interferes with the growing of grain crops to a much larger extent than the actual acreage of land occupied by the cane." She suggests that more appropriate and wholesome sources of sugar are the palm trees that grow freely on land unsuited for cultivation.[32] Much of what is called development, she says, leads in the long run to destruction. In schemes of this nature, she says, the interest of the people plays anything but a critical role. In the text of her writings her identity with India and with the landscape of the Himalayas is evident. "All this means," she says, "that we must not rest on our oars and think that, because we have won Swaraj, we are now safe from further exploitation. On the contrary, we have got to be very much awake, for this exploitation from within is even more dangerous than the former foreign exploitation, because it carries with it the glamour of apparent patriotism."[33] Our Mother Earth, she says, does her best to feed us all and we ought to serve her as dutiful children.[34]

Mira Behn's concern about the degradation of nature was integral to her concern for the villages. In her writings concerning the environment she became increasingly interested in the ecology of the hills, where the economic welfare of the villages depends perhaps most directly upon the condition of the forests. After living in the Himalayas for several years she observed that floods that occur in the North of India seem to be getting worse year by year. In an article in the *Hindustan Times* in 1950 she announced, "There is something radically wrong in the Himalaya, and that 'something' is, without doubt, connected with the forests." The problem, she argues, is not simply that the hills are being denuded, but that there has been a gradual but significant shift in the species of trees that cover these hills. The change, which she had observed over time, had been a shift from the Himalayan oak (called banj), to chir pine (also called chil pine). This change, she says, has been allowed to proceed, because the oak forests provide no revenue to the government while the chir pine is profitable, providing revenue both from timber and from resin for turpentine. She argues, however, that the profit from the timber and resin of the chir pine is hardly equal to the damage that has occurred from floods as a result of the loss of the oak. In one of her most well known ecological insights, she states: "The Banj leaves, falling as they do, year by year, create a rich black mould in which develops a thick tangled mass of undergrowth (bushes, creepers, and grasses), which in their turn add to the leaf-mould deposit and the final result is a forest in which almost all the rain water gets absorbed. Some of it evaporates back into the air and the rest percolates slowly down to the lower altitudes, giving out here and there beautiful sweet and cool springs. It would be difficult to imagine a more ideal shock-absorber for the monsoon rains than a Banj forest." She explains further that by contrast the chir pine produces a dry carpet of needles that absorbs nothing and prevents the development of significant undergrowth. "When the torrential rains of the monsoon beat down on these southern slopes of the Himalayas, much of the pine-needle carpet gets washed away with the water and erosion invariably takes place, because these needles, being non-absorbent, create no leaf-mould, but only a little inferior soil, which is easily washed out from the rocks and stones."[35]

The reason for the reduction of the oak and the spread of the pine, she says, is that the government has not adequately organized and controlled the lopping of the oak trees for cattle fodder. "When the Banj trees get weak and scraggy from overlopping, the Chil pine gets a footing in the forest, and once it grows up and starts casting its pine needles on the ground, all other trees die out."[36] Because the pine produces revenue, the government has little motivation to reverse this trend. She does not blame the villagers for the reduction of the oak. Their behavior is a predictable response to economic stress. She states that they fully understand the importance of the oak forests, without which their cattle would starve, the springs would dry up, and floods would devastate their terraced fields. But she argues that the problem is by no means beyond solution. If trees are lopped methodically, they could still provide a large quantity of fodder for the cattle. If the chir pines were pushed back to their ideal altitude of 3,500 to 5,000 feet, and if the oak forests were restored, then the stress on the trees would be reduced, and fodder available for cattle would increase. She points out that this strategy would by no means eliminate the revenue from the chir pine but only keep it within reasonable limits. Better management of pine forests, including the enforcement of tapping rules that mitigate the damage to the trees, would maintain a healthier pine forest and produce better economic results.

For Mira Behn, the banj forests are the center of nature's economic cycle on the southern slopes of the Himalayas. To consent to their destruction, she argues, is to cut out the heart of the whole natural structure. She acknowledges that because relations between the forest department and the peasantry are strained, the forest department cannot bring about these changes on its own. Her solution would require cooperation between the forest department and the villagers. She suggests that the forest department field staff should not only be increased but be given special training to engender a new outlook towards the peasantry. Constructive workers should organize village committees and village guards to work along with the forest department to protect and maintain the forests. By such means she envisions a long-term project to control the lopping of the trees and a gradual recovery of the banj forests. "The forests of the Himalayas," she says, "are the guardians of the Northern Plains, which, in their turn, are the Granary of India. Surely such guardians deserve the utmost care and attention that the Government can give them."[37]

Sunderlal not only read her many essays and articles but had the opportunity to discuss with her the many ecological observations and insights for which she came to be known. It would perhaps be not too much to suggest that during these days Sunderlal had become an apprentice to this remarkable woman. He refers to her thinking as critical to his own developing understanding of the relationship between the life of the villages and the life of nature. He described her influence on this life and work as comparable to that of Sri Dev Suman. He states explicitly that it was from her that he received his inspiration, "particularly the inspiration to serve the mountain villages."[38] Sunderlal understood the gravity of the ecological issues about which Mira Behn wrote and her understanding of the kind of true development that was needed in the hills.

Although Mira Behn was now residing in the Himalayas, she continued to take a keen interest in developments in other parts of the country, and she was far from pleased with all she saw. Yet she saw that community projects for rural development were being initiated, and she believed that a simplified experimental project oriented toward Gandhi's ideals could demonstrate his intention for rural India. She believed that from one such living example, Gandhi's methods of rural development could spread. This project would have more local control than other government-sponsored projects. At a gathering near Wardha, she had the opportunity to meet with Jawaharlal Nehru and put the idea before him of starting such a project with Gopal Ashram as its headquarters. Nehru readily agreed with her conception, and with his blessing she went to Delhi to work out the details with the Central Organization for Community Projects. With the approval of the central government she then went to Lucknow to the state government that administrates local community projects. There she sensed that the state government saw a challenge to their controlling power. But because the central government was willing to provide 1.2 million rupees (then about two hundred thousand U.S. dollars) in support of the project, she pressed her case with the state authorities and felt she had prevailed. She then returned to Tehri to work out the final details and the budget with the local authorities. She notes that the people of the Tehri Garhwal region took a keen interest in the project.[39]

Sunderlal states that she formed a working committee and appointed him as the project manager. His responsibility was to oversee the entire scheme and to guide the people in the application of Gandhi's principles to the project. Her hopes ran high. She states that on the day of the inauguration of the project, October 2, 1953, "villagers turned up from far and wide, most of them dressed in their own homespun and woven woolen clothes—hardy, simple people who had covered miles of rough mountain paths without turning a hair." She observed, however, that the government officials had more difficulty in reaching the place. Sunderlal points out that some of the officers had sustained injuries on the way, and it proved difficult for some of them even to sit with Mira Behn on the ground. Mira Behn gives more details: "The District Planning Officer had fallen off his mule and been taken back to Tehri hospital. The Divisional Forest Officer had fallen of his horse and arrived with a bandaged head, and afterwards the District Magistrate, on return to headquarters, spent a week in bed. Our project was not popular." But before long they began getting instructions from Lucknow that demonstrated to her that the bureaucracy was not about to let go its hold on the project. Mira Behn hurried to Lucknow for further talks and was assured that the project would be permitted to develop along the lines of her vision. But on her return to Gopal Ashram, she found the same problems emerging again. From these experiences and others like them, she drew her final conclusion. She states: "If this was, after all, to be just an orthodox project, and not the simplified, decentralized experiment that we had planned, then it was better to hand the whole thing over to the Government to run their own way. And that is what I did."[40] After a brief visit to Delhi, she returned to Gopal Ashram and in ten days had packed her belongings, distributed her animals, and departed. In Delhi she had come to know about new possibilities for the development of cattle breeding projects in Kashmir. She had decided to go there. Through her contact with the Kashmiri government, she selected a suitable site for her activities. She called the place Gaobal, from *gao* (cow), and *bal* (strength). It was the place for the well-being of the cow. She proposed a scheme to import Dexter cattle from England and to cross-breed them with the local cattle for a more hearty variety for the hills. After arranging for the transport of the Dexter cows, and after their arrival in India, her plan for this project came into full swing. With Gaobal located at an altitude of six thousand feet, she found good pastures for summer grazing at higher altitudes. The forest department first sanctioned her use of thirty acres at an altitude of seven thousand feet and then, in the third year, an additional open sweeping grassland of sixteen acres at eighty-six hundred feet. She exclaims, "And what a place that was! On the one side there was a clear view right down the Sind Valley, and on the other three sides there was a vast untrammeled forest of firs and pines intermixed with rich undergrowth."[41]

But just as the cross-breeding program was beginning to enjoy success, the animal husbandry policy of the state government underwent a change. Foreign breeds of cattle were no longer wanted. As her project came to an end, the Dexter cows were moved to Shimla in Himachal Pradesh, while Mira Behn and her small party returned to Tehri Garhwal. Through these experiences it became clear to Mira Behn that she could no longer be engaged with government projects. With little money left and her hopes for Pashulok, Gopal Ashram, and Gaobal all unfulfilled, she found a picturesque place in the Garhwal hills near Chamba. She called it Pakshi Kunj (grove of birds). There she turned to writing her memoirs, and there she began to recall the music that had moved her so many years before. Recognizing that the heat and malaria of the plains and the steep terrain of the hills was a challenge to her health, she resolved to return to Europe. She first went to England and then to Vienna, where she continued to campaign through her writings and lectures for the preservation of the Himalayan environment and the propagation of Gandhi's ideas.

Sunderlal remained in touch with Mira Behn through her travels to Kashmir, back to Tehri Garhwal, and to Europe. While she departed from India in 1959 disappointed with the projects she had begun, her legacy remains in the impact she left upon the lives of the people of the hills. There is perhaps no life upon whom this impact was more pronounced than that of Bahuguna himself. Following her departure, Sunderlal began to organize community groups and committees at the grass roots toward a common demand for the simple, decentralized, and sustainable society Gandhi had envisioned. One of the most important results of her work in the hills was the organization of labor cooperatives that eventually contributed to the emergence of a movement of the people in the 1970s known as Chipko. In 1981, his involvement with this movement brought Sunderlal Bahuguna to Europe where again he was able to meet with

Mira Behn, this time in Vienna. She was pleased to hear that her call to save the mountains was being voiced by the people. Sunderlal told her, "When you tried to awaken us, we still continued to sleep. Now when we are active you are so far from us." "Go to nature," she replied, "She will restore the Himalaya to its original glory."[42] The climate in Austria was cold, and Sunderlal did not have warm clothing. Mira Behn presented him with a jacket that provided for his need. He states that he accepted that gift as *prasad* and that he has kept it to this day. *Prasad*, he said, means divine blessing. He explained that when it comes from a patriarch or a matriarch, a gift is regarded as a blessing from the divine. Mira Behn died in Vienna on July 20, 1982.

Chapter 6

Marriage and the
Parvatiya Navjeevan Ashram

In his work with the Praja Mandal in Tehri, Sunderlal came into close contact with the emerging Congress Party. Many in the party had strong ambitions for Bahuguna in the political arena. But in the course of almost eight years as general secretary of the Praja Mandal, Bahuguna was not convinced that party politics would effectively bring about the kind of society that Gandhi had envisioned for the hills or for the nation. In 1954, as general Secretary of the local Congress Party, he began to organize meetings to spread Gandhi's constructive program and his message of social reform and to attract the youth to this work. Bharat Dogra points out that it was in the course of this organizational work that he met Vimla Nautiyal, a young woman of twenty-three. Having come from neighboring villages, they had actually known of one another from childhood. But now Vimla Nautiyal was working in the hills under the guidance of another celebrated European disciple of Gandhi, Sarala Behn.[1] Sarala Behn had already been a decisive influence in the life of this young woman, and her influence would soon have an impact upon the life of Sunderlal as well. A decisive change in their lives was about to take place.

Sarala Behn had come to India from England. Her original purpose, like that of Mira Behn, was to work with Gandhi in the cause of freedom. But her background, as Sunderlal explains it, was very different from that of Mira Behn. While Mira Behn had come from a privileged background, Sarala Behn was a woman of the common people. She was born in London on Good Friday in 1901 and was named Catherine Mary Heilemann.[2] In her autobiography she explains that her mother was British but that her grandmother was German. Her father was born in Switzerland but had immigrated to England by way of France. She states that for these reasons she grew up without a strong sense of belonging to an exclusive community or having a strong national identity. At the same time she grew up deeply affected by the teachings of Jesus, particularly his teachings of love and compassion, nonviolence, and the repudiation of hatred. During the First World War she was puzzled that the priests of her village invoked the name of God for victory over their enemies when she was sure that the priests of their enemies were doing the same. As a young adult she became increasingly uncomfortable with such attitudes and eventually joined an alternative community where people of differing backgrounds lived together. There she met two students from India who impressed her deeply. From them she began to learn about their country, its history and culture, and its freedom struggle. She read the works of such figures as Rammohan Roy, Swami Vivekananda, Rabinranath Tagore, and Mohandas Gandhi.

One day while walking in the forests of Surrey the thought of going to India came to her mind. After some reflection she wrote to Gandhi and received a reply from one of his colleagues. It stated that many people come to Gandhi's ashram but are not able to adjust to the tough living conditions and become a problem to others. Gandhi's advice was that she should not come. After writing to other prominent leaders and receiving similar replies, she determined that she needed a skill that would make her useful. She took training as a nurse and studied economics, social science, political science, and psychology. Eventually she received a letter from a man named Mohan Singh in Udaipur in Rajasthan, who invited her to join him to work in a new and revolutionary school. Although she insisted that she was not experienced in education, he assured her that her skills were needed. With difficulty she managed to get a visa for India and sailed from Liverpool in January 1932. It was in Udaipur that she was called Sarala Behn or Sarala Devi. While working with Mohan Singh she heard about another educational institution in Wardha, near Nagpur, dedicated to the education of women. In October of 1935 during a school vacation she decided to visit Wardha. Having received no reply to a letter she wrote to the institution, she sent a telegram before setting out. On her arrival at the station she was greeted by someone from the institution.

Having tried to catch a glimpse of Gandhi when he visited London for the Round Table Conference on India, and having missed him again when he visited Bombay for a Congress Convention, Sarala Behn now was about to visit his ashram near Wardha. She did not know that this visit would be the occasion for a face-to-face meeting with the man whose ideals had motivated her voyage to India. But Gandhi had seen her telegram and was waiting to meet her. Her meeting with him meant a decisive change in her life. It resulted in her departure from Udaipur, her joining the Sevagram Ashram near Wardha, her involvement with all aspects of the life of the ashram there, and especially with Gandhi's constructive program. But the heat of Wardha, like that of Udaipur, was difficult for her to bear, and her health suffered. Gandhi was concerned about her and suggested that a more appropriate climate for her work would be found in the hills. Thus, on her own, she began to explore to find a place where she could work, at an altitude where health issues would not be a problem. She found such a place in the picturesque hill station of Kausani, near Almora in the Kumaon hills, at an altitude of almost six thousand feet. There she also became aware of the challenges to the life and work of the women of the hills. One of the critical features of Gandhi's constructive program was the education of children. Sarala Behn recognized that hill regions had little opportunity for the education of children, and least of all for girls. In the course of time, she secured land and was given an old house as the venue for an educational institution for girls. Her ambition was to teach girls according to Gandhi's vision of what had been called *Nai Talim*, the New Education. Bahuguna informed me that during this time she also visited the homes of many freedom fighters jailed for their activities in the freedom movement and gave them her support. Because she was known to support the freedom movement, the local police viewed her as a dangerous person. Thus, before her plans for the institution had progressed very far, the local authorities placed her under house arrest. When she received their orders, however, she refused to be confined to her dwelling and declared that she would proceed with her activities as usual. For the violation of her house arrest, the authorities then sentenced her to a short term in jail. As a British woman jailed for activities in support of Indian independence, she impressed even her Indian jailers with her commitment to India's freedom struggle. She also became acquainted with many other freedom fighters. On her release the authorities informed her that there would be no further restrictions on her movements or activities. With that assurance she continued to develop her plans for an institution committed to the education and uplift of women. In 1946 that institution opened with a student body of six local girls, all the sisters and daughters of Indian freedom fighters. She called it Lakshmi Ashram.

Gandhi's idea of education for children was a radical departure from the system of education that came to India with the British. "Basic education," he said, "is meant to transform village children into model villagers. It is principally designed for them."[3] The inspiration for such education, he says, had to come from the villages themselves, and it is to the villages that the benefit of such education belongs. Gandhi also held that women in India had been suppressed under customs and laws in which they have had no hand. He held that "in a plan of life based on non-violence, woman has as much a right to shape her own destiny as man has to shape his."[4] Implementing these ideas, Sarala Behn developed an educational system that combined practical knowledge with academic learning, a form of education that would enable them to realize their freedom to work toward a free society. Here education included not only reading and writing but spinning and weaving for the production of clothing, as well as agriculture and the rearing of cattle to enable each village to which the girls would return to become self-sufficient in food, clothing, and shelter. As Sunderlal put it, it was education that combined the development of head, heart, and hands. Lakshmi Ashram, moreover, would be self-reliant and governed locally so that Sarala Behn would have the freedom to move about and work elsewhere as well. Her educational program also entailed outreach to local villages. She took students to the villages who educated the villagers by means of campfires with folk songs and plays on subjects such as respect for women, the equality of women, the dangers of alcohol, and the injustice of untouchability, dowry, and the selling of brides. Bahuguna states that through its education of girls and its outreach to villages, Lakshmi Ashram brought about an awakening among the women of the hills. In the course of time they became the pioneers of the *sharab bandi* (stop alcohol) movement and eventually the Chipko Movement.

Vimla Nautiyal from Malideval in Tehri Garhwal was one of Sarala Behn's first students at Lakshmi Ashram. Born in 1932, she was one of seven children of a forest officer from the Tehri Garhwal region, five of whom were daughters. Her father held progressive views on several social issues. He opposed discrimination against the lower castes and believed in the equality of women. He wanted to bring up his sons and daughters as equals. Her mother, who came from a family of royal priests, was remarkably open minded. When she taught Vimla to pay respect to her elders, she taught her to pay respect to the elders of the low caste families as well. When she addressed a male visitor as *bhai* (brother), she used the same term for a visitor of the lower castes.[5] Her father's assignments in various locations brought her family into contact with the broader issues in the political arena of the day. At an early age both of her brothers, Budhi Sagar and Vidya Sagar, were involved in the freedom movement, and both of them went to jail. When meetings of the freedom fighters were organized, Vimla went from house to house to collect donations and food for the meetings. Dedicated freedom fighters recognized that the task was now to reform society and reduce the burden of poverty. In the hills, this involved addressing discrimination against women and the hardship of their lives. Conditions required dedicated women activists to work in villages.[6] Sarala Behn founded Lakshmi Ashram to address such issues as these.

Even in her work with the freedom movement, Vimla came to see that social convention placed limitations on her activities. Thus when her older brother, Budhi Sagar, was released from jail and came home to tell her about a new school for women that had been founded by Gandhi's disciple Sarala Behn, she was intrigued. He told her that if she and others were interested, he would accompany them to the ashram. Vimla and three other girls from the region enthusiastically agreed. Thus in 1949, with her three friends, Vimla was admitted as a student of the Lakshmi Ashram. While the work of the ashram was an adjustment for the girls, they were impressed that Sarala Behn took an active role in the work as well. Sarala Behn was impressed with Vimla's intelligence, her industry and organizational skills, and her ready grasp of Gandhi's ideas. In the course of time she gave Vimla more and more responsibilities in the life of the ashram. As her activities and responsibilities increased, Vimla heard about the *bhoodan* (land gift movement) that Vinoba Bhave had been bringing to the attention of the followers of Gandhi.

Born in 1895, Vinoba Bhave was a student in Baroda when he first read about Gandhi.[7] In 1916 he resolved to join Gandhi's ashram in Ahmedabad, and when a school was added to the facilities of the ashram, Vinoba was appointed as religious instructor. His moral and spiritual development at Sabarmati won him such admiration from Gandhi that when a branch of the ashram was set up at Wardha in 1921, Gandhi sent Vinoba to Wardha to oversee the institution. Before the assassination of Gandhi, Vinoba Bhave had been among Gandhi's closest disciples, and after his death many followers turned to Vinoba for guidance and inspiration.[8] Vinoba Bhave wrote extensively on many subjects within the gamut of Gandhi's philosophy, including education, religion, and economics. He carried these ideas to the villages by means of *padyatras* (foot marches). Under British rule a system of land management called the zamindari system had assigned ownership rights over large tracts of lands to landlords. Landless peasants worked on land rented from a handful of landowning families who paid taxes to their colonial overlords. Many of the landless supported the national struggle for independence with the expectation that when the British departed, the land would be returned to the tiller.[9]

The basis of what Vinoba called *bhoodan* or land gift was the conviction "that the land is for all, and that no individual ought to exercise rights of ownership in it."[10] But his approach to this issue was derived from his commitment to Gandhi's doctrine of ahimsa or nonviolence, and his doctrine of trusteeship. In 1951 Vinoba inaugurated the *bhoodan* movement to persuade wealthy landowners to voluntarily donate land for distribution among the landless. The idea, however, was larger than simply a plan for the redistribution of land. Writing in 1955, he put it this way, "The basic idea of Bhoodan is that wealth, intelligence and every such thing which a man has, belongs to society and they should go to it. If somebody retains something, he is a trustee for it."[11] The program proved successful. In the course of six laborious years Vinoba and his workers succeeded in acquiring four million acres of land for distribution.[12] At the outset of this movement Vinoba had sent a call to Gandhian ashrams for volunteers to join him in this mission.

At the tender age of twenty Vimla was impressed with the strength of these ideas and consulted Sarala Behn as to whether she might take a leave from her responsibilities in Lakshmi Ashram to participate in this work. Sarala Behn was very supportive of this plan. She wrote the secretary of the *bhoodan* movement expressing her support for Vimla to spend a year working with them. Having received some basic orientation to the approach of the movement, Vimla was sent first to the region around Gaya in Bihar, where the exploitation of the landless was the most severe and where the response to the land gift movement was most hostile and intimidating. The procedure was to form small groups that would travel to remote areas to present the ideas of the *bhoodan* movement to the landholders of the region. Vinoba's approach to the landholder was to suggest that the land holder should think of him, the representative of the *bhoodan* movement, as a sixth son. If the land holder had five sons, he would naturally divide his land equally among them. Without depriving any of his sons of all their land, Vinoba suggested that he should consider donating the sixth part of his land to those who had been tilling the soil these many years. Vimla states that in some places the response was so hostile that the *bhoodan* workers would receive neither food nor a place to stay. In others they were treated warmly and received land gift papers from cheerful donors. Collecting these papers they would return to their base of operations to rest for another round of visits.[13]

Vinoba Bhave and his co-workers were impressed with Vimla's capacity for hard work in adverse conditions. Following her tour of duty in Gaya, she worked further in the area around Ranchi. After a year of work with the movement, she returned with enhanced vision to Kausani and to her work with Sarala Behn. These were meaningful days. She then began to travel with Sarala Behn from village to village raising consciousness among women, talking to people about the need to reduce inequalities and injustices and to realize true independence. During school vacations Vimla went with Sarala Behn and fellow students to visit villages where they would construct a stage and where they would enact plays, illustrating the social teachings of Gandhi and Vinoba. On one such occasion Sarala Behn took a group of her students to Tehri. Vimla was on her own home turf with relatives and family members in the audience. She was directing the play. In his capacity as secretary of the Congress Committee, Sunderlal was making announcements and introducing their guests from Kausani. Sunderlal was twenty-seven and not yet married. Having lost both of his parents early in his life, his elder brother, now a lecturer in the local college, was concerned that he should be married soon. His brother was sitting in the audience with Vimla's father, a retired forest officer. Vimla's father was proud of her work and of her achievements. But friends and relatives were reminding him that Vimla would soon be exceeding the appropriate age for marriage. The conversation between them turned to the question whether Sunderlal and Vimla might not be appropriate marriage partners for one another.

Sunderlal had been a freedom fighter in the area. He strongly supported the participation of women in social work. He had organized the meeting to which Sarala Behn and Vimla had come. In that context Sunderlal and Vimla had met and seemed to relate well to one another. Their families were from villages only a half kilometer from one another, and Sunderlal seemed to be poised for a successful political career. After the guests had left for Kausani, Vimla's father sent her a letter informing her that he had found the perfect marriage partner for her and informed her of the likely date for their wedding. Sunderlal recalls that when Sarala Behn received word of this proposal, she was furious. By now Vimla had become Sarala Behn's principal assistant. She had a deep emotional investment in Vimla. She had entrusted important responsibilities to Vimla with the expectation that she would continue to work with her in the hill villages and eventually succeed her as the leader of this work. Sarala Behn had come from a tradition in which women sometimes remained unmarried in order to devote themselves to a calling. She was not especially sympathetic to the practice of arranged marriages. Moreover, the demands of Vimla's work among the villages seemed to Sarala Behn to preclude the possibility of marriage and family life. She argued that Vimla "should remain single and work with me." While the celibate life for women was not unknown in the traditions of India, it was not widely practiced in the hills. After discussing the matter with Sarala Behn, Vimla indicated that she needed time to consider the implication of such a marriage for her work. Having already secured Sunderlal's consent to write Vimla with a marriage proposal, Vimla's father was embarrassed. Sunderlal remembers that her father became very sad and felt that he had been insulted by Sarala Behn's remark. It was an awkward situation. Sarala Behn wanted Vimla to remain single. Her father wanted her married and could not think of a better marriage proposal. Sunderlal and Vimla stood in the middle.

To this unsettling situation there came a mediating influence. Dada Dharmadhikari was a respected representative of Gandhi's philosophy who had arrived in the area to help spread his message to the people. Sunderlal explains that Dada Dharmadhikari was a descendent of a long line of professionals who were trusted in villages for their ability to render an appropriate verdict among disputing parties, particularly in matters touching religion. Born in 1899, he had left college in his second year to join Gandhi's noncooperation movement. Following that he had studied philosophy and especially the philosophy of Vedanta on his own. Having written many books on a range of topics in Gandhi's philosophy, he was highly regarded all over the country and considered one of the key exponents of Gandhi's philosophy of *sarvodaya*. From their engagement with Gandhi's *sarvodaya* activities Dharmadhikari also came to know both Sunderlal and Vimla and was in favor of their marriage. When he heard of Sarala Behn's disapproval, he was inclined to believe that Sarala Behn had not fully understood the positive impact that a marriage might have in the life of *sarvodaya* workers. While he acknowledged with Gandhi that women had long been oppressed, he did not believe that a life of celibacy was inherently a more effective arrangement than marriage for a social worker. His own viewpoint is perhaps best expressed in the short piece he wrote on the mutual fellowship of man and woman. He tells the story of a village school teacher who asked a class to punctuate a sentence that read: "Woman without her man is a savage." The girls punctuate the sentence, "Woman! Without her, man is a savage." When the boys punctuated the sentence it read, "Woman, without her man, is a savage." Vinoba's own opinion was that both the boys and the girls were right, but each only in part: "The honest truth," he says, "is that both man and woman are each a savage without the other. Both are only halves of an integrated human personality. Neither would be human or humane without the other."[14]

Concerning the present case, he stated that a couple who were compatible and could work well together could have a stronger impact on society than either working alone. Sarala Behn was not accustomed to a discussion concerning marriage in which the dialogue occurred only between the guardians of the couple. She suggested that the couple should also talk. "Let them understand one another," she said. "They should get to know each other and then decide." Finally it was decided that the couple should correspond with one another for the course of a year to determine whether they were sufficiently compatible to work effectively together. All parties were pleased with this resolution.

Over the following year, many letters passed between Vimla and Sunderlal. In the course of that time Vimla placed one critical condition upon their future marriage. It had two parts. The first was that Sunderlal must give up his career in politics. The second was that they must settle in a village in the hills and there together establish an ashram modeled after the ashram that Sarala Behn had founded in Kausani. This was to follow Gandhi's challenge that social activists should live in villages and work towards the uplift of the people. Having already become disenchanted with party politics, Sunderlal readily agreed to these conditions. Together they began to search for an appropriate place to start such an undertaking. They wanted to find a village in a remote and backward region where their work would have the most impact. They found it in Silyara in a picturesque valley on the Balganga River just twenty-two miles (thirty-five kilometers) to the north and east of Tehri, several miles from the nearest motor road. There with the approval of the villagers they acquired from the state government two and a half acres of common land. Long before their wedding Sunderlal arrived at the place and built a hut, where he resided with some of the students who were with him at Thakkar Bapa hostel in Tehri.

Their wedding on June 19, 1956, was an unusual event for the hills. Weddings in the region would normally involve a wedding band with music and dancing, an elaborate feast, and a dowry. This wedding would have none of those. Food was prepared by local people. There was no band, no marriage party, no special dress, and no dowry. The wedding was performed by a local Brahmin who administered the seven vows and the walk around the fire. Despite the absence of the usual wedding fanfare, the marriage was well attended. Sunderlal states that a large number of people came to see what was happening in such an unusual wedding. But for all who attended it was a meaningful event, and the total cost of the wedding was forty-nine rupees.

Bahuguna has often made the point that both he and his wife are products of the pioneering work of the two most celebrated English disciples of Gandhi: Mira Behn and Sarala Behn. The combined influence of both of these remarkable women and their contribution to the welfare of the people of the hills is evident in the activities that Sunderlal and Vimla began with their marriage. After their wedding, the guests departed: Sunderlal's relatives and Vimla's relatives to the region of Tehri, and Sarala Behn back to Kausani. Then with the facility of just two huts, Sunderlal and Vimla settled down together to establish an ashram dedicated to the education of the children of the region, especially the girls. They called it Parvatiya Navjeevan Ashram (ashram for new life in the hills). They chose not to take grants or subsidies from outside sources but to support their work from the contributions of local people and the labor of their own hands. To meet their own food needs they often worked in the fields of others for which they were given a share of the crop. While Vimla taught the village children, Sunderlal worked as a laborer. In the evenings he held classes for the boys. During the day he worked, among other projects, on an irrigation canal that brought water from the Balganga River to the fields. Both their days and evenings were filled with productive activity. Sunderlal also started a water mill to grind flour for the village people. In his work at the water mill, Sunderlal was able to hear about the needs and concerns of the village people.

In the period after India achieved independence, the principal priority of the new national government was development. But as Mira Behn had earlier observed, the kind of development they conceived of was not always along the lines that Gandhi had envisioned. More frequently they were projects generated at the top levels of political authority and passed down to the level of the people, many of whom were employed to work on such government projects. Working as a laborer, Sunderlal found that employment arrangements for such projects worked to the advantage of the contractors who were paid by the government but exploited the local people. Working with these people Sunderlal became a labor organizer. In response to the exploitative conditions he observed and, to which he too was subject, he organized the labor force into cooperatives that could negotiate directly with the government for work and wages rather than be subject to the exploitative wages and working conditions of the contractors. His skills as a community organizer would prove fruitful in future efforts to generate employment for the local people.

Bharat Dogra makes the point that the local people regarded the land that had been given for the ashram to be barren and unproductive.

Some of the local people told me that many believed it was haunted by evil spirits. Casting these considerations aside, Sunderlal and Vimla worked hard on this land turning parts of it into space suitable for cultivation. On other ground they planted and cared for trees that eventually became productive for food: guavas, walnuts, mangos, limes, oranges, and grapes. Later they planted Himalayan oak saplings among the chir pine to help stabilize the soil. With increasing green cover, the fertility of the soil improved. Thus through hard work and dedication they turned what was considered a barren site to productive land. Bharat Dogra states that living in such difficult conditions, they were able to demonstrate by example how a household with only a minimum of material goods could meet its nutritional needs by making the most efficient use of available resources. This practical demonstration of sustainability lent credence to their discussions with the villagers concerning health and nutrition and led the villagers to accept discussions on wider social issues: the desirability of education for girls, the improvement of the position of women in the community, the menace of liquor, and the need to maintain their forests. By their life and work, says Bharat Dogra, Sunderlal and Vimla Bahuguna demonstrated Gandhi's ideal of village self-reliance and resistance to injustice by nonviolent means.[15] With the help of donations from local people and donated labor, Sunderlal soon undertook further building work for living quarters and classrooms facilities. In a short time the number of children attending classes in the ashram increased to more than one hundred. In the midst of this new and developing venture, their own first child, Madhu, was born in 1957 and their second child, Rajiv, in 1961. Their third child, Pradeep, was born in 1965. In the absence of medical facilities in the area, they were blessed with the medical services of an elderly nurse, Besanti Devi. She was a widow and the sister-in-law of the freedom fighter Shankar Dutt Dobhal, an early associate of Sri Dev Suman. For her supportive and nurturing care to the community, Besanti Devi was known to all as *mataji* (mother).

Besanti Devi's contribution to the community was especially helpful in the light of a new phase of Sunderlal's work that was emerging at this time. Around this time Sunderlal and a small band of companions had begun to make *padyatras* (foot marches) to nearby villages to spread Gandhi's views concerning village self-reliance and rural development as it pertains to conditions in the hills. Sunderlal states that the inspiration for these undertakings came largely from the influence of Vinoba Bhave. Early in the 1960s, before and after India's brief war with China, the border regions of India became critical to national security. Part of the motivation for development, especially in the border regions, was the threat of Chinese military aggression. For this reason much of the development activity in the hills focused upon the perceived need for motor roads that could deploy troops to border regions. Vinoba Bhave had made the point that China was facing India not only with the force of arms but also with a philosophy that had addressed the poverty in their own country, the philosophy of communism. He argued that India too needed to fortify its border regions with a philosophy that would address the issue of poverty in the hills. That program, he argued, was Gandhi's nonviolent philosophy of *sarvodaya* (universal uplift). Sunderlal speculates that Vinoba may have come to know about his own activities from Sarala Behn. But Vinoba knew Vimla from her work with him in Bihar, and later, Vimla's younger sister Kamla was with Vinoba on another of his *padyatras*. Sunderlal told me that one day he received a message from Vinoba inviting him to join Vinoba in one of his *padyatras* near Arga. He explains that when Vinoba wanted to have a conversation with someone, he would invite that person to walk with him. He used to talk while walking. When he finally met Sunderlal, he made the point that China is not a tiger that can be driven away with a gun. China has a philosophy to address the poverty of its people. The Indian government has sent its armed forces to the border with guns but without a philosophy. Then he challenged Sunderlal with his words: "This old man (Vinoba) is straining his legs while you are sitting in an ashram?" In 1960 Vinoba Bhave thus entrusted Sunderlal with the responsibility of bringing the message of *satyagraha* (nonviolent resistance) and *sarvodaya* (universal uplift) to the border regions. With this motivation, Sunderlal began the program of walking from village to village in the border regions spreading Gandhi's philosophy of universal uplift.

In the course of time, the reach of Sunderlal's *padyatras* increased. With him were a number of colleagues who played a critical role in later activities: Dhoom Singh Negi, Kunwar Prasun, Ghanshyam Sailani (the famous folk singer), Surender Datt Bhatt, Bhavani Bhai, and others. Eventually Sunderlal was spending long periods away from Silyara, often returning only to begin planning for another *padyatra*. Between 1960 and 1965 Sunderlal undertook *padyatras* over all the hill districts of what was then the state of Uttar Pradesh. One of the most ambitious was a journey of 120 days covering 1,300 kilometers. When I inquired about the strategy of the *padyatra* as a means for spreading the message of Gandhi, Sunderlal explained that in India the *padyatra* has a long and impressive history. It was through his *padyatras* that Shankaracarya spread the message of Vedanta that divinity is present everywhere and in everything. It was through his *padyatras* that the Buddha preached the message of nonviolence and compassion. He reminded me that when Jesus spread his message of love for all mankind, he never had the benefit of a vehicle. Sunderlal explains that in the *padyatra* one can meet the people and talk with them directly. In the *padyatras,* he said, Vinoba had recovered a dignified and effective strategy to reach the people.

In the course of these *padyatras* Sunderlal and his colleagues came to see that one of the most pressing of social problems in the hills was the consumption of alcohol. With the advent of factory-made liquor in the hills, the men would squander much of the money they had earned through labor. This habit deprived their families of the benefits of their income and often led to family violence. Road accidents from drunk drivers had sent busloads of passengers to their death on narrow and treacherous mountain roads. However, the government was generating revenue from the auction of the right to open new liquor shops in the hills and additional revenue from taxes on the sale of the liquor. Between 1965 and 1971 many Gandhian activists in the hills saw this benefit to the state to be inimical to the interests of the local people and began programs of nonviolent opposition to the opening of new liquor stores. It came to be known as the *sharab bandi* (stop alcohol) movement. In this important movement, Sunderlal and Vimla took a leading role. A critical part of their work with the villages became raising awareness of the menace of alcoholism and empowering women to raise their voices against this peril.

Around this time Sunderlal and Vimla received word that a new liquor store would be opening in the town of Ghansyali, also on the Balganga River, only a short distance from their ashram in Silyara. When he heard about it, Sunderlal thought again of the scavengers' community in Tehri where the men would drink to excess and would fight and cause injury to one another. Sunderlal wrote Vinoba Bhave to inform him of these developments and to express his deep concern. He and Vimla had established an ashram that was teaching and propagating Gandhian principles. Sunderlal was now traveling to villages addressing community issues that included the consumption of alcohol. In a neighboring town a liquor store was about to open. Sunderlal suggested that he might take a break from his travels to undertake a nonviolent protest against the opening of this store. Vinoba supported Sunderlal's plan. He pointed out that while China had effectively conquered the menace of opium, it was ironic that India should be enslaved to alcohol. "How can India with its liquor," he asked, "combat China, which has become free from opium?"

Sunderlal walked to the site of the proposed liquor outlet in Ghansy-ali and began a session of peaceful sitting protest, known among Gandhi-ans as *dharna*. This silent protest lasted several days, during which time he received much support from influential people in the community. On one occasion he had taken a bath in the river near the site and was sitting almost naked in the sun to dry, wearing only an undergarment. People had begun to gather to learn about his protest. On that occasion a retired session judge (the equivalent in the American system of a district court judge) came to the place. Surendra Datt Nautiyal was a respected man who lived very close to the people. He used the occasion to make a point to the people. He addressed the gathered people: "Do you know why this man is sitting here naked?" Immediately he had attracted their attention. "He is sitting here naked," he said, "to tell you that you too will be naked if this liquor shop is opened. Your income will go to the purchase of liquor, and you will be fleeced out of everything." He told them that the consumption of liquor means a horrible life for women on whom the welfare of the family depends. Liquor precipitates family violence especially against women and children. Bal Krishna Nautiyal, a retired subdivisional magistrate (the equivalent in America of a municipal court judge) also joined the movement. With the support of men such as these, the women of the community also came forward to protest the opening of liquor outlets. Eventually the government was forced to reverse its decision to open a liquor outlet in Ghansyali and also in the nearby town of Lambgaon. But the movement did not end with this achievement.

By 1971 the movement had gathered strength, and the protest now moved from Ghansyali to Tehri. Here the demonstration was directed not only against establishment of new liquor stores, but against established liquor outlets as well. Along with women from Ghansyali and other towns, many women from Tehri also came to be involved. For most it was their first time to participate in public life. Sunderlal now undertook a fast of sixteen days to express solidarity with those who wanted the liquor stores closed. Public support was enormous; thousands participated in the protest. The demonstration finally came to an end with the arrival of the state police. They arrested Sunderlal and hundreds of protesters. Those arrested included Vimla, her elderly mother, and her youngest son, Pradeep, then only six years old. To further intimidate the protesters, the police took thirty of the women to a jail in Saharanpur, many miles to the west of Haridwar. Yet the arrests and detentions only enlarged public support for the movement. Sunderlal tells the story of a former student, Chandra Singh, from the Thakkar Bapa hostel who was posted as subdivisional magistrate (the equivalent in America of a municipal administrator) in the town in which the women were jailed. He went to visit the protesters in jail. There he saw Pradeep. Thinking that a jail is no place for a child, he took the young Pradeep on his lap and suggested he bring him to his home. To this the jailer exclaimed, "You cannot do that! The child is a prisoner!"

Sunderlal refers to the protest that ended with the movement against alcohol outlets in Tehri as their first major success of the antiliquor movement. It put the issue of alcohol consumption at the forefront of social issues facing the hill communities and helped to turn public opinion against the consumption of alcohol. The protestors were released after fourteen days. Late in 1971 the state government finally imposed a ban on liquor outlets in five hill districts, three districts adjoining the Chinese border—Uttarkashi, Chamoli and Pithoragarh—and two others adjoining these—Tehri Garhwal and Pauri Garhwal.

Sunderlal states that during the days of the protest against liquor, he received much moral support from the influential Vedantic saint, Swami Chidananda. Born to a prosperous Brahmin family in South India, in 1916, Swami Chidananda had taken an interest in spiritual things from a very early age. During his undergraduate studies at Loyola College, he had encountered and studied the Bible, which he found to be as living and real as the Vedas, the Upanishads, and the Bhagavad Gita. His breadth of spiritual vision enabled him to see Jesus in Krishna and not instead of or in opposition to Krishna. In 1943 he had joined the ashram of the famous Swami Sivananda, the founder of the Divine Life Society in Rishikesh. After Swami Sivananda passed away in 1963, Swami Chidananda had succeeded him as president of the society. From the insight of Vedanta philosophy that all are one in God, Chidananda was drawn to the service of those suffering from disease, and particularly to lepers. In the ashram his first responsibility was to take charge of the dispensary. Recognizing no distinction between himself and others, he was concerned with a number of critical social issues. He sympathized with the plight of the poor and worked to address sources of conflict in their lives.[16] When Sunderlal began his *padyatra* of 120 days through the hills of Uttar Pradesh, Swami Chidananda was present to inaugurate that *padyatra* with his blessing. For him the proliferation of liquor stores in the hills was a critical cause of family and social conflict that also interfered with the human aspiration toward spiritual development. Sunderlal points out that Swami Chidananda was present to lend his support to the protest against the liquor stores in Tehri and worked with him in a critical protest against the opening of a liquor shop near the ashram of the Divine Life Society in Rishikesh.

As Sunderlal continued his regimen of *padyatras* in the hills regions, he utilized his skills as a labor coordinator to establish a number of local organizations to generate employment and support the development of sustainable village economies in line with the Gandhian ideal of village self-reliance. Each of these was a block-level organization called a *sangh*. Sunderlal explains that a block consisted of perhaps fifty to sixty villages. Reflecting their commitment to Gandhi's ideal of village self-reliance and village self-rule each was known as a *swarajya sangh*, emphasizing the idea of *swaraj* (self-rule). Because they were committed to the Gandhian ideal of village-level development each was called a *gram* or village organization. In 1964, Sunderlal's colleague Chandi Prasad Bhatt founded such an organization in the region of Dashauli called the Dashauli Gram Swarajya Sangh. In the years to follow, this organization received considerable media attention. Bahuguna emphasizes that other such organizations were active in similar ways in other areas. In this context he mentions the Gangotri Gram Swarajya Sangh, the Kailash Gram Swarajaya Sangh, and the Badrinath Gram Swarajya Sangh. During this period he wrote to Vinoba again drawing his attention to another threat to the hills besides the threat of international invasion and the menace of alcohol. That was the threat of floods. Observing the landscape over time, he could see, as Mira Behn had pointed out, that that the increased flooding of the region was related to the condition of the forests. This, he believed, could only lead to disastrous consequences for the local people. Thus in the period to follow, two themes became prominent in Sunderlal's activism. One was the establishment of community organizations to support the ideal of sustainable village independence; the other was the condition of the forests upon which such economies would depend.

Chapter 7

Embracing the Trees

There is perhaps no cause with which the name of Sunderlal Bahuguna has been more widely associated than that of the Chipko Movement, the grassroots environmental movement that from 1973 began to receive international attention. During the time of their conversations, Indira Gandhi referred to him as Chipko Bahuguna to distinguish him from H. N. Bahuguna the then chief minister of the Indian state of Uttar Pradesh. It was in the glow of the Chipko Movement that Bahuguna became an internationally recognized environmental activist traveling with the chipko message to Europe, to Africa, and to the United States. In some writings he is referred to as the founder of the movement or as its leader. Sunderlal flatly denies both of these claims. Against the opinion of some researchers, he holds that Chipko was and remains largely a movement of forest women. He refers to his own role in the movement as a messenger of the movement, a person who supports the concerns of the movement and who has carried its message first to the villages, and second to the larger public arena. To understand the nature of his role in this movement it is appropriate to reconstruct some of the background of the movement and some of the critical events that brought the movement to national and international attention. In doing so, I acknowledge the very significant contribution of a number of specialists who have offered thorough discussions of the context and development of the Chipko Movement. In writing this and the following two chapters I am dependent in particular upon the research of Ramachandra Guha and Thomas Weber, whose monographs covering the Chipko Movement I recommend, and upon a number of other scholars who have given specific accounts of particular developments and specific events within the larger movement.[1] My purpose is not to add to these very thorough studies but to discuss Bahuguna's own understanding of this movement, his activities in the context of this movement, the background of these activities in the influences on his early life, and the significance of these activities in the light of Bahuguna's own philosophy of nature. To do this effectively it is necessary to understand a little of the geographic and cultural context in which this movement took place.

In his study of ecological change and peasant resistance in the Himalayas, Ramachandra Guha begins with an insightful discussion of the people of Garhwal, and of their economy and culture as it appeared largely before colonial expansion into the region. Several of his observations are germane to the present subject. In the first place, he points out that, along the river valleys, cultivation of wheat, rice, and millet was limited by the steepness of the land and by the difficulty of irrigation. Yet he notes that throughout the nineteenth century, two or sometimes three harvests produced a surplus of grain sufficient for export to Tibet in the north and to the plains in the south. With their usual six-month supply of grain stock and their diet supplemented by fish, fruit, vegetables, and meat, Guha finds strong support for the claim of Henry Ramsay, commissioner of the region, from 1856 to 1884, that the hill cultivators were "probably better off than any peasantry in India."[2] He comments that European travelers to the region were frequently given to lyrical descriptions of peasant life in the mountain villages, comparing them to those of England and Ireland.

Guha observes, second, that the land-tenure system that the British inherited differed significantly from that of the plains. He notes the observation of G. W. Traill, the first commissioner of the region, that in at least three-quarters of the villages the actual proprietors were the cultivators of the land.[3] In Tehri Garhwal the holding of land was by hereditary rights. It could be gifted to religious endowments or leased to tenants. But, according to Guha, there were few large landowners. Rather, "the agrarian system was dominated by peasants cultivating their holdings with the help of family labor."[4] The texture of colonialism in the hills, according to Guha, differed significantly from its more characteristic features on the plains. "The absence of a class of 'feudal' intermediaries," he says, "further reinforces the image of an independent peasantry firmly in command of its resources." Comparing these hills to the stratified villages of the Indo-Gangetic plain, he finds it much closer to the peasant political ideal in which the king and the peasantry are the only significant social forces.[5]

A third distinctive feature of the hill culture was the role assigned to women. In the difficult terrain of the hills, according to Guha, a single economic activity was usually insufficient to sustain a household. He states that a typical household was supported by a "basket" of economic pursuits that required the equal participation of women. Here he cites the work of Ramesh Chandra, who states that the work of women in the hills was no less valued than that of men. He states that women worked equally with men in the fields, and in the care of domestic animals. With the exception of plowing, there was virtually no activity the wife did not do. Guha asserts that in addition to their work in the fields, the women were also exclusively responsible for the household chores of cooking and cleaning, rearing children, and collecting fuel, fodder, and water. Some researchers see the signs of sexual oppression in this disproportionate share of labor. Others have looked to education for the solution to what appears an unnatural division of responsibilities.[6] Whatever response this condition might evoke in the mind of the viewer, the features of the life of the hills we here observe supports one very general observation that Bahuguna has often expressed. It is that before, during, and since the colonial period, the people of the hills were and remain an extremely hard-working and productive people. Reflecting on his own accumulated knowledge of the region, Bahuguna states that prior to industrial and economic expansion into the region, the people of the hills were happy, healthy, and prosperous.

During the colonial period the British had taken a strong interest in the forest resources of India. Early in the nineteenth century the teak (*Tectona grandis*) forests of Malabar were a vital resource for the burgeoning ship-building industry in the British Isles. By the middle of the nineteenth century, the hardwood trees of the Himalayas proved essential for the expansion of British commerce and industry in India, facilitated by its developing and far-reaching railway network. The building of railways required a colossal supply of railway ties, what the British call sleepers. While the supply of timber for this purpose was soon stressed in other parts of India, the region of Tehri Garhwal, with its abundant forests of the finest deodar trees (*Cedrus deodara*) proved opportune.

Bahuguna told me that the exploitation of timber in the princely state of Tehri Garhwal began with the career of a young British soldier who abandoned his position in the colonial armed forces to seek his fortune in the hills. Having deserted the army, Frederick Wilson traveled to the Bhagirathi Valley where he shot game and shared the meat with the local people. He also shot birds with colorful plumage and was able to sell them to merchants in Mussoorie for the market in Britain. The skins and feathers of these exotic birds fetched a high price in the international market, as did the exotic musk from the musk deer of the local forests. Wilson gained a handsome return for his exploits. His gifts of meat also brought him the good will of the people. Because the Brahmins of the area were in the habit of consuming a nonvegetarian diet, they were especially fond of the flesh of the birds he shot. The Brahmins also supported a community of drummers who played their instruments at a variety of local festivals. They provided housing for Wilson in the community of the drummers. Eventually he was married to a young woman from the area, the daughter of a local drummer, and settled near the pilgrimage town of Gangotri, near the source of the Bhagirathi River. Because of his popularity with the local people, they suggested that he should go to meet the raja of the princely state. Presently, he set out to Tehri to do so. Sunderlal states that when this tall Englishman in the clothing of a local man of the hills met the raja of Tehri, he saluted him with the appropriate prostrations and presented him with an offering of several gold coins that he had earned from the sale of the plumage of the exotic birds and the musk of the deer of the area. In a region where such currency was rare, the raja was amazed to meet a man in possession of so many gold coins. When he inquired how Wilson had managed to acquire them, Wilson explained that he had been making his living by shooting local birds and selling their skins and feathers and the musk of the local deer to dealers in Mussoorie for the fashion market in Europe.

The king was impressed with both Wilson's ambition and his enterprising spirit. According to Bahuguna, the raja is reputed to have placed his hand on the young man's head and exclaimed, "You are my golden bird!"

Wilson was an amiable and resourceful young man. Sunderlal states that Wilson then explained to the raja that there was much more gold to be gained from the Bhagirathi Valley, and he proceeded to explain how. "Allow me," he said, "to cut the trees of the valley and float them down to Haridwar where they can be sold for railway ties in the timber market. A high return will be brought to the coffers of the royal household." D. P. Joshi states that in 1840 and for a very nominal fee Frederick Wilson received a lease on the forests of the Tehri state including the Yamuna and Bhagirathi valleys that permitted the shooting of wild game and the exploitation of their products. For the years 1850 to 1864, the state renewed this lease to include major timber products for a fee of a mere four hundred rupees per year.[7] Guha refers to Wilson as a pioneer in the water transport of timber, a critical innovation in the development of the forest industry. In 1865, after Wilson's lease expired, the government of the

Northwestern Provinces negotiated with the British a twenty-year lease for all of the forests of the state for an annual fee of ten thousand rupees. This agreement was renegotiated with further provisions for another twenty years in 1885 and again in 1905. Because these agreements were intended to facilitate the extraction of timber for railway ties, it curtailed the rights of local people to utilize the forests for their own needs: for food, fodder, fuel, fertilizer, and fiber. From 1902, in lieu of an annual rental fee, the raja received 80 percent of the net profits of the forest revenue. Between 1869 and 1885 the new industry extracted deodar trees from the forests of Tehri Garhwal sufficient for 6.5 million railway ties. Says Guha, "At the time when the rate of forest destruction imperiled further railway expansion, the forests of Tehri Garhwal proved a strategically valuable resource for British colonialism."[8]

In the course of time, revenue from timber extraction became an ever-increasing stream of income for the ruler of the princely state, eventually constituting the largest supply of revenue from any single source. Extraction of timber from these hills, particularly through the two world wars was considerable. Government management of these resources developed only after logging and the river transport of timber was already effectively developed. When forest management came into being, it was largely to regulate the extraction of timber to insure adequate reproduction of revenue-producing species. Increasing commercial forest management by the state reduced the traditional access of village people to the forests. Forest management directed toward assuring the supply of revenue-producing species eventually endangered the diversity of the forests.[9] These dynamics constituted a significant feature of a tension between the interests of the newly formed forest department that administrated forest resources for commercial purposes and the needs of the village people. The needs of the local people and the condition of the forests upon which they depended were the emerging foci of Sunderlal's forest activism.

In 1815, following the British war with Nepal, the British occupied Kumaon and much of the Garhwal region. At this time Garhwal was divided. The eastern region, the land east of the Alakananda River, came under direct British rule, while the western region became the princely state of Tehri Garhwal under the sovereignty of the raja who could trace his ruling authority for more than a thousand years.[10] The kingdom of Garhwal, says Guha, was by far the oldest in northern India. The king of Garhwal was also regarded as the religious head of the Badrinath temple near the source of the Alakananda River and was known by the title "Bolanda Badrinath" (speaking Badrinath, or the deity personified). The king's administration, however, was mediated by royal officials, whose power was often subject to abuse. Given his semidivine status, popular dissatisfaction with his administration was rarely expressed in acts of hostility toward the king or toward the institution of kingship, but more often against subordinate officials. From before British influence in the region, the customary means of peasant protest was the *dhandak*, a strategy by which the peasantry could draw the attention of the monarch to the wrongdoings of his officials.[11] Typically the people would refuse to cooperate with new rules an official was imposing. While reserve forests were sometimes set on fire, the demonstrations were usually nonviolent. Sometimes an official would be seized and insulted but rarely harmed. Guha explains that a mass gathering would usually be initiated by beating of drums. People from surrounding villages would gather at an appointed place, normally a shrine. The people would resolve not to conform to new regulations, not to pay new taxes. From that location they would undertake a march to the capital where they would demand an audience with the king. With the appearance of the king and his promise of redress, the crowd would usually disperse. The *dhandak* represents, says Guha, "a right to revolt traditionally sanctioned by custom." Once the offending official was identified and appropriately punished, the uprising tended to subside.[12]

Guha states that the people's dissatisfaction with increasing restrictions on their access to the forests was for a long time expressed in this form. But a decisive departure from this custom occurred in 1930. Bahuguna states that it would long be remembered as a symbol of tension between the government and the village people. Officials who had served in British India were often unable to comprehend the tradition of the *dhandak* and took any large demonstration as an act of hostile rebellion. Such an official was Chakradhar Juyal, who according to popular opinion had been appointed as *dewan* or chief minister to the king more for his flattery than for his competence.[13] With the imposition of new forest restrictions based upon the recommendations of the German forest expert Franz Heske, the people of Rawain in the western part of Tehri Garhwal expressed their dissatisfaction with the customary *dhandak*. In an economy dependent upon sheep and cattle rearing, the villagers understood that a new restriction would limit each family to ten head of sheep, one cow, and a buffalo. Villagers were to be taxed on animals exceeding that limit. They would also no longer be permitted to cut the lower branches of trees without a permit. The people felt that land available to them outside the reserved forests, the forests reserved for the use of the state, was already insufficient for their needs. The *dhandak* soon spread to the neighboring region of Jaunpur. Alarmed by the protest, Juyal conveyed orders to the local magistrate to arrest the leaders of the uprising. In response, the magistrate requested that two of them proceed to Barkot, a place on the banks of the Yamuna, where their grievances would be heard. On their arrival, officials handcuffed the two and took them partway to Tehri, leaving them in the custody of the local police. While the officials were returning to Barkot they met a group of peasants who were taking food to the arrested men. A quarrel ensued in which one of the officials fired on the group, killing two men and wounding two others.[14] This episode added fuel to the *dhandak* that now appointed a single leader who designated himself as prime minister to the king. They met for a rally at Tilari, a level plain overlooking the Yamuna. On May 26, Juyal ordered the state forces to march on the protesters. When the commander, Colonel Sunder Singh, refused to march on his own people, Juyal himself took charge of the troops and began the march toward Rawain. He sent two villagers to the protesters inviting them to surrender. They replied that they would respond only when their president returned. Weber states that on May 30, 1930, Juyal and his army met the protestors at Tilari. He states that the troops surrounded the protestors on three sides and fired, killing seventeen and wounding many others.[15] This breakdown in the traditional form of redress among the people of the hills had important consequences for the protest against forest policy that occurred in the following years.[16] Bahuguna told me that after independence, May 30 came to be observed as Van Diwas or Forest Day in memory of those killed in the confrontation.

While the expansion of the timber industry in the late nineteenth century gradually depleted the diversity of the forest cover of the hills, and restricted local access to the forests, the middle of the twentieth century brought new perils to the forests and the interests of the local people. To many it seemed that, in the wake of the Chinese war with India in 1962, the development of motor roads to the border regions would bring new opportunities for economic development of these forest areas. Forests of chir pine, a species once considered economically unprofitable, was now being cut for timber. Economic opportunists also found in the sap of the chir pines a resource they could turn to profit in the production of turpentine. For the villages, the problem was that the new industries were conducted much like other development projects, arrangements to which Sunderlal had objected in his work as a labor organizer in Silyara. Contractors negotiated with the state government for rights to cut timber and to tap resin, and the contractors came to the hills with their own labor force to execute the contracts. Employment in the hills remained scarce because the contractors tended to hire their laborers from outside the region. The challenge for one committed to Gandhi's vision of village self-reliance was to wrest the sources of employment from the contract system to provide employment for village men. I stated earlier that in the course of Sunderlal's *padyatras* in the hills, he established a number of organizations or *sanghs* to generate employment and support the development of sustainable village economies. Sunderlal established such organizations to address this condition. He and other *sarvodaya* workers believed that as people of the hills they should be able to make their living from the natural resources of the forests rather than conceding this employment to outsiders and descending to the planes to earn a living. The basis for a viable economy of the hills, he argued, was to entrust the handling of forest products to such local cooperative societies, eliminating the need for a middle man. At this time he was calling for more forest industry to bring prosperity to the hills.[17] To this end, the government formed a forest corporation with which these labor cooperatives could negotiate for work. In 1964 Chandi Prasad Bhatt founded the Dashauli Gram Swarajya Sangh (DGSS) for the purpose of developing village level industries based on the natural resources of the forests. A previous labor organization in the region had enjoyed limited success in gaining contracts from the Public Works Department for building sections of road. The DGSS was now interested in setting up local forest industries to provide employment for the local people. According to Bahuguna, they set up a small woodcraft unit to process ash wood logs for producing sporting goods such as cricket bats on the plains and to produce agricultural implements for local use. But the accepted method for the distribution of forest resources was also a system that originated in colonial times. The State Forest Department often auctioned whole stands of forests to the contractors. Thus when the DGSS tried to set up small forest industries it had to acquire timber resources through the auction of forests resources conducted by the State Forest Department. Vested interests quickly perceived their emerging power as a threat. Contractors bid high for their forest resources and often supplemented the expenditure by illegal felling.[18] Such strategies put the DGSS at a distinct disadvantage. The DGSS then turned to collecting medicinal herbs from the mountains for pharmaceutical manufacturers in the plains. But here they found that the greater share of the profits went to those who marketed the herbs to the drug manufacturers. The DGSS then began to negotiate directly with the drug manufacturers in Delhi,

Punjab, and Bombay. This led to a successful flow of income for about 1,000 villagers for the period from 1969 to 1972.[19]

Along with other organizations for village self-reliance, the DGSS set up its own small turpentine factory in the town of Gopeshwar in the Chamoli district and began to bid for the raw material, called *lisa*, the sap of the chir pine, for the production of turpentine. It was one of eight such factories which Gram Swarajya Sanghs were operating in the region. The difficulty was that the distribution of *lisa* was in the hands of the forest department, and most of the supply was designated for established resin and turpentine factories on the plains. The forest department provided *lisa* for only five of the eight local units and only enough to keep them operating for three to four months of the year. Even this supply was given at a cost 30 percent higher than what was charged to the established factories on the plains in which the government had a large financial interest. The factories that received no allocation of *lisa* had to buy it at higher prices on the open market.[20] In October of 1971, under the leadership of Sarala Behn and Chandi Prasad Bhatt, the villagers in Gopeshwar organized a large demonstration in protest of these discriminatory policies. They argued that they themselves had nurtured forest growth and should be given preference in the allotment of raw materials. Guha points out that a demonstration of this size had never before been seen in the district of Chamoli.[21] During the following year, Bahuguna undertook *padyatras* through the villages of the region to explain the injustices to which the villages were subject and the importance of the nontimber forest products upon which their lives were dependent. Chandi Prasad Bhatt brought the grievances of the people to the state capital in Lucknow and to Delhi. In December 1972 at the site of the martyrdom that occurred in May 1930, Bahuguna launched a new massive demonstration. Then with Ghansyam Sailani the poet and folk singer of the movement and with Chandi Prasad Bhatt of the Dashauli Gram Swaraj Sangh, he proceeded by bus to Uttarkashi and Gopeshwar where together they launched further demonstrations.

Because of Bahuguna's many contacts in the media and his experience in mass communication, this protest now had the support of two large daily newspapers. In November 1972 they carried reports of the work of the DGSS over the past twelve years and the discrimination they encountered from a forest policy that favored vested commercial interests.[22] The villagers demanded an end to the contract system, the restoration of their traditional rights to forest products, and an equitable provision of raw materials, especially of *lisa* for local industries.[23] Bahuguna refers to this protest as the first phase of what eventually came to be known as the Chipko Movement. Here the dissatisfaction of the local people centered upon the injustice of discrimination against local forest industries by government contract policies and resource distribution policies that favored vested interests over the local communities.

But while discrimination against small local industry was the focus of this protest, other concerns were not off the agenda. The concern of the women for the condition of the forests upon which their household needs depended was related to their recognition of another threat to the local environment. Guha points out that from the 1950s there is a clear record of local indignation about timber sales to outside contractors and the evident dissipation of forest resources.[24] This indignation had come into clear focus in 1970. That year, in a devastating flood in the Alakananda Valley that brought disastrous loss of life and property, the villagers began to recognize the ecological consequences of the destruction of their forests. That flood inundated 100 square kilometers (38.6 square miles) of land. It marooned 101 villages and destroyed 604 homes, six motor bridges, sixteen foot bridges, and 500 acres of crops. It destroyed cowsheds and watermills and killed 142 head of cattle. In the violence of its flow 55 people died. It destroyed houses as far away as Rishikesh. Its effects were seen as far away as Haridwar, 300 kilometers (186 Miles) downstream, where the Upper Ganga Canal was silted to a depth of two or three meters for a length of ten kilometers, cutting off irrigation to a significant portion of the eastern region of the state of Uttar Pradesh.[25] Guha describes this flood as a turning point in the ecological history of the region. The villagers whose lives were the most affected by the damage could see the relationship between the deforestation that was taking place in their midst and the resulting landslides and floods. Some of the villages most damaged by landslides lay directly below forests in which significant felling had been undertaken.[26]

Most of the accounts of the origin of the Chipko Movement discuss a confrontation that occurred between the DGSS and the Symonds Company, a sporting goods manufacturer based in Allahabad. At the beginning of 1973, the turpentine plant which the DGSS had begun in Gopeshwar was idle, and its woodcraft unit was without raw materials. The DGSS made a request to the forest department for its usual allotment of five ash trees. The forest department refused this request. Nevertheless it awarded a contract to the Symonds Company to extract ash trees for the production of sporting goods. Ash trees were to be taken from the Mandal forest only thirteen kilometers from Gopeshwar. At this time the office of the DGSS became the center for discussions of an appropriate response. Bahuguna explains that ash trees were important to the people of the hills for two critical reasons. In the first place, because it is a light but strong and durable wood, it was useful for the production of agricultural implements, such as the yoke that is used to attach a bullock to a cart or a plow. Second, it produces leaves that are a critical source of fodder during the scarce season. Weber points out that the DGSS did not object to the allocation of ash wood for the manufacture of sporting goods so long as their own needs for ash wood could be met. They believed that the extraction of such products from the forests could address their own concern for local employment.[27] Bahuguna explained to me that Chandi Prasad Bhatt's proposal was that the ash wood logs should be processed in the DGSS woodcraft plant in the hills. There they could be fashioned into "half-made" cricket bats to be finished in the Symonds plant in Allahabad. He points out, however, that the minds of the local women were on the question of how their cattle would survive the loss of the ash trees on which they depended for fodder. Nevertheless, the allocation of a forest of ash trees to the Symonds Company and the denial of the same resources to the DGSS became the occasion for a protest against forest policies that worked against the interests of the local industry.

Over thirty years after the Chipko Movement drew national and international attention to the environmental crisis in the Himalayas, the actual origin of the movement remains less than clear. An examination of the principal published sources discloses inconsistencies that challenge the presumption that the movement can be traced to a single genesis. Thomas Weber (1988) refers to two accounts of how the movement began. One version has it that at a meeting in the office of the DGSS in Gopeshwar the local activists committed themselves to prevent the Symonds Company from felling the trees. The question they were pondering was how. According to this version, it was after some debate that Chandi Prasad Bhatt, "in a fit of inspiration," made a decisive proclamation: "Let them know," he said, "that we will not allow the felling of ash trees. When they aim their axes upon them we will embrace the trees."[28] Guha (1989) seems to be supporting this version when he states that the injustice that the government was perpetrating led the DGSS to organize several meetings in Mandal and Gopeshwar to discuss possible action. Two alternatives that were presented were (1) to lie down in front of the timber trucks, or (2) to burn the resin and timber depots as was done during the quit India movement. He states: "When Sarvodaya workers found both methods unsatisfactory, Chandi Prasad Bhatt suddenly thought of embracing the trees. Thus 'chipko' (to hug) was born." He states that, under the leadership of their headman Alam Singh Bist, the villagers of Mandal resolved to hug the trees "even if axes split open their stomachs," and that "young men cemented the oath with signatures in blood."[29] But according to Weber, the discussion of "the form the direct action would take" occurred three days later in a public meeting in the courtyard of the office of the DGSS in Gopeshwar. Here, he says, "Many suggestions were put forward, ranging from preventing the Company's workers from entering the forest, through lying in front of the trucks as they were about to remove the felled trees, . . . to felling and removing the trees themselves or even burning the trees so that the company could not use them."[30] It seems possible that the term "chipko" and the strategy of hugging the trees came to be recognized in a variety of situations. But the discrepancy in the principal sources does tend to cast doubt upon the claim of Weber that the Chipko Movement was born on March 27, 1973.

The other version of the story to which Weber refers differs significantly. This version was expressed in a study of the Chipko Movement by Bharat Dogra in 1980. It claims that during the discussion of possible strategies, an elderly village woman stood up and said, "When a leopard attacks a child the mother takes his onslaughts on her own body." Then after a brief silence another shouted, "Yes, that is it, we'll hug the trees when the Simon's agents comes to axe them."[31] Bahuguna acknowledges an element of truth in both accounts, but he attaches great significance to the story of the woman protecting her child from the attack of a leopard. From his own life in the hills he understood the role of the forests in providing for the needs of villagers, and he understood the role of women in gathering wood, food, and fodder to meet the material needs of their families. For Bahuguna, the Chipko Movement was a women's movement, not by any means to the exclusion of men, who worked tirelessly and courageously for the protection of the trees, but in the sense that the issues of forest protection that the Chipko Movement addressed were issues of first importance to the women. In this sense it belongs to the long history of local protest against commercial interests in the hills that conflicted with those of the local people. For Bahuguna, the Chipko Movement was an expression of the program of rural development for which Mira Behn and Sarala Behn had worked, an expression of Gandhi's vision of economically independent, self-governing, and self-reliant villages.

While the precise date and circumstances of the birth of Chipko may remain a matter of dispute, the location of the events that brought it to public attention is less ambiguous. The agents of the Symonds Company, who had been allotted ash trees, were forced to depart from the Mandal forest without felling a single tree. At a further meeting on May 2, 1973, the DGSS began to articulate concerns that went beyond the protection of just one stand of timber. At this meeting under the auspices of the Uttarakhand Sarvodaya Mandal, the organization for village uplift which Sarala Behn had founded in 1961, it demanded that local people be included in the administration and management of the forests and that local forest industries be given priority in the allocation of forest resources. As the most visible of *sarvodaya* activists then working in Uttarakhand, Sunderlal Bahuguna expressed high appreciation for the resolve of the people. He affirmed that Chipko is a natural extension of Gandhi's idea of nonviolence as a social force. He also pointed out that the forests had to be protected from wasteful exploitation by the villagers themselves. On the following day in an expression of solidarity with the ideals of this movement, Sunderlal together with the folk singer Ghanshyam Sailani and a number of others set out to take the message of Chipko to the villages.[32]

The emerging force of the Chipko Movement and the breadth of its concerns, however, were yet to be recognized by the government. In June of the same year the forest department allotted trees to the Symonds Company in another location, near the village of Phata in the Mandakini Valley, on the pilgrimage route to the famous Kedarnath Temple near the source of the Mandakini River. When word of this contract reached the DGSS, it organized, despite heavy rainfall, another massive demonstration. At this demonstration the people passed a resolution that if the loggers should come to cut the trees, they would embrace the trees to save them. When the agents of the Symonds Company arrived at the forest, they witnessed the determination of the protestors and their resolve in the preparations of their action committee. The people had appointed guards on the roads where the sound of a conch shell would alert the villagers to the approach of the company's men. In this situation, a confrontation developed between the villagers and the agents of the Symonds Company that continued for three days. By the end of that time, the Symonds agents recognized that the protesters were not about to abandon their cause, and they gave up hope of taking the trees they had come for. The company's agents returned to Gopeshwar complaining to the District Forest Office that, even after depositing money in pledge, they were unable to take away any of the trees they had been promised.[33]

In June 1973 the Forest Department announced the end of its policy of discrimination in the pricing of *lisa* for small local turpentine plants. But by now the Chipko Movement was gaining strength, and the range of

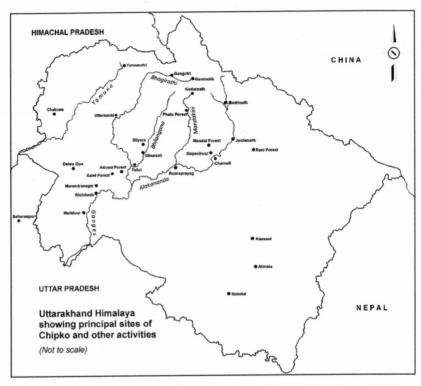

Map of Uttarakhand Himalaya Showing Principal Sites of Chipko and Other Activities

its concerns could no longer be limited to the price of raw materials for local industry. Its appeal at the grass roots was also spreading. At this time the Uttarakhand Sarvodaya Mandal, the organization that Sarala Behn had founded and in which Sunderlal and his wife Vimla were active, came to be closely identified with the interest of the Chipko Movement in protecting the forests. As a longtime worker in Gandhi's constructive program, Bahuguna was increasingly troubled by the condition of the forests and the significance of the condition of the forests for the villages. Thus on October 25, 1973, on the centenary of the birth of Swami Ram Tirtha, a saint who had lived in the Uttarakhand region, Sunderlal embodied his role as messenger of the movement, by setting off on a *padyatra* of yet another 120 days through the hills of Uttarakhand to bring to the village people there the message of the Chipko Movement.[34] Weber points out that while Bahuguna had undertaken many *padyatras* in the past, they were now taking a more visible form. As larger numbers of young people began to participate, they became veritable rallies.[35] In these *padyatras* Sunderlal's role as messenger of the movement was supported by his skills as a public speaker who could articulate complicated economic and ecological issues in terms the rural people could understand and act upon. His credibility with the people was supported by his acknowledged role as a *sarvodaya* worker devoted to nonviolence, a person who had renounced political aspirations to commit himself to the uplift of the local people. Often he was able to express his ecological insights in slogans that would sometimes emerge spontaneously in his interaction with the people. In these journeys he came to be so identified with the movement that to many he came to be regarded as its leader. As I have said, he denied that claim. Yet his charisma was sufficient to inspire many young people of the hills to take up the cause of the protection of the forests and to participate in the movement in visible ways.

The spread of the Chipko Movement, however, did not immediately alter the most critical features of prevailing government policy. By the middle of June in 1973 the government had ended its discrimination against small industries in the distribution of *lisa*, but they continued their planning for the annual government auction of forests in November of 1973. One of the plots marked for sale was the Reni forest near Joshimath, in the Alakananda Valley, an area in which the memory of the devastation of 1970 was especially vivid. There two thousand trees had been designated for felling. Chandi Prasad Bhatt recommended the strategy of embracing the trees, and chipko activists organized a massive demonstration. On this occasion the government resorted to deceit. On the promise of a meeting with the conservator of forests, Chandi Prasad Bhatt remained at Gopeshwar. On the promise of compensation long overdue for lands appropriated by the Indian army after the Chinese invasion of 1962, the men of Reni and the surrounding villages had journeyed to Chamoli. With the leadership of the DGSS and the local men out of the way, the contractor's men avoided contact with Reni village and proceeded directly to the forest to begin felling the trees. On their way a young girl saw them and reported their presence to Gaura Devi, the head of the village women's organization. Gaura Devi mobilized the women of the village, who proceeded to the forest and implored the lumber men not to fell the trees. At first the women were met with threats and verbal abuse. But the women remained firm in their purpose. According to one report, when one of the men leveled his gun at her, she replied,

"Shoot and then only you can cut this forest which is like a mother to us."[36] When it was clear that the women would not be intimidated, the men departed from the forest. The women guarded the path to the forest through the night and for the following four days. On the return of the men, the village planned a massive demonstration. March 31, 1974, saw the largest demonstration that had ever been seen in the hills with men, women, and children converging from the many neighboring villages. With the strength of this demonstration, for the moment at least, the Reni forest was saved.[37]

Guha states that the protest at Reni is of historical importance for two reasons. One is the fact that this was the first occasion in which women participated in the movement in a major way. The other was the fact that the government could no longer treat the movement simply as the reaction of local industry to policies that deprived it of raw materials.[38] The Reni protest was an expression of the importance of the environment upon which the local domestic economy was dependent, a concern centered largely on the lives of the village women. Gaura Devi herself explains that the protest occurred spontaneously. "We wanted to make the people understand," she said, "that our existence is tied with the forests."[39]

On April 24, 1974, after the protest at Reni, H. N. Bahuguna, the chief minister of the state, himself a man from the Garhwal region, invited Chandi Prasad Bhatt and Sunderlal Bahuguna to a meeting in Lucknow for discussions. The chief minister eventually set up a committee, under the direction of the botanist Dr. Virendra Kumar to investigate the grievances of the people. Following the Reni protest, chipko activists successfully opposed the auction of forests in the Chakrata division forest in Dehra Dun, in the Chamyala forest, near Bahuguna's ashram at Silyara, at Loital, and at Amarsar. By similar strategies they stalled much other scheduled felling.[40]

In August 1974 members of the Uttarakhand Sarvodaya Mandal, gathered in the town of Garur in Almora to demand a ban on green felling and an end to the practice of resin tapping that was destroying their chir pine forests. They also demanded an end to the contractor system and a fair wage for forest laborers. Eventually the scene of protest moved to the places where the auctions were conducted. Weber states that at one of these demonstrations youths entered the auction hall, took over the microphone, and announced that the auction was cancelled. Demonstrations like this were held against forest auctions in Dehra Dun, Nainital, Kotdwara, Uttarkashi, and Tehri. During an auction at Uttarkashi on October 3, 1974, Bahuguna entered the hall where the auction was being conducted and made an impassioned plea to the officials to put an end to the proceedings. When his appeal did not prevail, he proceeded to the neighboring Hanuman temple where he undertook a fast of two weeks to protest the exploitation of laborers and the indiscriminate contract felling of trees. Following the agitation against the forest auctions the chief minister of the state set up another committee, the Swaminathan Committee, to undertake a comprehensive study of the abuse of forests of the region. At this time the state imposed a moratorium on the auction of forests to outside contractors pending the report of the Swaminathan Committee. Felling operations would now be undertaken under the authority of the Forest Corporation, and where the Forest Corporation had not yet been implemented, smaller forest lots could be auctioned so that local industries could legitimately compete. Raw materials would now be made more readily available to small-scale forest industries. In November 1974 the state passed minimum wage and other welfare legislation to improve the condition of forest laborers.[41] Eventually the Virendra Kumar committee concluded that the deforestation of the Alakananda Valley was the major cause of the flood of 1970, and the government imposed a ten-year ban on commercial felling in the upper catchment of the Alakananda River and its tributaries.[42] In terms of its mobilization of local people, the Chipko Movement had in the course of two years become the most celebrated forest movement that the Himalayan region had ever seen. In terms of the changes it brought about in established forest policy, it would, in the course of time, also become the most effective.

Chapter 8

Modes of Chipko Resistance

In his study of peasant resistance in the Himalayas, Ramachandra Guha undertakes an analysis of the Chipko Movement from the perspective of the sociology of social movements. In doing so he draws attention to its pattern of leadership, its forms of mobilization, the emergence of its codified ideology, and the relationship of the leader and the led. He also tries to comprehend the transformation of meaning it brought about in the lives of its participants and its relationship with past movements that concern the relationship between peasantry and state.[1] His analysis does much to explain the political impact of the Chipko Movement. In the course of my many conversations with Sunderlal, I heard repeatedly about a number of features of the Chipko Movement that, from his perspective, contributed largely to the achievements of the movement. To call them strategies or methods might imply that they were procedures contrived and deployed to address the villagers' condition. I call them modes of chipko resistance. While each had its own origin and development, they emerged organically in the context of the Chipko Movement and together reveal its integrity and character. There were three such modes of chipko resistance that stood out prominently in these conversations, and a fourth, about which Bahuguna said little, but that judging from press reports and other literature had a strong impact on the moral credibility of the movement. Foremost among them was the *padyatra* (foot march).

I stated earlier that as a means of spreading the message of Gandhi, the idea of the *padyatra* had come to Bahuguna from Vinoba, but it had an impressive history in the work of the Buddha, Shankaracarya, Jesus, and Gandhi. Because communication among the villages of the region was limited, the method of the *padyatra* was especially congenial to conditions in the hills. During a foot march the activists could meet the people. "Jesus," he reminded me again, "spoke to people face to face." The *padyathra*, as Sunderlal practiced it, was an especially exciting venture. Frequently Sunderlal would begin it on a date of special significance that tended to highlight its importance. May 25, 1974, was the anniversary of the birth of Shri Dev Suman. On this date several young people began a historic *padyatra*, traversing the entire region of Uttarakhand from the village of Askot on the border with Nepal in the east, to Arakot on the border with Himachal Pradesh in the west. Sunderlal was with them for a good part of the journey. With the accompaniment of musicians and singers, they entered each village with songs and slogans that provoked a gathering of interested and curious villagers. Their message was about the importance of the forest for their own welfare, the threats to the forest from government policy, and the need to protect them. The visitors would then invite the villagers to an evening meeting in which they would tell the story of the Chipko Movement and of the success it had achieved. The following day, with a letter of introduction from the headman of the village, they would proceed to their next destination. They repeated this regimen for forty-four days. Because the *padyatra* is a pilgrimage, it evokes a strong religious sentiment. It tended to provoke both a festive mood and a sense of the seriousness of the issues that provoked it. Weber points out that they were sometimes organized by students, sometimes by the women. Often they were to areas especially affected by landslides and floods. To the people they brought insight into the causes of these conditions and the strategy needed to address them. From 1973 to 1975 Sunderlal Bahuguna is known to have walked forty-two hundred kilometers.[2] Much of the success of the demonstrations that brought about real change in policy was related to these efforts in bringing the chipko message to the villages of the hills.

A second critical mode of chipko resistance was the folk song. I indicated earlier that on May 3, 1973, when Sunderlal set off on his first *padyatra* in support of the Chipko Movement, the Garhwali folk singer and folksong writer Ghanshyam Sailani was with him. During this and other *padyatras*, Sailani's inspiring songs put the message of the movement to music and verse. It was in a song composed during one of these journeys that the word "chipko" itself gained currency among the people. At this time forest activists wanted to raise a memorial at Tilari to those who had lost their lives in the firing in 1930 on a group of village people protesting government control of the forests. Sunderlal explains that on the journey from Tilari to Gopeshwar, he was traveling by bus with Ghanshyam Sailani and Chandi Prasad Bhatt. He states that Sailani always

traveled with his harmonium, an accordionlike musical instrument, which
he played while he sang for all who would listen whenever the bus would
stop. At one such stop at Rudraprayag at the confluence of the Alakananda
and the Mandakini rivers, Sailani climbed with his harmonium to the top
of the bus, where he began to play and sing. There he extemporaneously
composed and sang the song later entitled "Chipko," which became the
rallying cry of the movement. Roughly translated it goes like this:

> Brothers and Sisters let us awake!
> The Forest Department has proven the killer of the forest
> Embrace (Chipko) the Trees
> Save them from felling
> The wealth of the forests
> Don't let it be looted.

Because Sailani participated actively in many of the protests, the
influence of the folk song became gradually more prominent as the movement developed. In the course of time, he was widely identified with
Chipko. Having accompanied Sunderlal on many of his *padyatras,* he
had become for many the voice of the movement. Bahuguna states that
because he was well known to the people, his songs attracted people to
the demonstrations while supporting the cause that provoked them. The
songs of Ghanshyam Sailani told about the importance of trees and the
ruthlessness of government forest policy, the importance of the protection
of trees, the hazards of deforestation, and the need of planting new trees.
In doing so, they often appropriated references to trees in the religious
literature of India, in which trees are the objects of worship, in which
one tree is said to be equivalent to ten sons, in which trees are praised
by Krishna and admired by Rama, and in which the forest is hailed as
the birthplace of the Vedas and Puranas. Often just a phrase or a seg-
ment of the larger song became slogans that would be repeated at rallies,
on *padyatras,* and during demonstrations. Bahuguna states that a talk or
lecture to the people confers a meaning to the people, but the practice
of the folk song makes that meaning their own.

> Sisters and brothers
> Let us awake!
> Save the forest
> From the government's plans
> Embrace the trees

Save them from felling
The conservator of forests
Is now the forest's foe.

In the songs of the movement, subtle plays on words often deepen the impact of the message. In the folk song rendered above, the words "conservator of forests" are an English translation of the Hindi and Garhwali *aranya pal*. In the next line of the song *aranya pal* is juxtaposed with *aryana kal* (killer of the forest). Many of Sailani's songs drew attention to the many gifts of the trees: air, water, soil, energy, food, clothing, shelter, medicine, fodder, and shade. Sailani and other singers taught these songs to school children who shared them with others. They sang verses extolling the virtues of the trees that often ended with a refrain in which the women and children would join in chorus with, "Don't cut, don't cut!" Eventually their lyrics were on the lips of thousands of women and children of the hills. The folk song itself, as Sunderlal explains, is the product of the social situation it depicts.[3] Often even without a formal title folk songs expressed a sense of urgency that is difficult to appreciate outside the context in which they were originally sung. The translation of this song by Govind Raturi, Ghanshyan Sailaini's elder son, comes close to communicating in English the desperate situation they express:

Oh! save them! save them!
From fatal axe
Towering pines, rhododendrons and oaks
The flowing canals, the running streams
Smiling flowers and gurgling springs. Save them . . .
The gentle winds, the pattering rains
Curled green twigs on these mountains. Save them . . .
Trees have milk in their leaves
Cool and fresh water in their roots
Protect them from the Brutes. Save them . . .
The hacking of trees has created turmoil
Now who shall hold the trickling soil. Save them . . .
The life of man and animal are the trees
How can heaven be thought of without them.
Save them! Save them!
From the fatal axe.[4]

It is hardly a wonder that Bahuguna saw the folk song as the most effective method to spread the chipko message among the people. For him

Ghanshyam Sailani was the heart and inspiration of the movement. While the cadence, meter, tone, and rhyme of these songs are unfortunately lost in translation, the prevalence of contrasting imagery nevertheless survives. In the following untitled song, the sacred significance of the forest and its meaning for the life of the people are starkly juxtaposed against the attitude reflected in the policy of the government that administrates it:

> To weave garments for barren earth
> Plant new trees and make new forests.
> To save the earth from impending danger,
> Come one come all and get together.
> Forests are our life and soul
> They are the source of rivers all.
> Rains and springs are created in them
> The soil, water and air are because of them.
> Trees are blessed even by God
> He came once to save them from the odds.
> They are worshipped by mankind
> Without considering their safety all planning is blind.
> Apricot, apple, walnut are their treasure
> We derive from them fodder wood and water.
> Once Uttarakhand was heaven on earth
> Where in deep forests, Vedas and Puranas took birth
> To drive away the ruthless cutters
> Come one, come all and get together.
> Now it has become our religion
> To save the forests from destruction.[5]

Bahuguna makes the point that more than half the credit for the popularity of this movement belongs to the singers of folk songs, and among them especially to Sri Ghanshyam Sailani.[6]

In one of the best known of his songs, "The Appeal of a Tree," a forest tree speaks in the first person to the people and to the government. Here the poet draws a contrast between the thoughtless destruction of the forest and the benefits she offers to the people and their progeny. As Weber states, it calls for a harmonious relationship with nature and advertises the movement:

> I have been standing for ages,
> I wish to live for you.
> Do not chop me, I am yours.

I wish to give you something in future.
I am milk and water for you.
I am thick shade and showers.
I manufacture soil and manure.
I wish to give you foodgrains.
Some of my kind bear fruits.
They ripen for you.
I wish to ripen with sweetness.
I wish to bow down for you.
I am the pleasant season.
I am spring. I am rains.
I am with Earth and life.
I am everything for you.
Do not cut me, I have life
I feel pain, so my name is tree.
Rolling of logs will create landslides
Remember. I stand on slopes and below is the village.
Where we were destroyed,
Dust is flying there.
The hill tops have become barren.
All the water sources have been dried up.
Do not cut us, save us.
Plant us, decorate the Earth.
What is ours, everything is yours.
Leave something for posterity.
Such is the Chipko movement.[7]

While much has been written about Chipko, most of the available publications devote little attention to the religious and spiritual dimensions of the movement. Bahuguna has often made the point that the common people of India and especially those of the hills are religiously devoted.[8] In an environment in which the prevailing approach to forestry saw nature in exclusively material terms, he suggests that the religious devotion of the local people was the secret of the success of the Chipko Movement. He states: "We tried to interpret religion in its real sense. Ritual has done so much harm to religion in India that people have forgotten the real spirit of religion. The body is there, but without any heart. We have to revive the real spirit of the religion. That is what we did in Chipko movement."[9] The *padyatra* has a strong religious dimension because it is a form of pilgrimage the like of which had long been practiced in the religious traditions of India. We suggested earlier that while it awakens a festival mood, the *padyatra* evokes a strong sense of the seriousness of the issues being raised. It also develops, as those who have studied the pilgrimage have affirmed, a strong sense of community among the participants.[10] The folk songs that accompanied them also evoke a strong sense of the religious in their frequent reference to trees in the religious traditions of India.

It is in the third mode of resistance that the religious and spiritual dimension of the Chipko Movement is perhaps most prominent. Most of the sources that document the Chipko Movement describe a demonstration that occurred in 1977 in the Advani forest in the Hemvalghati region just south of Tehri. Between December 13 and 20, 1977, large numbers of women from fifteen villages guarded this forest. During this time, according to one report, they listened to discourses on the role of forests in Indian life from ancient texts.[11] According to another report, the activists organized readings from the Bhagavad Gita.[12] Curious about these readings and discourses, I inquired from Bahuguna and others about their content and the persons who undertook them. When I raised this question with Bahuguna, he acknowledged that verses from the Bhagavad Gita might have been recited as they would at the outset of any momentous communal undertaking. But he stated emphatically that the ancient discourses that were heard over the seven days of the demonstration were not from the Bhagavad Gita. They were Bhagavat Kathas. Others explained to me that the women of the hills would have no knowledge of Sanskrit and that to them the Bhagavad Gita would be practically unknown. Bahuguna states that in addition to the folk songs, the Bhagavat Katha was one of the principal methods by which the activists spread the chipko message. Kathas are narrative tales of the actions of divine beings from which practical moral lessons are derived. Bhagavat Kathas are moral lessons taken especially from the ancient stories about the earthly life of Lord Krishna. He explained that the *kathas* that were recited over the seven-day vigil in the Advani forest were from the ancient stories of the entire life of Lord Krishna. While Bahuguna was not himself the main practitioner of the Bhagavat Katha, he frequently made arrangements for this practice and recognizes it, like the folk song, as one of the most important supports of the Chipko Movement.

In the course of the Chipko Movement, the best known of the practitioners of the Bhagavat Katha was the woman activist, Indu Tekekar. While she was not present at the week-long vigil that occurred in the Advani forest in December 1977, her teaching through the Bhagavat Katha instilled a strong sense of the religious and spiritual grounding for forest activism, among those who participated in that demonstration. Known to her fellow workers as Indu Tai (*tai* meaning auntie), she was an energetic participant in the Chipko Movement delivering lectures and discourses from the ancient texts in which she found values that gave strong support to a mutually supportive relationship of human beings with nature. Her insight into the ancient texts was supported by a strong academic preparation in Indian philosophy. Born in 1934 she was inspired by the teachings of Dada Dharmadhikari, Vinoba Bhave, Jayaprakash Narayan, and others. With the inspiration of their thought and actions, she went on to earn her doctor's degree from Banaras Hindu University in 1967 with a focus on Gandhi's philosophy of *sarvodaya*. In the course of her career, she wrote more than a dozen books and innumerable articles in Hindi, English, and her mother tongue, Marathi. She taught at several colleges affiliated with the University of Poona and Shivaji University in Maharashtra. Her meeting with Vinoba Bhave in the late 1960s was the occasion for her, like Vimla Bahuguna, to become an active participant in the land gift movement. From the 1960s she became a close associate of Sunderlal and his wife in the *sharab bandi* movement. In this period she helped organize women and inspired them with examples of women's power in many of the Puranas. In 1968 she left her academic career to settle in an ashram, Ujeli, on the banks of the Bhagirathi River in Uttarkashi. Combining spiritual consciousness and social responsibility, she recognized the unity of all religions. Thus while she believed that the scriptures of all the great religions express ecological truths, she found the lessons in ecology from the Puranas of special relevance to the people of the hills.

Forests and trees have always played a significant role in the religious life of India. This is no less the case in the villages of the hills than in universities where scholars study the great scriptures of the Hindu tradition. Admiration, respect, and recognition of the value of trees can be found in all the great religious documents of India: the Vedas, the Upanishads, the Mahabharata, Ramayana, and the Puranas. In the remains of the Indus Valley civilization, the earliest of the Indian subcontinent, we find references to trees as the objects of religious worship.[13] For the people of the hills there was perhaps no document more relevant to their struggles than the Bhagavata Purana known also as the Shrimad Bhagavatam. Book 10 of that Purana was especially relevant to the struggle to protect the forests. It tells the stories of the birth, the childhood, and the adolescence of lord Krishna as he grew up among the *gopis* (cowherds) of Vrindavan. Sunderlal indicated to me that the life and adventures of

Krishna in the forests of Vrindavan are known in Garhwali translations from the ancient Sanskrit text and were especially popular in the villages of the Garhwal hills. In the many demonstrations to save the forests, these stories, which Indu Tai and others recited, were rich resources for reflection upon the moral and religious significance of the forests that were now desperately endangered.

The Bhagavata Purana contains the story of the miraculous escape of the infant Krishna from the evil king Kamsa across the Yamuna River and of his childhood under the care of his adoptive parents, the cowherd Nanda and his wife, Yashoda. It tells the stories of the sons of Kubera who learned humility by being incarnated as trees, eventually liberated by Krishna; of Krishna's swallowing a forest fire; and of Krishna's raising of Mount Govardhana, to shelter the gopis and their cattle from the storm arising from the jealous anger of Indra, the ancient Vedic god of rain. It contains the popular tale of the compelling sound in the night of Krishna's flute and of the response of the enchanted gopis who stole away from the security of the homes of their fathers and husbands to dance with Krishna in the moonlight. In the telling of these stories it becomes evident that forest protection is not an issue from which the divine is removed. Krishna is present in the forest of his childhood home. He is present in the forests of the Himalayas. One especially striking story in this *purana* tells of an occasion in which a demon by the name of Dhenuka had occupied a forest in which Krishna and his companions wanted to play and enjoy the fruit of the trees, and where they wanted to lead their cattle to graze. The chapter begins with the recognition of Krishna's love for nature and of its resplendent beauty. Here we read of his delight in the songs of the birds, the hum of the bees, and the sounds of the cattle. Noticing how the grasses and the green shoots in the forests embraced the feet of his divine brother Balarama, he observes, "How blessed are these little plants. They kiss your feet so that the state of ignorance, which was responsible for their birth as trees, might cease. Surely, they were holy men in their past lives."[14] As they are admiring the beauty of this setting, their companions tell them of a man-eating demon that was jealously guarding a forest of palmyra trees and preventing them from entering the forest, a situation that mirrors the plight of the village women who needed food, fuel, and fodder from the forest to provide for their families. The story celebrates Krishna's defeat of Dhenuka and of his opening of the forest so that the people could enjoy its fruit and their cattle could graze on the grass in the shade of the trees. The women of the forests could identify with the plight of Krishna and his friends. From the stories of his life in the forest, they found support for their struggle to survive. Bahuguna states that Indu Tai made the Srimad Bhagavatam her medium "to raise spiritual and ecological consciousness among the mass."[15] Vimla explains that Indu Tai interpreted the Bhagavata Purana in the modern context to explain the need to establish cordial relationships among the human being, the inner-self, society, and nature, providing the opportunity for education in ecology and the strategies of *satyagraha*.[16] She states that in the Puranas, she found the lessons of ecology in allegorical, mythical, and historical stories. She refers to Indu Tai as a powerful orator who had the capacity "to arouse and inspire common humanity and activate it for social transformation." Her message, however, was not just one of support through identification with the mythical heroes of the past. She believed in what she taught. "The present crisis of civilization," she argued, "is not just ecological or economical, it also has moral and spiritual aspects."[17] In the stories of Krishna in the forests of Vrindavan, she found authoritative grounding for the moral significance of the forests and the obligation of the people to be involved in their protection.

I stated that the practice of the Bhagavat Katha was especially prominent in a demonstration that occurred in the Advani forest in December 1977. There were a number of factors that prepared the way for this critical demonstration, factors that made this one of the most decisive demonstrations of the movement. An understanding of some of these factors will prepare us to understand a fourth critical mode of chipko activism. For one thing chipko activists were disturbed not only by the auction of trees to outside contractors but also by the results of the tapping of chir pines for resin. While the chir pine was of little use to the local people, they had come to realize that forest cover was vital for life in the hills, and they moved to protect them. The government committee that had been formed to investigate the practice had found that standard rules regulating the length, width, and depth of the cuts from which resin was extracted were rarely followed. The health and life of the trees were endangered. On May 30, 1977, known as Van Diwas (Forest Day), chipko activists in the Tehri district had informed the Forest Department that they intended to enter the forest to bandage the chir pines that had been damaged by inappropriate overtapping. A procession of activists entered the forest of the Hemvalghati region of Tehri Garhwal and applied mud and sack plasters to the wounds of the pines. As abusive tapping continued and the forest department did nothing to address the problem, the villagers began a program of direct action. On another historic occasion, July 25, 1977, the anniversary of the martyrdom of Sri Dev Suman, villagers began removing the iron blades inserted into the trees to bleed off their resin. Following this action, forestry officials eventually arrived to inspect the area. Observing the effects of abusive tapping and the results of the work of the villagers, one of them remarked that the village people had done precisely what the Forest Department should have been doing all along. Soon afterward, the Forest Department revoked the contracts for all resin tapping in these forests.[18]

Another factor that made this demonstration especially significant was the fact that, in terms of public awareness, 1977 was already a significant year for the environment in India. On October 15 of that year, the government of Uttar Pradesh accepted the final recommendations of the committee it had appointed after the Reni protest to study the claims of the chipko activists concerning environmental conditions in the Alakananda Valley. It supported the earlier ten-year ban on tree felling in the 1200 square kilometer (463 square miles) catchment of the Alakananda River and its tributaries, now saving the 2451 trees of the Reni forest indefinitely.[19] That year Sunderlal Bahuguna brought together a number of nationally recognized leaders in the Gandhian tradition who issued a public appeal supporting the demands of the Chipko Movement for the protection of the Himalayan forests and calling for a fundamental change in forest policy. These included the *sarvodaya* leader Jayaprakash Narayan and Kaka Kalelkar, the famous disciple and associate of Gandhi who had been influential in the freedom struggle in finding common bonds among diverse religious traditions of India. The same year also saw the passage of the forty-second amendment to the Indian constitution, which imposed obligations on the state and its citizens to protect the environment. One article stated specifically, "The State shall endeavour to protect and improve the environment and safeguard the forests and wildlife of the country" (Article 48A). Another stated: "It shall be the duty of every citizen of India to protect and improve the natural environment including forests, lakes, rivers and wildlife, and to have compassion for living creatures" (Article 51A).[20]

It is remarkable that with the success of the Chipko Movement in halting the felling of trees, the new amendments to the constitution, and the evident concession by government officials to some of the concerns of the chipko activists, the most critical feature of government forest management had not changed. Despite an earlier temporary moratorium, the policy of the forest auction was still very much in effect. In October 1977, at Narendranagar, the town in which Sunderlal had been incarcerated during the freedom struggle so many years before, a government auction sold 640 trees of the Advani forest and 273 trees of the Salet forest in the Hemvalghati region of Garhwal for contract felling. During the proceedings, Sunderlal undertook a fast and appealed to the district authorities and the forest contractors not to give up the forest to felling. Despite popular opposition, the auction proceeded, and the Advani forest was scheduled for felling in the first week of December 1977. Now, under the leadership of Bachni Devi, a woman whose husband was a village headman and a forest contractor, large numbers of women came forward to prevent the felling of the forest. Hundreds of women took a pledge to protect the trees even, if necessary, at the cost of their own lives. Dhoom Singh Negi, the most visible local chipko activist in the region, undertook a fast of five days to make the people fearless.[21] According to Vandana Shiva the women tied sacred threads to the trees as a token of a vow of protection. It was during the protest against the felling of the Advani forest that one of the most persuasive ecological slogans of the protesters came to be identified with the Chipko Movement. Differing versions of this incident are recorded in different sources. One of the strategies of the women of chipko was to carry lighted lanterns in the light of the day. This was to symbolize the wisdom of the forest women, as opposed to the knowledge of so-called scientific forestry. Vandana Shiva states that forest officials then arrived to intimidate the women and found them holding lighted lanterns in the light of the day. Out of curiosity, a forester asked them about their intentions. The women stated, "We have come to teach you forestry." To this he uttered the dismissive reply, "You foolish women, how can you who prevent felling know the value of the forest? Do you know what the forests bear? They produce profit and resin and timber." She states that the women immediately sang back in chorus:

> What do the forests bear?
> Soil, water and pure air.
> Soil, water and pure air
> Sustain the earth and all she bears."[22]

While a variety of sources express the slogan in slightly different terms, it seems to be this confrontation more than others that identified this slogan with the movement. Bahuguna himself put it this way, "What do the forests bear? Soil, water, and pure air! Soil, water, and pure air! These are the basis of life."

The protest in the Advani forest draws our attention to a fourth critical mode of resistance in the activism of the Chipko Movement. One of the practices of chipko activism that always drew media attention, and always raised public awareness, was Bahuguna's resort to the fast. Sunderlal's fast in the context of the demonstration in the Advani forest was not the first of his career, and it would by no means be the last. Along with the *padyatra*, the folk songs, and the Bhagavat Kathas, the fast became over time a prominent feature of the movement. But it was a form of protest that not everyone was able to practice. While Bahuguna was not the only person to engage in this practice, Richard St. Barbe Baker, the famous man of trees, once made the point that to the best of his knowledge Sunderlal Bahuguna was the only person to undertake a fast to death to save trees.[23] In the context of protests against life-threatening policies of the government, the fast underlined the gravity of the concerns of the movement. The fast demonstrated that the issues with which Chipko was concerned were matters of life and death.

I stated earlier that in October 1977, during the proceedings in which the Advani and Salet forests were auctioned, Sunderlal undertook a fast and appealed to district authorities and contractors not to give up the forest to the ax. Later, Dhoom Singh Negi undertook a fast in support of the women who undertook the week-long vigil in the Advani forest. Recognizing the strength and determination of the women during the vigil in the Advani forest, the contractors eventually departed. But they returned on February 1, 1978, now accompanied by two truckloads of armed police. The contractor's intention was to blockade the forest in order to undertake felling operations without the interference of the people. But the chipko activists had already entered the forest and made their case to the laborers. When the contractors arrived with the police, they found chipko volunteers guarding every tree they had marked for felling. Before nightfall the police again withdrew.[24]

In December 1978 *sarvodaya* workers learned that the State Forest Development Corporation was planning felling operations in the area of Badiyargad midway between the Bhagirathi and the Alakananda rivers. Guha reports that Dhum Singh Negi, Kunwar Prasun, Pratap Shikhar, and Vijay Jardari went from village to village to inform the people of the government's plans and its harmful ecological effects. Vimla Bahuguna and other women of the movement mobilized the women of the villages. On January 9, 1979, his fifty-second birthday, Sunderlal again began a fast. Conducted in an abandoned shepherd's hut and in the depth of winter, this fast became the focus of the agitation. Guha states that more than three thousand people participated in the protest.[25] Opponents of the Chipko Movement eventually burned down the grass hut in which he had taken up his fast, but he continued his fast in a nearby cowshed. In the middle of the night on January 22 the police arrested Sunderlal and took him to Tehri jail, the same jail in which Sri Dev Suman had suffered and died after a fast of eighty-four days on July 25, 1944. With the leadership of Ghanshyam Sailani and a respected priest named Khimad Nand Shastri, thousands of men, women, and children then occupied the Badiyargad forests. From January 26 the protesters again undertook readings from the ancient texts and listened to Bhagavat Kathas as they guarded the forest from the cutters. After eleven days the contractors admitted defeat, abandoned felling operations, and withdrew. Sunderlal was released from jail on January 31 1979, but did not break his fast until February 2 when the state government issued an order to the effect that no new auctions or felling would be carried out until such time as Bahuguna could meet to discuss the matter with the chief minister of the state.[26]

Because of the attention the fast seemed always to receive in the press, and because of the attention it brought to the movement, it is difficult to underestimate its importance. Yet stories in the press and studies of the movement provide little insight into the background of the fast, its meaning, or its purpose. For this reason, it is useful to examine this mode of resistance in some detail. In some cases, press reports and studies of the movement refer to the fast as a hunger strike. Bahuguna considers this designation both inaccurate and misleading. What then were the background, the meaning, and the purpose of the fast as a mode of protest in the context of the movement to save the forests of the Himalayas? In my conversations with Bahuguna, its background in Gandhi's philosophy of *satyagraha* became especially clear. Gandhi's view of the meaning and purpose of the fast was the ideal to which Sunderlal's engagement with the fast aspired. But it was not with his study of Gandhi that his knowledge of the fast began. As we suggested earlier, Sunderlal's first acquaintance with the fast came from his mother. We noted that as part of her religious practice she regularly undertook a fast on the full moon of each lunar month. But during the days of her fast she allowed herself no reduction in the work she had to do. When her husband died she did not abandon the practice, but increased its performance twofold. From an early age Sunderlal understood her fast as a profound expression of personal commitment to God. His repeated insistence that the fast is not a hunger strike but an act of devotion is rooted in this early experience. It was during his tutelage to Sri Dev Suman that Sunderlal began to understand the gravity of the fast and its power in the context of nonviolent resistance against injustice. It was Sri Dev Suman's commitment to nonviolence that stood behind his fast of eighty-four days in the Tehri jail that ended in his death.

But it was during his days in Sikhanwala, the remote town in Punjab where he spent a year underground, that Sunderlal committed himself to the writings of Gandhi. It was there that he came to understand Gandhi's experience with the fast and its place in his philosophy of *satyagraha*, which enabled Sunderlal to understand the meaning of the fast for Sri Dev Suman. It was here that the meaning, gravity, and power of the fast became apparent to him. During this year underground Sunderlal himself began to experiment with fasting and proceeded to reduce his diet to one meal a day. On his return to Tehri when the police of the princely state refused him admission to the town, Sunderlal undertook his first experiment in *satyagraha*. There he undertook a fast of almost a week at the Iron Bridge at the entrance to the town. And there his experiment in *satyagraha* prevailed. The success of this experiment, he says, strengthened his resolve for future acts of nonviolent resistance. Throughout Sunderlal's career it was Gandhi's recognition of the importance of fasting that determined the meaning the fast would have for him and the role it would have in the arsenal of this devotee of nonviolence. To understand the significance of the fast for Bahuguna, it will be instructive to look briefly at Gandhi's experience with fasting.

In his autobiography, Gandhi points out that as a child of a Vaishnavite family, and of a mother who was given to keeping religious vows, he himself came as a matter of course to observe a fast on Ekadashi and other holy days. But he states that in doing so he was only imitating his mother and seeking to please his parents. He states that later he undertook fasting now and again for reasons of health. But during his days in South Africa, he found that his friend Hermann Kallenbach deployed the fast in support of his *brahamacarya* vow. Gandhi states that when he heard about it, he followed Kallenbach's example and began to keep a fast on Ekadashi for the purpose of achieving self restraint.[27] He states: "I was anxious to observe *brahmacharya* in thought, word and deed, and equally anxious to devote the maximum of time to the *satyagraha* struggle and fit myself for it by cultivating purity."[28] Passion, he states, is generally coexistent with a hankering after the pleasures of the palate. Recognizing this weakness in himself, he had already begun to exclusively eat fruit. Thus on Ekadashi, when the Hindus generally allow themselves milk along with fruit, he observed a complete fast, permitting himself only water. Eventually he came to attach greater importance to fasting and began to deploy it on almost any occasion for penance.

A particularly striking occasion for penance presented itself in what he calls "the moral fall" of two of the students in the school at one of his ashrams. While he does not state the nature of the offence, he indicates that, for him, it was a "fiery ordeal." The news, he states, "came upon me like a thunderbolt." He acknowledges that his wife had already warned him in the matter, but he states that "being of a trusting nature, I had ignored her caution."[29] He immediately undertook a train journey to the ashram to address the matter and states that in the course of the journey his own responsibility for their behavior became as clear to him as daylight. If he was to be their real teacher and guardian, he must find a way to touch their hearts. He states: "I felt that the only way the guilty parties could be made to realize my distress and the depth of their own fall would be for me to do some penance." He imposed upon himself a fast for seven days and a vow to have only one meal a day for four and a half months thereafter.[30] Gandhi did not believe that a teacher should resort to the fast at every moral failing of his student, but believed that this was a situation that called for such a drastic measure. He also states that unless there is true love between the teacher and the pupil, unless the pupil's delinquency has touched the very being of the teacher, and unless the pupil has genuine respect for the teacher, the fast is out of place and may even be harmful.[31] For a fast to be effective, he states, one must be in possession of clarity of vision and spiritual fitness.

For Gandhi, the decision in favor of a fast came as a relief. It meant, he says, a heavy load off his mind. "The anger against the guilty parties subsided and gave place to the purest pity for them." While he acknowledges that his penance caused some pain, he states that it cleared the atmosphere. "Everyone came to realize what a terrible thing it was to be sinful, and the bond that bound me to the boys and girls became stronger and truer." It was a case in which, as he puts it elsewhere, a "genuine fast cleanses the body, mind and soul."[32] He states that the circumstances arising from this incident compelled him a little later to undergo a further fast of fourteen days through which he learned some of the techniques for conducting an effective fast. In his discussion of this case, he mentions the efficacy of *ramanama*, the repetition of the name of God, and he emphasizes the importance of drinking plenty of water. It is also significant that during his fast he regularly listened to readings from the Ramayana and other sacred books.[33] Another striking occasion in which Gandhi resorted to the fast is also instructive. It occurred during the strike of the textile workers in Ahmedabad. Gandhi had received word about the working conditions of the mill workers from their principal organizer, a woman named Anasuya Behn. Wages were low, and the laborers had been agitating for a raise in pay. Gandhi had the desire to guide them in their efforts but felt he could not do so from a distance. He decided to make the journey to Ahmedabad. Because Gandhi was on friendly terms with both the laborers and the owners of the mill, he describes the situation as delicate. He recommended that the laborers resort to a strike. But he explained to them the conditions necessary for such a strike to be effective. He states that they must (1) never resort to violence, (2) never molest the strike breakers, (3) never depend upon alms but earn bread during the strike by other honest labor, and finally (4) remain firm in these commitments no matter how long the strike should continue. He states that the leaders of the strike understood and accepted these conditions, and at a general meeting the laborers pledged not to resume work until their terms were accepted or until the mill owners agreed to refer the dispute to arbitration. During the strike, thousands of laborers attended meetings in which Gandhi reminded them of their pledge and of their duty to maintain peace and self-respect. In daily peaceful processions through the streets of the city, they carried a banner bearing the inscription "Ek Tek," meaning "One Resolve." As the strike proceeded, Gandhi consulted with the mill owners, entreating them to do justice to the workers. But his entreaties failed to move them.[34]

He states that for the first two weeks of the strike, the mill workers showed great courage and self-restraint. But then they began to show signs of flagging. Attendance at the daily meetings began to decline, and on the faces of those who did attend he saw signs of despair. Their attitude toward the strike breakers became more and more menacing, and Gandhi began to fear an outbreak of violence. He states that he felt deeply troubled and began to think furiously to comprehend his duty. His thoughts are informative: "The mill-hands had taken the pledge at my suggestion. They had repeated it before me day after day, and the very idea that they might now go back upon it was to me inconceivable. Was it pride or was it my love for the labourers and my passionate regard for truth that was at the back of this feeling—who can say?"[35] Presently the answer came. At one of the meetings of the workers, Gandhi suddenly saw the light. He states: "Unbidden and all by themselves the words came to my lips: 'unless the strikers rally,' I declared to the meeting, 'and continue the strike till a settlement is reached, or till they leave the mills altogether, I will not touch any food.'" The laborers, he says, were "thunder struck." The eyes of Anasuya Behn, the organizer of the laborers, were filled with tears. The laborers announced it was they rather then he that should fast. They begged his forgiveness for their lapse and promised to be faithful to the end. He replied that there was no need for them to fast but only remain true to their pledge. He stated that his fast would continue until the strike was settled.[36]

Gandhi's fast placed him in a delicate situation because he had enjoyed a close and cordial relationship with the owners of the mill. As a practitioner of *satyagraha* he didn't want them to be coerced by his fast, but by the strike of the mill workers alone. "My fast was undertaken," he writes, "not on account of lapse of the mill-owners, but on account of that of the labourers in which, as their representative, I felt I had a share."[37] To fast against the mill owners, he explains, would amount to coercion. Finally he recognized that his fast would inevitably put pressure on them as well, but he felt that this was something over which he had no control. His duty to fast, he says, was clear. He states that Anasuya Behn and a number of other colleagues chose to fast with Gandhi on the first day, but he dissuaded them from continuing it further. The result, he says, was an atmosphere of good will. The hearts of the mill owners were touched, and they set about to find the means for a resolution. The opposing parties agreed upon an arbitrator and after twenty-one days, they reached a settlement. The strike ended after only a three-day fast.

These cases exemplify some of the principles that governed Gandhi's practice of the fast, principles to which Sunderlal also always tried to adhere. In the first place the fast is nonviolent. In 1947 in the publication *Harijan*, Gandhi states that the fast is "the last weapon in the armoury of the votary of Ahimsa."[38] Second, because it is nonviolent, a genuine fast permits no harmful intention to be harbored toward the wrongdoer. Ahimsa requires, says Gandhi, "not injuring any living being, whether by body or mind." In undertaking the fast he was not to hurt the wrongdoer. He could not bear ill will toward him causing him fear or mental suffering.[39] On the contrary, the practitioner of the fast must have pure benevolence for the offender. Third, because it entails no harmful intention toward the wrongdoer, it accepts the imposition of suffering upon oneself. As Bart Gruzalski points out in his book on Gandhi, the suffering to be born is not to be imposed on those whose actions the *satyagrahi* wants to change but by the *satyagrahi* himself. "Ahimsa," says Gandhi, "requires deliberate self-suffering, not a deliberate injuring of the supposed wrong doer."[40] The objective of the fast, therefore, is not to embarrass, coerce, or manipulate the offender. Its objective is not to coerce but to convert. Finally the fast is not directed even to the reason of the offender. It is directed to the heart. Gandhi argues that all true change comes from within. A nonviolent action is intended to open the inner understanding of the man. According to Gandhi nonviolence is the greatest force "because of the limitless scope it affords for self-suffering without causing or intending any physical or material injury to the wrongdoer. The object always is to evoke the best in him. Self-suffering is an appeal to his better nature, as retaliation is to his baser. Fasting under proper circumstances is such an appeal *par excellence*."[41] As Gandhi said elsewhere, "any change brought about by pressure is worthless."[42]

It is significant that Gandhi also acknowledges, as was the case in the mill workers' strike, that it is not always possible to be certain that undue pressure or a sense of coercion may not result from the fast. He also acknowledges that the fast can be subject to abuse when it is used for a selfish purpose. But while he acknowledges that the dividing line between selfish and unselfish purposes is often very thin, he urges that "a person who regards the end of a fast to be selfish or otherwise base should resolutely refuse to yield to it, even though the refusal may result in the death of the fasting person." Nevertheless he states that as a weapon in the armoury of *satyagraha,* the fast cannot be given up simply because of the possibility that it may result in a sense of coercion or because of its possible abuse.[43]

In October 1977, when Sunderlal undertook a fast at Narendranagar, his action was not intended to coerce or embarrass the government that was selling 640 trees of the Advani forest and 273 trees of the Salet forest. It was not against the laborers, whom he considered his brothers, nor against the contractors. While he appealed to the district authorities and the forest contractors not to give up the forest to felling, his action was not intended to manipulate them. His purpose was to participate in the suffering of those who were to lose the benefits of the forests upon which they depend for their very survival. In this case his effort was like the effort of Gandhi to reveal to the offending students in the ashram the depths of suffering their actions brought about. For Gandhi, "fasting is a spiritual act and, therefore addressed to God." The desired effect is that their sleeping conscience is awakened.[44] Likewise in January of 1979, during the fast that became the rallying point of the villages around Badyargarh, Sunderlal's intention was to identify with the suffering of the village people. While he intended no coercion, the pressure the authorities felt was evident in his arrest and incarceration in the Tehri jail. But it is clear that the hearts of the state authorities were eventually moved. This is evident in their resolution not to carry out any new felling or auction before Bahuguna discussed the issue with the chief minister of the state.

It is also significant that for Gandhi the fast is not the first weapon of the votary of nonviolence, nor is it simply one weapon among others. It is the last weapon. While we cannot draw explicit analogies between fasts that are conducted by different people at different times with differing purposes in mind, it is significant that when Gandhi undertook his fast in the situation of the erring students in his ashram, he felt that the only way the guilty parties could be made to realize his distress and the depth of their own moral failing was for him to undertake some penance. He felt that he had a share in their failing because he was their teacher and guardian. Sunderlal was neither the teacher nor the guardian of the Forest Department. Nevertheless he was both the son and the son-in-law of forest officers. Moreover, as a longtime *sarvodaya* worker who had committed himself to the uplift of the villages of the hills, he shared the same ostensive goal to which the Forest Department itself was also ideally committed, the welfare of the people. Like Gandhi, he felt he was implicated in their policies and their actions. As a representative of the people of the hills, he had attempted to impress the depths of the suffering of the people upon these officials by various means, by peaceful protests, by demonstrations, and by impassioned speeches to the officials themselves. And like Gandhi in the situation of the erring students, he felt that only one path remained open. In the situation of the striking mill workers, Gandhi's fast was not against the mill owners. It was not their lapse but the lapse of the mill workers that provoked his fast. His action was in support of the mill workers which, as their representative, he felt he had a share. It was a voluntary participation in their suffering. Again he felt it was the only option available to him. Weber records the words of Bahuguna when he undertook this fast: "When all our proposals, requests and people's representation failed to persuade the U.P. State Government to stop green felling in the hills and felling of trees started in full strength in the sensitive catchment of the Alaknanda in spite of people's protests. . . . [I] started this self-imposed penance to awaken the sleeping spirit of the conservationists to save Himalayas and ultimately the flood devastated country."[45] As Gandhi puts it "when human ingenuity fails, the votary fasts."[46]

In discussing his fasts with me Sunderlal emphasized that the fast is not a hunger strike, but an act of devotion to God. The hunger strike is a protest in which you have some anger against your adversary. "You know," he said, "the soldier of non-violence takes pains upon himself. There is a difference between that and a violent struggle. In a violent struggle you accuse the other side. In a non-violent struggle you search inside yourself, that whatever wrong is happening is due to our sins. And taking responsibility for those I have to repent."[47] At another time he said, "Here you believe that there is God inside everybody. And so you pray to the God to awaken the God inside him to make him realize that he is making a mistake." These fasts, he said, were prayerful fasts. "A fast is a prayer to reach the heart of the other person whom you think that is doing wrong. Fast means that you want to improve him also. You know there is difference between this and an ordinary struggle in which you want to eliminate your adversary. Here you want to change his heart."[48] And as with Gandhi the fast is the last strategy in the arsenal of the devotee of nonviolence. He states that when all his worldly efforts have failed, the votary of nonviolence finally leaves the affairs of the world where they stand and puts himself under the protection of God. His fast is the expression of his faith. When nobody listens to you, he said to me, then you can sit in prayer so that the almighty will listen to you. Here there is no longer any anger. Rather, one is fully satisfied. One is completely surrendered to the pleasure of the almighty. "If God so chooses, the body can be taken away."[49]

Chapter 9

A Permanent Economy

I stated earlier that from the beginning of his engagement with the Chipko Movement there were two central themes that occupied Sunderlal's attention. One was the establishment of community organizations to support sustainable, economically independent villages; the other was the condition of the forests upon which such village economies and local households depend. The one concern was related to issues of village social disintegration brought about by what Sunderlal calls a money order economy, wherein able-bodied men left the villages in the hills to find employment in the plains, from where they sent money orders home to address the basic needs of their families. The other was related to the needs of local households, the principal responsibility of the village women. In the course of time, these two sets of concerns came into conflict. From as early as 1973 the DGSS was effective in pressuring the Forest Department to end its policy of discrimination in the distribution of raw materials to local forest-based industries. Weber notes that by 1975 the state government had formed a Forest Corporation with the purpose of undertaking felling operations without the auction of forests to outside contractors. "Raw materials were made more readily available to small-scale industries and smaller forest lots were auctioned so that local industries had a better chance of competing where the Forest Corporation had not taken over."[1] By that time the government had implemented minimum wage legislation and other measures to improve the condition of the forest workers. From his experience especially with the protests in the Hemvalgati region and his observation of forest destruction from his many forest *padyatras*, it eventually became clear to Sunderlal that it makes no difference whether outside contractors were cutting down the forests or whether local forest cooperatives were doing the job. In both cases forests upon which local

Gaumukh, the Source of the Bhagirathi River, Where in 1978 Sunderlal Bahuguna Took the Pledge to Protect the Himalayas in All Aspects

household economies were dependent were being destroyed. Even local turpentine plants required the burning of two kilograms of pinewood as fuel to produce one kilogram of resin.[2] For Sunderlal the destruction of forest cover would be disastrous for the people of the hills and ultimately for the nation. In May 1978 at Gaumukh, where the Bhagirathi the northernmost tributary of the Ganges has its source in the Gangotri Glacier, Sunderlal Bahuguna took a pledge to devote himself to the protection of the Himalayan environment in all its aspects. He found support for this perspective in Gandhi's view of rural self sufficiency in which villagers lived in a nonexploitative relationship with nature in harmony with their natural surroundings. He believed that forest-based industries that destroy the trees were not necessary to address the economic needs of the villagers and concluded that the villagers could meet their needs for food, fodder, fuel, fertilizer, and fiber without cutting down the trees.

There were a number of persons and publications that supported this change in Bahuguna's perspective. During the Chipko Movement Sarala Behn had introduced him to a new book by the renowned British economist E. F. Schumacher. The book *Small Is Beautiful* (1973) was then an international best seller whose scholarly merit might be concealed by its eye-catching title and its popular appeal. It was a broad critique of the science of economics as it was currently understood in the Western world and practiced internationally. In it Sunderlal found intellectual support for many of the concerns and emerging objectives of the Chipko Movement. Its subtitle, *Economics as if People Mattered* made sense in light of the prevailing conflicts between the forest contractors with the support of a government policy of the economic exploitation of the forests and the survival needs of the local people. In his introduction to the book, Theodore Roszak makes the point that the work "belongs to that subterranean tradition of organic and decentralist economics," whose major spokesmen include both Prince Kropotkin and Gandhi, authors of the two pamphlets which, under the guidance of Sri Dev Suman, Sunderlal had read at age thirteen. Schumacher was a close student of Gandhi whose economics started and finished, as Roszak points out, with the people.[3]

Schumacher agrees with other economists that the main subject of economics is "goods." But he argues that one of the most striking antinomies of the prevailing economic system is the tendency to reduce the consideration of all goods to goods of a single kind. While it does distinguish between consumers' goods and producers' goods, it fails to recognize the crucial distinction between primary goods, that is, those that are taken from nature, and secondary goods, those that are manufactured. Once any goods have appeared on the market, he says, "they are treated the same, as objects for sale, and economics is primarily concerned with theorizing on the bargain hunting activities of the purchaser." He argues that the distinction, between primary and secondary goods, is critical "because the latter presupposes the availability of the former." The human being, he says, is not the producer but only the converter of goods. Moreover, the power to convert depends upon energy, which "immediately points to the need for a vital distinction within the field of primary goods, that between non-renewable and renewable." He argues that among secondary goods there is also a vital distinction to be recognized between manufactured goods and services. "The market," he says, "knows nothing of these distinctions. It provides a price tag for all goods and thereby enables us to pretend that they are all of equal significance." But clearly they are not of equal significance, because the primary goods are not in unlimited supply. "Since there is now increasing evidence of environmental deterioration, particularly in living nature, the entire outlook and methodology of economics is being called into question."[4] He states that in the interest of the ever-increasing production of goods, the present economic system considers short-term gains economically viable, while the long term tends to be left out of account. "This means that an activity can be economic although it plays hell with the environment, and that a competing activity, if at some cost it protects and conserves the environment, will be uneconomic."[5] Because economics deals with goods in accordance with their market value, even the priceless is given a price. "To the extent that economic thinking is based on the market," he says, "it takes the sacredness out of life." He argues, therefore, that "if economic thinking pervades the whole of society, even simple non-economic values like beauty, health, or cleanliness can survive only if they prove to be 'economic.' "[6] The same rules that apply to manufactured goods are applied to those goods that human beings must win from nature. "All goods are treated the same, because the point of view is fundamentally that of private profit-making, and this means that it is inherent in the methodology of economics to *ignore man's dependence on the natural world.*"[7]

According to Schumacher, this economic system has tended to resist change and revision, because "until fairly recently the economists have felt entitled . . . to treat the entire framework within which economic activity takes place as *given*, that is to say, as permanent and indestructible."[8] It has become a religion with its own rules of conduct. "If a buyer refused a good bargain because he suspected that the cheapness of the goods in question stemmed from exploitation or other despicable practices (except theft), he would be open to the criticism of behaving 'uneconomically,' which is viewed as nothing less than a fall from grace." For Schumacher, "The religion of economics has its own code of ethics, and the First Commandment is to behave 'economically.' "[9] Materialist economics, he says, has "built a system of production that ravishes nature and a type of society that mutilates man."[10]

While Schumacher speaks broadly about what he calls "modern" or "materialistic" economics, his point is that it is not the only possible economic system. Against it he juxtaposes what he calls "Buddhist economics." He explains, however, that the choice of Buddhism is purely incidental and that the teachings of Christianity, Islam, Judaism, or any of the great traditions of Asia offer a similar, compatible, and viable alternative to the prevailing system. In other parts of the book, in fact, he draws heavily from the classical Christian virtues. He does not equate Buddhist economics with the economy of any particular Buddhist country, many of which he acknowledges to be increasingly enamored with the economic system of the West. He does not claim that a Buddhist economics has been explicitly articulated, but from his knowledge of Buddhist teachings and the kind of life he has observed in Buddhist countries, he envisions what such an economy would mean. "While the materialist is mainly interested in goods," he says, "the Buddhist is mainly interested in liberation." He explains further, however, that Buddhism is the middle path between the

extremes of self-indulgence and asceticism and in no way is antagonistic
to physical well-being. "It is not wealth that stands in the way of liberation but the attachment to wealth."[11] For him, the keynote of Buddhist
economics is simplicity and nonviolence. What he sees as the marvel of
Buddhist life is the "amazingly small means leading to extraordinarily
satisfactory results." He states that while materialist economics considers
consumption to be the sole end and purpose of all economic activity,
Buddhist economics regards the ownership and consumption of goods as
the means to the end of human well-being.[12] He states that the effort to
sustain a way of life so ordered "is likely to be much smaller than the effort
needed to sustain a drive for maximum consumption." From the point of
view of Buddhist economics, he says, production from local resources for
local needs is "the most rational way of economic life, while dependence
on imports from afar and the consequent need to produce for export to
unknown and distant peoples is highly uneconomic and justifiable only
in exceptional cases and on a small scale." The Buddhist economist would
hold, he says, "that to satisfy human wants from faraway sources rather
than from sources nearby signifies failure rather than success."[13] Thus
while a materialist economics results in the harsh and imprudent treatment of those things upon which we ultimately depend, especially water
and trees, the teachings of the Buddha enjoins an attitude of reverence
and nonviolence towards all sentient beings but to trees in particular.
He points out that the follower of the Buddha is enjoined to plant a tree
every few years and look after it until it is safely established. A Buddhist
economist can demonstrate, he says, "that the universal observation of
this rule would result in a high rate of genuine economic development
independent of any foreign aid." He suggests that much of the economic
decay of Southeast Asia and many other parts of the world is the result
of "a heedless and shameful neglect of trees."[14]

Sunderlal was impressed with many of the insights of this unusual
economic treatise. It is not surprising that he found Schumacher's ideas
relevant to a protest against the extraction of trees from the hills to serve
the interests of a distant market. He could see that the economics that
the British had introduced to India and that had remained in place after
independence stood in stark disjunction from the economics reflected in
the life of the villages. He could see that the life and well-being of the
people of the villages were not a viable consideration in the calculus of
the religion of economics. But he also saw that Schumacher's insights into
the situation of the villages were not altogether new. Gandhi had made
many similar points. Years before, Sunderlal had read *The Economy of*

Permanence by J. C. Kumarappa, the Gandhian economist whom Schumacher cites in support of his understanding of a Buddhist economics. Like Schumacher, Kumarappa had drawn distinctions among a number of kinds of economies. In light of Schumacher's distinction between the materialist and the Buddhist economics, they are illuminating. Kumarappa's typology distinguishes between five distinctive kinds: (1) a parasitic economy harms if it does not completely destroy the source of its benefit, (2) an economy of predation attempts to achieve its own benefit without contributing to the benefit of others, (3) an economy of enterprise motivated by ambition and enlightened self-interest desires to benefit co-workers, as well as others if possible, (4) an economy of gregation (his own coinage) is motivated by the common interest of the group rather than that of the individual member, and (5) an economy of service is based on love and the desire to serve without reward. He holds that just as individuals can pass from one kind of economy to another, so a group of individuals can advance collectively from one kind of economy to another. These economies generally correspond with what he sees as the three stages of civilization: parasitic and predatory economies belong to what he calls the primitive or animal stage of civilization. He states that an economy dependent on colonial production or on exploited labor is a parasitic economy. They are transient and violent. Economies of enterprise and gregation belong to the modern or human stage. They are also transient with a pronounced element of violence but also with "a growing desire for permanency and non-violence." The economy of service belongs to the advanced or spiritual stage of civilization which strives for peace, permanence, and nonviolence. "Here," he says, "the sense of duty, not only to those of the group, but to all creatures, pervades the whole atmosphere." While he can identify the first four economies in history and especially in the history of India, he states that he has yet to find a large social group that exemplifies the economy of service. He states that it was toward this stage of civilization that Gandhi was pressing, and that only if it should succeed could we see the establishment of a nonviolent economy of permanence.[15] Sunderlal told me that after reading Schumacher's book, he felt that Schumacher had done a commendable job of presenting Gandhi's economic ideas to a Western readership. In it he found an idiom by which he could relate the struggles of the Chipko Movement to a larger public. Schumacher's claim that a viable economics depends upon the recognition of the importance of ecology and Kumarappa's recognition of the importance of permanence over a transient economy led Sunderlal to coin a slogan for which he came to be widely known. From his encounter with Schumacher, from his reading of Gandhi and Kumarappa, and from his engagement with the economic issues in the villages of the hills, he came to recognize that ecology is permanent economy.

Weber suggests that another reason for the clarification of Bahuguna's viewpoint and his emerging emphasis upon ecology may have been related to his meeting with Richard St. Barbe Baker, the famous British forester who at the time had been touring the world raising consciousness about the hazard of the loss of what he called the earth's green mantle and motivating people the world over to become involved in its restoration. Sunderlal gives high praise to this pioneer in forest restoration. In an article written in 1979 he states that his first meeting with St. Barbe Baker was on November 20, 1977. At the age of eighty-eight, St. Barbe Baker was in New Delhi to participate in an International Vegetarian Congress. Two months earlier Sunderlal had written to him through the *Ecologist Magazine* in England, giving him a brief account of the Chipko Movement and requesting that he devote some time to the Himalayas on his arrival in India. St. Barbe Baker never received that letter. What Sunderlal had read of his life and thought inspired such a sense of veneration that he decided to make his way down to Delhi "as if on a pilgrimage" to see this man. Finally they met. At his meeting with this man, Bahuguna states, "I felt as if I was in the presence of a heavenly soul."[16] Elsewhere he pointed out that as soon as St. Barbe Baker heard about the Chipko Movement in the Himalayas he decided he wanted to go there. To Sunderlal he said, "I want to go on a pilgrimage to that place."[17] Sunderlal points out that some of the important people in Delhi tried to dissuade him. They told him that considering his age and the state of his health, he should not take the risk of traveling into such rugged terrain. St. Barbe replied that at the most it would cost him his life, and that if he should die in the cause of the Himalayas it would be the most glorious event of his life. Sunderlal points out that his own opposition to what was widely regarded as a scientific approach to the felling of trees had made him an unpopular person. But when they asked their guest how long he had known the man with whom he would be traveling in the Himalayas, he replied that they had known each other for many lives![18] Other officials encouraged him to go. Sunderlal told me that as a guest of the government of India, St. Barbe Baker was to give a lecture at the Forest Research Institute in Dehra Dun. Sunderlal accompanied him to that institute and from there to the Garhwal hills. St. Barbe Baker states that when he decided to go with Sunderlal to visit the chipko people, he received the support of one minister of the central government, the minister of chemicals and petroleum, himself a man of the hills, who was interested to hear St. Barbe Baker's impression of the Chipko Movement and its demands for a moratorium on green felling of the forests of the Himalayas.[19]

Between Sunderlal and St. Barbe, as he was known to his friends, there was an instant and profound rapport. St. Barbe traveled with Sunderlal to Tehri Garhwal, visited the sites of many of the chipko demonstrations, and met many of the chipko activists. For Sunderlal one of the most memorable events on this journey occurred when they came to see the Advani forest already marked for felling the following month. There, he says, St. Barbe requested the vehicle to stop. He bowed his head, closed his eyes, and offered this simple but profoundly moving prayer, "I pray for these trees that they might live!"[20] For St. Barbe, one of the most engaging experiences was his visit to the hill campus of Garhwal University, where he delivered three lectures and where the students kept him with their questions beyond midnight. Sunderlal also took him to visit the now elderly Vinoba Bhave from whom Sunderlal received the inspiration for his many *padytras* in support of the Chipko Movement. When I asked Sunderlal about St. Barbe's ideas of forestry and how they differed from the kind of forestry that had been practiced in the Himalayas, he stated that the traditional foresters managed forests for timber. "For St. Barbe," he said, "the tree does not mean timber: the tree means oxygen, the tree means water, the tree means soil." And especially in the hill terrain the tree contributes to the stability of the landscape. He believed, therefore, that all the hill slopes should be covered with trees. He stated that St. Barbe's viewpoint was quite different from the traditional view "because he was a humanitarian, and he had worked among the tribal people in Africa. So he knew the relationship of forests with human beings. He was a far sighted man. And he knew that the future of humankind lies in saving the forests."[21]

By the time of this visit to India and to the Himalayas, Richard St. Barbe Baker had already lived a life for which the term "remarkable" would be an understatement. Born in Hampshire, England, in 1889, St. Barbe relates in his autobiography (1970) that he had felt the call to his lifelong mission of saving trees when, alone and at the age of five or six, he first ventured into a forest near his home.[22] The experience reminds us of a similar experience in the childhood of Mira Behn. As he set out on what he calls "that greatest of all forest adventures," he soon found himself in a dense part of the forest where the path was lost in the bracken beneath the pines. Soon he was completely isolated in the luxuriant, tangled growth of ferns, which were well above his head. His response was neither panic nor fear. He states that he wandered on as though in a dream, having lost all sense of time and space. Although he could see only a few yards ahead of him, he had no sense of being shut in. The sensation was exhilarating. He states, "I began to walk faster, buoyed up with an almost ethereal feeling of well-being as if I had been detached from the earth. I became intoxicated with the beauty around me, immersed in the joyousness and exultation of feeling a part of it all." Soon he entered a clearing where the dry pine needles covered the forest floor with a soft brown carpet. The rays of light that pierced the canopy of the forest were illuminated in the ground mist and appeared as glorious beams interlaced with the tall shafts of the trees. He states: "I had entered the temple of the woods. I sank to the ground in a state of ecstasy." He refers to this encounter as his "woodland rebirth," an experience that followed him, he says, through all his years.[23]

St. Barbe's autobiography is replete with fascinating details of his vision and mission that offer insight into the depth of his encounter with Sunderlal. At school he was enthralled with the sciences of botany and forestry. His father made his living as an arborist, a specialist in the planting and maintenance of trees, but he was also an enthusiastic evangelical worker. He had built a mission hall on his property and held meetings on Sunday afternoons and evenings. From a young age Richard was interested in this ministry. From the age of twelve he would occasionally substitute for his father as the preacher and director of the meetings. His home was the meeting place of a number of influential evangelical preachers, including the revered Melville Churchill, cousin of the later Sir Winston, and General William Booth, later the founder of the Salvation Army. While at school he happened to hear a talk from a man who had just returned from Canada and decided he must go there. Then a missionary pioneer from the western prairies of Canada encouraged him to make the journey to western Canada to undertake a ministry to the settlers on the prairie. He sailed for Canada in 1909, where he homesteaded to support himself while attending Emmanuel College of the University of Saskatchewan, where one of his classmates was John Diefenbaker later prime minister of Canada. During his time as a student and part time minister he could see that the agricultural practices of the European settlers, especially the plowing of prairie grasslands and the cutting of natural scrub trees, were leading to soil degradation. Later, working in a lumber camp near Prince Albert, Saskatchewan, he was disturbed by the unnecessary waste of trees. He observed what he called "a desert in the making."[24] After three years he returned to England to prepare for ministry at Ridley Hall, Cambridge.

But these plans were interrupted by the outbreak of the First World War. He enlisted and served in France in a field artillery unit and was wounded on three occasions. Following his last injury he was discharged from the military, and after the war he returned to Cambridge University where he earned a diploma in forestry.

His first assignment as a forester was in 1920. Under the Colonial Office he went to Kenya, where he observed that centuries of land mismanagement, including the clear felling of trees, was leading to the devastation of large tracts of land. With meager funds to address the problem, he consulted with the elders of Kenya's Kikuyu people to see how they might participate in a program to restore the region's natural forest cover. There in 1922 he set up a tree nursery and a program for the voluntary planting of trees. In answer to his challenge three thousand Kikuyu Warriors came to his camp. With the help of their chief, Josiah Njonjo, he founded *Wau wa Miti* (Men of Trees). In a way that reminds one of Sunderlal's pledge to protect the Himalayas, the volunteers took a pledge before N'gai, the high god, that they would protect the native forests, plant native trees every year, and protect and care for all trees everywhere.[25] Two years later he returned to England to found the Men of Trees, England, which engendered organizations of similar nature in countries around the world. From 1924 to 1928 he served as assistant conservator of forests for the southern provinces of Nigeria, where he initiated other programs of forest restoration and undertook forest planning on the Gold Coast. His work with the colonial government in Nigeria came abruptly to an end when he defended a Kikuyu worker against an assault by a British official. This action put an end to his career in the Colonial Service, but supported his credibility among the Africans. In his biography he states that his discharge from the Colonial Service liberated him for greater work in reforestation and the regeneration of the earth in other parts of the world.[26] In 1931, at the invitation of its governor designate, Sir John Chancellor, St. Barbe went to Palestine to assist in launching a program that united the differing religious communities of the country in a tree planting project for the benefit of all.[27]

It is interesting that while Richard St. Barbe Baker is little known in the United States, he played a decisive role in saving the California redwoods. Touring the United States and Canada in the early 1930s he became aware of the threat to the redwoods by the lumber industry. St. Barbe believed that it was necessary to set aside an area large enough to maintain their health and growth. With funding from Men of the Trees in England, he raised interest in this plan by lecturing extensively across the United States and England. The American public responded with contributions of more than $10 million that resulted in the setting aside of twelve thousand acres of redwood forests to be preserved for all time.[28] Later, at the height of the Great Depression he worked with President Franklin D. Roosevelt to establish the Civilian Conservation Corp, which provided employment for some six million men. In Africa, beginning in 1952, St. Barbe began an effort involving twenty-four African countries to reclaim fertile land from the expanding Sahara through the planting of trees, what he called a "Green Front" against the encroachment of the desert.[29]

When St. Barbe arrived in India in 1977 he was hardly a stranger. He had been coming to India intermittently since 1931. He had met Jawaharlal Nehru and other important figures, drawing their attention to the declining tree cover across the country and the advance of the deserts in the drought-prone regions.[30] In 1957 he had given lectures at the famous Forest Research Institute of India in Dehra Dun. Now at age 88 he was a celebrity whose autobiography *My Life, My Trees* was internationally known. Bahuguna points out that his arrival in November of 1977 was at the height of the Chipko Movement. St. Barbe states that after his tour of the villages where chipko activities had taken place, he received word of yet another auction of forests to timber contractors. This was the auction of the Advani and Salet forests in the Hemvalghati region that provoked massive demonstrations. St. Barbe was there and observed. He got back to Delhi in time to keep an appointment for a lecture at the Gandhi Museum in Delhi. There again he met with the minister of chemicals and petroleum who had supported his visit to the chipko people. To him he expressed support for the chipko demand for a ten-year moratorium on tree felling in the forests of the Himalayas to enable them to recover from the severe felling they had undergone during the war years, and from which they had never been allowed to recover.[31] In his writings and in his conversations with government officials, St. Barbe gave strong support to the Chipko Movement. He spoke with respect and admiration of Sunderlal's fast that began on January 9, 1979, and that continued even after his arrest. His impression, as he put it, was that "there can be no more dedicated protectors of their forests than the villagers of the Himalayas except perhaps the Indians of the Amazon Forests, who are sacrificing their lives in thousands to protect their native habitat of the tropical evergreen forests."[32]

From his encounter with St. Barbe, Sunderlal Bahuguna derived much benefit. For one thing he came to understand that the problems of the Himalayan people were not simply matters of local concern but had global dimensions. He came to see that all over the world, forests were being devastated at alarming rates. For Bahuguna, as for St. Barbe, these developments could only have disastrous consequences for human beings and for life on the planet. St. Barbe had a deep appreciation for the ancient wisdom of the people of the Himalayas and of the indigenous peoples around the world, who saw the earth as a living being. Looking at this wisdom from a scientific perspective, he states that the forest cover of the earth is like the skin of a human body. If a man loses one-third of his skin he cannot survive. If a tree loses one-third of its bark, it dies as well. St. Barbe submits that if the earth should lose one-third of its natural tree cover, it too will die.[33] In his autobiography he states that he learned early "that the forest is a society of living things, the greatest of which is the tree." His understanding of the value of the forest stood in stark contrast to that of the prevailing forest industry of India. For him the true value of a forest was not just in the revenue it could generate, but in its permanence, its capacity to renew itself, and its ability to store water. Besides this, he acknowledged its many biological functions, which include its capacity to provide a valuable ground cover, and the most adaptable of all raw materials, its wood.[34] Second, Sunderlal came to see that that it was not just in the Himalayas but in other parts of the world that local people were suffering from the degradation of the forests upon which their lives and livelihood depend. St. Barbe had seen this in South America, in Canada, in New Zealand, in Africa, and elsewhere. Third, he saw that like the people of the Himalayas, with their traditional wisdom, indigenous people in places around the world had been the guardians of the forests upon which the world's supply of oxygen depends, and that in locations around the world local people were rising up to oppose the policies of governments that were insensitive to their needs and oblivious to the global implications of their policies. Because Sunderlal was opposed to what the forest industry had been calling scientific forestry, many forest officials regarded Bahuguna as an opponent of science. Because St. Barbe was distinguished as a man of science and an acknowledged international authority on forestry, his association with Bahuguna did much to strengthen Bahuguna's public credibility. In addressing a gathering of forest officials, he once stated to them, "You are interested in forestry." Then referring to Sunderlal, he said, "What this man is saying, that is real forestry!"[35] St. Barbe also had an intuitive appreciation for the spiritual traditions in which Sunderlal found support for the intrinsic as well as the instrumental value of nature and support for his activism in support of the environment. In the words of St. Barbe: "I believe in the oneness of mankind and of all living things and in the interdependence of each and all." He stated also that unless we play fair to the earth, we cannot exist physically on this planet. "Unless we play fair to our neighbour, we cannot exist socially or internationally." To this he adds that unless we play fair to our better self, there is no individuality and no leadership.[36] From St. Barbe, Sunderlal also received the prayer with which his name is widely associated. It was composed on a train journey in India on December 1, 1977. St. Barbe was not simply a man of science but also a man of deep spiritual sensitivity. But his spiritual sensitivity was not separate or ancillary to his scientific environmental concerns. It was integrated within it. Sunderlal told me that his prayer has been translated into many languages and that it has even been seen on signs along motorways in India, a most practical way to raise consciousness of the sacred significance of trees as the creation of God. Sunderlal states that the appeal of this prayer is to the hearts of the people, and if we want to save the remaining forests of the earth, it will be possible only by going to the heart. He reminds us of the view of Gandhi that it is according to the dictates of the heart that human beings will act.[37] The words of that prayer are a worthy subject of reflection and meditation:

> We thank Thee God! for thy Trees,
> Thou comest very near to us through thy Trees.
> From them we have beauty, wisdom, love,
> The air we breathe, the water we drink,
> the food we eat and the strength.
> Help us, Oh God!
> to give our best to life
> and leave the world
> a little more beautiful and worthy
> for having lived in it.
> Prosper thou our planting
> and establish thy kingdom of love
> and understanding on the Earth.[38]

On his last visit to India St. Barbe expressed appreciation that during his fast of January 9, 1979, Sunderlal had read his autobiography, *My Life, My Trees*. Sunderlal called it the companion of his fast and stated that it gave him the inspiration he needed for the ordeal.[39] Richard St. Barbe Baker died in Canada in 1982. In 1989 Sunderlal made the journey to an international conference in Reading, England, where he offered his homage to St. Barbe. There, for the way in which St. Barbe combined the ideals of a humanitarian scientist, a social activist, and a conscientious man of letters, Sunderlal called him a *vriksha sant* (forest saint). I stated earlier that Sunderlal always refers to Sri Dev Suman as his guru. In one sense and by tradition there can be only one such person, for a guru is one who gives the disciple something of himself that no one else can give. The guru dispels the darkness giving direction, guidance, and purpose to the life of the one who follows. It is interesting that to acknowledge his importance to Sunderlal's life, his centenary tribute affectionately extends this title to St. Barbe as well.[40]

But if Sunderlal derived benefit from his encounter with St. Barbe, it is clear that St. Barbe received tremendous benefit from his encounter with Sunderlal as well. In the course of his visit in India, Sunderlal told St. Barbe the story of Amrita Devi of the Bishnoi sect of Rajasthan. In a famous incident in 1731, Amrita Devi led a group of Bishnois to resist the decision of the maharajah of Jodhpur to cut down their khejri trees for use in a lime kiln for a new royal palace. The Bishnois were committed to the protection of nature, and to the khejri tree (*Prosopis cineraria*) in particular. This tree provided food and fodder, as well as building materials for fencing and other purposes. For the Bishnois the tree was sacred. On this occasion they embraced the trees in order to prevent the ax men from cutting them down. In the protest, 363 men, women, and children lost their lives.[41] In the dedication and sacrifice of the people of the Chipko Movement, St. Barbe found the kind of commitment to the environment upon which the future of the planet depends. He commented that more girl children should be named after Amrita in commemoration of the sacrifice of the Bishnois people. When St. Barbe returned to India for the last time on August 10, 1980, he stated on his arrival in Bombay, "Sunderlal Bahuguna is to my knowledge the only man in the world who went on a fast unto death for saving trees."[42] On that visit he made a second journey into the Himalayas to see Sunderlal again and to see again the brave chipko people of the Himalayas. There, he says, they met him on a mountain road with a band and with one their most haunting songs:

> What do the forests bear?
> Soil, Water and pure Air,
> Soil, Water and pure Air:
> These are the basis of Life!

Ron Rabin, a social activist from Oregon, describes a meeting with St. Barbe in the spring of 1980 at the fiftieth anniversary of St. Barbe's first encounter with the redwoods. Standing in the light costal rain, the small group of people gave prayers of thanksgiving for the many gifts of the forest. Turning to Rabin, St. Barbe said, "What do the forests bear? Soil, water and pure air–soil water and pure air are the basis of life; this is the slogan of the Chipko (Hug to the Trees) women in India—those who work with Sunderlal Bahuguna to save the forests of the Himalayas. Sunderlal is my Guru."[43]

Chapter 10

Chipko Ecology

Shallow or Deep?

It might be suggested that Bahuguna's commitment to the protection of the Himalayas in all its aspects represents a shift from what has been called a *shallow* to a *deep ecology*. This suggestion is complicated by the fact that the term "deep ecology" is used in different ways. It also depends on the interpretation of the views and practices of Bahuguna and of those who opposed him.[1] In any case, Bahuguna's commitment to the protection of the Himalayas in all its aspects meant not only a conflict with the views of the forest industry and the government agencies that support it, but also conflicts with some of the other participants of the Chipko Movement. During his fast that began on January 9, 1979, the press was actively presenting their understanding of his demands, the response of the government, and the reaction of other chipko workers. As it was expressed in the *Indian Express,* his demands included the declaration of the Himalayan forests as protected forests; a ban on green felling; the formulation of a policy for mass plantation with priority for trees providing food, fuel, and fodder; the people's participation in forestry operations; the immediate recall of the axe men and saw men from the sensitive catchment of the Alakananda River; and the utilization of already felled trees to meet local needs. N. P. Tripathi, secretary of the Uttar Pradesh State Forest Department, responded that "an irrational moratorium on felling would lead to sizable unemployment, dearth of timber in short supply, denial of raw materials to import-based forest industries like paper, matches, resins, etc, and consequent adverse effects on the economy, especially of the hill areas."[2] Nevertheless, the following day the government announced a complete and unconditional ban on all felling, and Sunderlal ended his fast.

I stated earlier that, according to Weber, Sunderlal ended the fast on February 2, 1979, with the announcement by the state government that no further forest auctions or felling would occur until such time as Bahuguna should meet to discuss the matter with the chief minister. That chief minister left office on February 28, 1979. In a footnote Weber points out that the moratorium remained in force until April 1980 when it was rescinded following press reaction and the criticism of the "development oriented Chipko supporters."[3] This press report raises the question of the identity of these "development oriented" chipko supporters. During the 1960s Sunderlal Bahuguna was active in organizing forest laborers into cooperatives that could enable the local people to achieve economic independence through forest work independent of outside contractors. Weber states that throughout 1977 chipko activists undertook activities either to spare trees in sensitive catchment areas or to stop the Forest Corporation from felling the trees until local industries had been established. "Gradually," he says, "Bahuguna moved away from this latter view; Chandi Prasad Bhatt and the workers of the DGSS did not." Bhatt and his colleagues in the DGSS believed that local forest industries were necessary to address economic conditions in the hills. They cooperated with government programs of reforestation and welcomed their willingness to provide them with resin and other raw materials for their industries. They were also willing to allow felling in areas it did not consider critically sensitive. "By contrast, in mid-1977, Bahuguna and others gathered at Dharam Ghar, home of then seventy-seven-year-old Sarala Devi, and demanded an ending of the commercial exploitation of green trees in the Himalayan forests for at least ten years."[4]

Bahuguna's fast and the subsequent government ban on felling of all trees for any reason punctuated a rupture between these two active branches of the Chipko Movement. Following the announcement of an unconditional government ban on the felling of all trees, one of the papers announced: "Sunderlal Bahuguna breaks fast—and the people lose their rights."[5] Newspapers were efficient in reporting the criticism of a number of chipko leaders, including that of Chandi Prasad Bhatt. Bhatt stated his opposition to the abridgement of any of the peoples' rights. The paper also quoted an anonymous *sarvodaya* worker to the effect that "no environmental policy can succeed if it ignores the people in that environment, who are as much a part of it as the trees, rivers and mountains."[6] This statement by Bhatt and the anonymous *sarvodaya* worker could have come as easily from Bahuguna himself. As he explained it to me, his fast was not intended to curtail the rights of the people for which he had been working for many years. His fast was not against but in support of the rights and the welfare of the people threatened by the commercial exploitation of the forests.[7] Weber suggests that the decision of the government to impose a ban that exceeded the chipko demands was a political maneuver calculated to alienate supporters of the Chipko Movement and to make Bahuguna the enemy of the people. He indicates that, after the newspaper reports that focused on the abrogation of the peoples' rights, Bahuguna stated that the government had eliminated concessions to the local people in order to discredit the Chipko Movement and to bring about a countermovement congenial to vested interests. Bahuguna pointed out, he says, that the aim of the movement "was to safeguard and guarantee the rights and concessions of the local people as they 'are the real protectors of the forests' "[8]

Some writers suggested that in the course of time, the representatives of these two viewpoints came to constitute distinct branches of the Chipko Movement that were active in different regions, the one centered in the Alakananda Valley under the leadership of Chandi Prasad Bhatt, the other centered in the Bhagirathi Valley with Sunderlal as its principal representative. The difference in their viewpoints and their leadership has been the subject of much debate in literature about the Chipko Movement. Some have described them in terms of differences in personal style, methods, or approaches to leadership, while others have claimed momentous differences in their respective philosophies of nature. While I found no open hostility between the two leaders or the two groups, I found that writers who favor one tended to neglect the other or to characterize the leader of the other as representing its opposite. Weber points out that Anil Agarwal, in his famous publication *The State of India's Environment 1982: A Citizen's Report*, summarized the differences between the two in terms less than sympathetic to Bahuguna.[9] Agarwal saw the difference between the two largely as a difference in operational styles. He characterized Bhatt as "a grassroots worker" who "believes in organizing the people" and praises him and the DGSS for having "organized the country's largest voluntary afforestation programme." He saw Bahuguna as "a journalist" and a "publicist par excellence," whose main focus has been on spreading the chipko message. He claims that Bahuguna "tends to dismiss" reforestation as irrelevant at this stage of the movement against deforestation and "concentrates all his writing and speaking power against the forest departments."[10] In their essay, "Chipko: Rekindling India's Forest Culture," Jayanta Bandyopadhyay and Vandana Shiva describe such a characterization of Bahuguna as "mischievous" and state that it "deflects attention from the very real differences in philosophies of development, technology policy, democratic values, self help and survival strategies, concepts of productivity and efficiency, which are of extreme significance and which need serious analysis."[11] To distinguish these differences Ramachandra Guha develops a chart in which he characterizes the two leaders in terms of their respective historical influences, their respective identification of the agents of deforestation, their understanding of the underlying causes of deforestation, their respective methods of work, their personal style, their relation to the Gandhian movement, and their respective understandings of a solution to the forest crisis both local and global. He calls it, "Bahuguna versus Bhatt: Personality and Ideology."[12] While some of the oppositions he develops are instructive and have clear support, others are less than convincing. For instance, because Bhatt was an early disciple of Bahuguna, who stands in the same history of protest, it is hard to imagine that the historical influences of the one would differ significantly from that of the other. Guha states that for Bahuguna the agents of deforestation are "representatives of the forest department in league with timber contractors." It is hard to see much difference between this and the view he attributes to Bhatt, for whom the agent of deforestation is "forest policy influenced by commercial interests." It is also questionable whether Bahuguna's view of a solution to deforestation at the global level actually implies, as Guha claims, a return to a preindustrial economy. Bahuguna is a known advocate of solar energy, wind energy, geothermal energy, and other ecofriendly technologies.

Weber sees their difference in terms of what he calls their basic worldviews. Guha seems to agree with this. Guha states that, for Bahuguna, commercial forestry and the close links between contractors and forest officials are responsible for the deteriorating condition of the Himalayan environment. But he points out that for Bahuguna, "shortsighted forest management is but the symptom of a deeper malaise—the anthropocentric view of nature intrinsic to modern industrial civilization." Thus, and here he quotes Bahuguna, "the ecological crisis in Himalaya is not an isolated event. It has its roots in the [modern] materialistic civilization, which makes man the butcher of Earth."[13] The followers of Bhatt presumably think otherwise. It is interesting that Guha had to insert the word "modern" to this quotation from Bahuguna. From my own conversations with Bahuguna it became clear that his understanding of the root cause of the ecological crisis in the Himalayas is not modernity as such but the materialism it has engendered. In the booklet Guha cites, Bahuguna points out that the tribals living in perfect harmony with nature are more civilized, "in the sense that they do less harm to the environment as their use of nonrenewable resources of nature is negligible." But then he raises the question, "Can we in Himalaya evolve a strategy of development in which science and technology may help in maintaining this harmony?" This, he says, will not be possible until the community is strengthened in its native lifestyle. But for such a strengthening of this native lifestyle, he says, the youth have an important role to play by implementing programs of mass education through *padyatras*. The thrust of his concern is that "the present trend of earning easy money by exploiting the nature is very dangerous."[14] For Sunderlal materialistic civilization has generated a mistaken notion of development whose goal is the accumulation of "an abundance of things." It has produced a temporary prosperity "by exploiting the centuries old treasures of Nature with the help of technology." The worldwide environmental problems we face today, he says, are the gifts of this civilization. For what he calls *aranya* culture, the civilization of the Indian forests, the objectives of true development are permanent peace, happiness, and prosperity, and these lead naturally to a stage of satisfaction. The difficulty is that "we have sacrificed peace and happiness to achieve temporary prosperity."[15] As Weber puts it, "While the DGSS workers claim that man is the centre of any ecosystem and that the fruits of the ecosystem should meet the demands of the local economy, Bahuguna sees man not as the centre of anything but as part of an indivisible whole."[16]

In 1987, in another effort to articulate the differences and similarities among the two branches of chipko, Bandyopadhyay and Shiva focus upon their philosophical standpoints. "Bahuguna believes that development as practiced today in official programmes, is going to be unsustainable if ecology is not considered as imperative." They state further that for Bahuguna, the material basis of economic development "cannot be divorced from the productivity of the ecological endowments and their stability. Thus economic development in the Himalayas must be based on the expansion of trees and not of agriculture." They go on to state that Bhatt, though his philosophical standpoint is not as well articulated, "strongly favours the introduction of a modern development package in these regions." They state further that he "firmly believes that the acceptance of the present modes of resource utilization with a new emphasis on the location of manufacturing activities in the hill areas and a strengthening of their raw material base will lead to development and fight poverty."[17] Bhatt's model, they state, "is easily subsumed by the dominant development paradigm with minor environmental adjustments." The difference between the two, they argue "is universally faced as the difference between deep ecology and environmentalism. It is a difference that is inevitable in any serious ecology movement and has nothing to do with personalities as is commonly made out." The program of ecological development that Bahuguna propounds "requires a serious change in consumption patterns and a reorganization of interest groups in society." Bhatt's program "can be realized within the present social structure and is commonly known by the name 'eco-development.' " They go on to state that the work strategies of the two are complementary and not contradictory. "Bahuguna believes in spreading the idea of ecological development in all parts of India since his model requires a fundamental change in public opinion and political alignments at the national level." Bahuguna, they say, has not been a grass-roots activist in the narrow sense but has encouraged activists in all parts of the country. Bhatt, whom they describe as the best example of local activists whom Bahuguna has encouraged, "believes in concentrating in his region of influence and working towards consolidation."[18]

This article provoked a strong response from Ramachandra Guha, who found it to be a partisan stance in favor of Bahuguna. He states that their presentation "is marred by the need to present Bahuguna's wing as the more 'radical' of the two" and that "this leads them to make serious errors of fact and interpretation." Among other things he points out that in the events leading up to the first chipko agitation in the village of Mandal, it was Chandi Prasad Bhatt who suddenly thought of embracing the trees. Likewise, he states, "the Reni episode was made possible by the meetings held by Bhatt and his associates from the Dasholi Gram Swarajya Sangh . . . at the village of Reni, when the women first heard of the 'Chipko' technique." He points out that "after the first movements at Mandal and Rampur Phata, Sunderlal Bahuguna himself visited the Alakananda valley, and warmly praised Chandi Prasad Bhatt as the 'mukyha sanchalak' (chief organizer) of the Chipko movement."[19] He argues that the claim that Bhatt favors the "modern development package," and that he accepts the present mode of resource utilization with the qualification that industries should be relocated in the hills, gives the impression that Bhatt places uncritical faith in industrialization and modern science. He finds these claims "gratuitous and insulting, referring as they do to a man who has spent the better part of his lifetime advocating and implementing ecologically sound technologies." He is also critical of the neglect of a third group within the Chipko Movement, the Uttarakhand Sangharsh Vahini that was active in Kumaun between 1974 and 1978, and he is critical of what he calls "an overestimation of the Gandhian influence on Chipko."[20]

Bandyopadhyay and Shiva responded to this critique with the recognition of their own dispensability to chipko and the irrelevance of debates about what is the "real chipko" and about who is the "real leader."[21] Chipko, they say, "has no centralized leadership, and therefore cannot be divided into 'camps,' 'led' by personalities." Chipko, they insist is the property neither of Bahuguna nor Bhatt. "Movements do not belong to individuals. Individuals belong to movements." For them neither Bahuguna nor Bhatt is at the center of the movement. Both are followers of a popular upsurge.[22] For this reason the actual birth of Chipko is hard to identify with a particular temporal event in a particular place. Did the Chipko Movement begin in 1968, when village communities around Tilari took a renewed pledge to save their forests at the cost of their lives? Were the martyrs who died there in 1930 the pioneers of the Chipko Movement? Did chipko begin with the composition of the song by Ghanshyam Sailani in which the word "chipko" first appears? Did it begin with the first mass demonstrations in Uttarkashi and Gopeshwar in December 1972 or with the protests in the Mandal forests in April 1973? In making this point they refer to many other times and places in which the origin of Chipko might, with justification, be located. In their words, "We do not deny Bhatt's important role. We merely insist it was one of the many other pioneering roles of many other visible and invisible people, that Bhatt was part of a collectivity, part of a historical process and in that lay his effectiveness."[23] To the claim that their earlier article overestimates the influence of Gandhi on Chipko, they reply that Guha "misrepresents our reference to *satyagraha* by extending it to 'nationalism,' the 'Congress,' and 'Gandhism' as an 'ideology.'"[24]

An issue of the most critical importance to Guha was the claim by Bandyopadhyay and Shiva that a change in the demands of Chipko occurred in May 1977 in various parts of the Garhwal Himalayas. "It is very important to note," they say, "that it was no more the old demand for higher allocation of forest products to local industries, but the new demand for ecological control on forest resource extraction in order to ensure a regular supply of water and fodder."[25] Guha understands their interpretation of this change as the "move from an economic to an ecological perspective, carried out under Bahuguna's leadership," an interpretation he finds among other "partisans" of Bahuguna. He sees this as "a tendentious rewriting of history" and points out that "from its inception Chipko drew an intimate connection between commercial forestry, deforestation, landslides and floods."[26] In their reply Bandyopadhyay and Shiva recognize that "in the popular space Chipko has always been ecological." They also point out that the voluntary organizations that the *sarvodaya* network set up throughout Uttarakhand during the 1960s "related to forests on a cooperative but commercial basis, not as life support systems. For them forests were suppliers of raw materials like resin and timber." These organizations included the DGSS and many other such organizations. They go on to point out that during the early 1970s the interests of these organizations converged with the interests of the villagers to put an end to the contract system. While the village communities who depended upon the forest for their survival had no interest in the forest as the source of raw materials, the local forest-based industries did. "Thus while the villagers drove away contractors to protect their forests for survival, the organizations like Dasoli [Dashauli] Gram Swaraj Sangh were interested in protecting their raw material base." What they call the distinction between the ecological and the economic interests of Chipko is the distinction between the imperatives of the survival economy of the people and the commercial economy of local industries. They state: "When we wrote that Chipko became ecological in 1977 we implied that for the first time the messengers of Chipko wholly shared the perspective of the community, especially the women, in seeing forests in their life-support function, not merely as raw material for industry. And with this transition came a split." The decisive nature of this split can be seen in a meeting that followed the Advani protest, in which the activists suggested the new demand of a ban on green felling for commercial purposes. After initially supporting this agreement, Bhatt withdrew his support for this demand "because it ran into conflict with the raw material needs of the wood processing and resin unit at Dasoli [Dashauli] Gram Swaraj Sangh."[27]

It is remarkable that the writers who discuss this debate seem to agree that an unfortunate antipathy between two branches of the Chipko Movement has existed for a considerable period of time. They also seem to agree that the antagonism is not among the participants but among journalistic and academic writers, urban intellectuals, and environmentalists who support one or the other side. Ironically, the authors of each of these pieces refer to journalistic writers, scholars, and academics but not to themselves as partisans of one or the other side. They see the antipathy as arising from somewhere else. Perhaps it is in the nature of journalistic and academic discourse to view things in terms of contrasting positions, to write in terms of oppositions, and to compare positions in terms of their perceived merits. Perhaps it is human nature to do so. Perhaps it is also human nature to identify with the person or position with which one feels the deepest affinity and to disavow what is perceived as *the other*. It certainly is human nature to believe that the position one has examined thoroughly enough to affirm is the most reasonable position one can take.

Bahuguna himself does not see the economic interest and the ecological interest of the Chipko Movement as standing in opposition to one another. This is the meaning of the slogan that affirms: Ecology Is Permanent Economy. Bahuguna speaks today in positive terms of Bhatt's leadership and his prodigious work of reforestation. But he remains firm in his view that the forests must not be cut down but must be preserved to provide food, fodder, fuel, fertilizer, and fiber for the local economy. He believes that the economic needs of the people of the hills can and should be met by cultivating the forests of the hills for this purpose.

Sunderlal's fast of January 9, 1979, ended on February 2, 1980, with the announcement by the government of U. P. of an immediate moratorium on felling of trees in the hills of Uttar Pradesh. St. Barbe recalls that the central government was then making efforts towards a moratorium on all felling for ten years, but that the states that were getting revenue from tree felling continued to cut trees.[28] He states that the Uttar Pradesh government's moratorium that coincided with the end of Sunderlal's fast remained "in effect for some time but they again started felling trees and the Chipko fight to save their trees continues."[29] Weber states that the moratorium stayed in force until April of that year.[30] In March 1980, at the launching of the World Conservation Strategy in India, Indira Gandhi the then prime minister, made an impassioned speech concerning the environment. To this initiative of the International Union for Conservation of Nature and Natural Resources, the United Nations Environment Program, the World Wildlife Fund, and other organizations, Indira Gandhi gave her explicit support. In this speech she pointed out, "In his arrogance with his own increasing knowledge and ability, man has ignored his dependence on the earth and has lost his communion with it."[31] She pointed out that concern for the conservation of nature is not a sentimental interest but a truth well known to the ancient sages of India. "The Indian tradition teaches us that all forms of life–human, animal, and plant–are so closely inter-linked and that disturbance in one gives rise to imbalance in the others." In this speech she drew attention to the Himalayan foothills in particular and pointed out that "the manner in which we are encroaching upon our forests and mountains, and are permitting the indiscriminate cutting of beautiful and useful old trees is alarming." She stated that "one of our immediate tasks is to restore the eco-systems of the Himalaya and other mountain ranges."[32] In a speech to the Central Board of Forestry in August 1980, she pointed out that "the reckless and indiscriminate felling of trees, especially on our Himalayan slopes for immediate profit either of contractors or in the name of development has proved hazardous. Trees are cut all over the world but quite some time ago most countries evolved policies whereby this would not denude their forests, affect their climate or create other problems." Whether or not she fully appreciated the details of the plight of the forest people, she pointed out that "forests must provide food, fodder and fuel," and that "apart from the timber they yield, they can be a good source of earning for those living in and around them."[33] Weber states that in 1980 the Central Government recommended a moratorium on green felling but that the government of Uttar Pradesh did nothing to implement it. On the following republic day, January 26, 1981, the Government of India named Bahuguna recipient of the prestigious Padma-Shree award for service to the environment. While Bahuguna first welcomed the award as recognition of the achievements of the Chipko Movement, he decided eventually to refuse it because, as he put it to me, "the Himalayas were still bleeding." Weber records his words as they appeared in the press at the time: "I don't deserve it till the flow of flesh and blood of Mother Earth, that is the fertile top soil of India, ceases. I wrote back to Rashtrapatiji [the president] and humbly refused it." It was during this period that Sunderlal was given the opportunity for the conversation with the chief minister of Uttar Pradesh that had been promised during his fast of January 9, 1979. Sunderlal explained to me that the chief minister summoned him to his office in Lucknow, where he complained that his activities of hugging the trees was disturbing the forest industry and curtailing the flow of revenue to the state. Forest officers had complained that because of the mischief of this man they were unable to carry on their work. Sunderlal explained that it was not him but the women of the villages who were hugging the trees. He was only their messenger. He further explained that the women were objecting to the felling of the trees because they needed the trees to meet the domestic needs of their families, for food, fodder, and fuel. While the forest officers see the forest in terms of timber, resin, and foreign exchange, the women see it in terms of soil, water, and pure air! The chief minister's reply was that while he was sympathetic to their concerns, he was the chief minister of a very large state with many interests to consider.

Following this conversation, Sunderlal took the initiative of making the journey to Delhi to visit with Indira Gandhi herself. In her he found a strong ally whose concern for the environment had begun with the advent of her political career. Eventually she summoned the chief

minister for conversations about the condition of the hills and the interest of the chipko people. When the chief minister explained to her that
the cutting of trees provided a principal source of revenue for the state,
he was surprised to find that Indira Gandhi's sympathies were with the
people of Chipko. She replied ironically that she could then withhold all
central government grants, and he could run the state on revenue from
the felling of trees! Weber states that five days after Sunderlal's refusal of
the Padma-Shree award, the state government put a stop to the felling
of trees and appointed another committee under the leadership of Dr.
K. N. Kaul to review the protection of forests and the maintenance of
environmental balance in the hills. It also imposed a new moratorium on
the felling of green trees above the altitude of one thousand meters and
on slopes with a grade of over thirty degrees. This moratorium applied
to all eight hill districts of Uttar Pradesh.[34] Through her intervention the
government of Himachal followed with a similar ban on green felling
for commercial purposes at altitudes of over one thousand meters and
on slopes of over thirty degrees. Indira Gandhi also lent her support to
Sunderlal's next project in raising the environmental consciousness of the
people of the hills, the most ambitions *padyatra* he had ever undertaken.
It is one thing for state governments to enact resolutions to protect the
environment, but it is another thing for those resolutions to have the
support of the people and to be carried out. St. Barbe makes the point
that after his fast of January 1979, Sunderlal felt that his struggle was only
beginning. He describes it as "a race between education and disaster."[35]

Chapter 11

Srinagar to Kohima

An Educational Mission

It was an overcast day in Srinagar, the capital of the Indian state of Jammu and Kashmir, when with one companion, the seventy-two-year-old Rattan Chand Dehloo, a *sarvodaya* worker from Himachal Pradesh, Sunderlal Bahuguna set out on a journey by foot to the town of Kohima in Nagaland almost five thousand kilometers to the east. Sunderlal decided to undertake this ambitious journey after a prayerful fast of eleven days in Uttarkashi, in which he reflected on the best method to spread the chipko message. He states that in April 1979 he was isolated for standing by the hill women's slogan, first articulated in their demonstrations in the Advani forest: What do the forests bear? Soil, water, and pure air! This slogan, he says, became the inspiration of a small group of activists who hoped to save those sectors of humanity that are threatened by the horrors of air and water pollution, desertification, and other ecological disasters. He felt he should spread this message far and wide. Through his reflections, he decided on a method he had used many times before. He states, as he had stated before, that the great teachers of mankind, and their unknown disciples, walked thousands of miles to spread their message, and it is because of their hard penance that these humble messengers of faith still reign over the hearts of the people. On April 12, 1981, when he announced his plans for this ambitious journey, his decision came to many as a surprise. He states that he could understand this reaction among the armchair social workers. But he noted also that many who regarded themselves as activists had difficulty digesting the idea. Thus while many people admired his endeavor, hardly anyone was willing to share the hardships and hazards of such a march. Sunderlal was not deterred by the isolation. From years before he had learned to accept the hazards that fall to one who swims against the tide. He found strength in the famous words of Bertrand Russell: "An adventure seeker must be able to withstand isolation, neglect and ridicule, to overcome oppression, tyranny and exploitation, to withstand hunger, thirst and fatigue. At times he must be prepared for dynamic dangerous living whether it be on the cornice of a mountain or a battle for the defense of his convictions."[1]

Bahuguna's purpose in undertaking this *padyatra* was threefold. First, he wanted to get an overall picture of the condition of the Himalayas, the degree of ecological damage already done to the forests, and the results that can be expected if policies are not changed. Second, he wanted to publish and publicize his findings, especially to the decision makers who had the best hope of undertaking changes in forest policy. His third purpose was also the most personal. This, he expressed most explicitly to a group of Bhutanese villagers midway through the trip: "The foot march is to share our anguish with our brothers and sisters in the Himalayas from Kashmir to Kohima, anguish caused through the distress of Mother Earth in this region."[2] In an interview he gave during his travel through Bhutan, he develops this purpose further. "Many people see Chipko as a localized movement, restricted to Garhwal, we wanted to give a wider perspective and to widen the base of this movement to other regions in Himalayas."[3] The two set out without a single rupee between them. Their fortunes and their sustenance would be dependent upon the hospitality and good will of the villagers they would meet along the way. Two weeks before the journey, he and Rattan Dehloo had met to arrange for contacts along the way and the route to be taken. The evening before their departure, they had requested and received the blessing of Sheikh Mohammed Abdullah, then chief minister of Jammu and Kashmir. When the chief minister met the two, he inquired whether they would be able to make the journey all the way to Kohima through such difficult terrain. Sunderlal replied that if God was willing, He would give him the strength needed for the journey.

They left on May 30, a commemoration of the martyrdom of forest protestors at Tilari in 1930. On that date in 1968 Sunderlal and others had taken a pledge to work toward a harmonious relationship between the forests and themselves. They began their journey after a short farewell function organized by the Kashmir Ecological Society. It had begun to drizzle as the two, accompanied by two young students from Uttarkashi, departed, rucksacks on their backs, down the national highway. The first question that they heard as they departed from the city was one that Sunderlal would hear all the way to Kohima: "Why are you walking?"

He gave the answer to everyone who asked: "We are distressed with the wounds on the body of Mother Earth, specially in the shape of landslides and soil-erosion. The situation in the Himalayas is critical. We could not bear it. But we had nothing except our legs to walk and backs to carry the luggage, so we set out with Chipko message to share our anguish with our hill brethren. If we do not check this situation, our survival in the hills is in peril and people living down in the valleys and plains are also suffering due to floods and scarcity of water for irrigation and power. This is not a local but a global problem and if we solve it here, others will also be inspired."[4]

During the planning of the journey, they had laid out the *padyatra* in four phases in order to avoid the hazards of the monsoon and the perils of winter storms at high altitudes. During the intervals between these phases, Sunderlal would remain at work to draw attention to conditions they had witnessed and the plight of the people they had met. The first phase of the *padyatra* proceeded from Srinagar in Kashmir to Chamba in Himachal Pradesh. The *padyatris* (the participants in the *padyatra*) soon left the main road for a route that took them through the picturesque Kashmir Valley in the watershed of the slow-flowing Jhelum River. Sunderlal comments on its enchanting beauty with saffron and paddy fields, with willow, poplar, and mulberry trees along the roadsides, and the ornamental trees in old Mughal gardens. But as they approached the hills, they saw the ghastly scenes of flooding streams that had turned the paddy fields on both of their banks into heaps of sand and pebbles. They saw overgrazed brownish mountain slopes and conifers loped for fuel. Similar scenes greeted them as they made their way to the first of many villages where they would remain for a night. We get an idea of their reception by the local people from an account provided by Bharat Dogra:

> It is dusk, and just as the people of a sleepy village located in the interior, remote parts of the Kashmir Valley are preparing their evening meals, two elderly men awkwardly find their way into the village. They are strangers, and the villagers' initial response is one of suspicion, if not open hostility. The strangers talk to some elderly villagers, and explain the purpose of their visit. A group of villagers gather. A school-teacher is summoned. The strangers take out their diaries and tape recorder, containing introductory letters and messages from prominent dignitaries. Then suddenly the teacher remembers something and rushes to shake hands with the strangers. He

tells them he had seen the programme featuring them on TV, and also heard the praise showered on them by the Chief Minister and the Governor. Reassured of their antecedents, the villagers now talk to them with trust and confidence. Soon the initial hostility has melted down, and the villagers listen to the visitors with respect.[5]

The watershed of the Jhelum River ends with the hazardous Symthan Pass, at an elevation of 12,414 feet (3,783 meters). Even before they began their journey, they had been warned of the threat of avalanches and had been told that they would be risking their lives if they tried to cross the pass at that time of year. When they persisted in their resolve some courageous officials and some local people agreed to accompany them. On June 6, they crossed from the Kashmir Valley over the Symthan Pass in deep snow into the watershed of the Chenab Valley. There their guides departed to return to the Kashmir Valley, leaving the two to find their way alone. On this leg of the journey Sunderlal collapsed and suffered a fall but quickly recovered and made it to a rest house, where they were able to recuperate and to prepare for the journey ahead.

In his account of the journey, Sunderlal explains that the Chenab Valley was once regarded as the richest treasure of forest wealth. When commercial exploitation of the valley had begun a century before, the lower accessible areas had been clear felled. With the disappearance of the larger trees the younger ones were the victims of snow and avalanches. What they witnessed there was what he calls a graveyard of fir, spruce, and other conifers. A picturesque valley had been turned into a highland desert. At higher altitudes a new generation of contractors was at work.[6] In the days that Sunderlal had spent underground in Lahore, he had learned Urdu with difficulty. He saw that it was the language of the people he was meeting in Kashmir. His knowledge of this language quickly established his credibility in these predominantly Muslim villages. It also enabled him to discuss from the Quran the need to save their forests. In this region they organized a large number of meetings in which they talked about the harmful effects of deforestation, the common problems of the hill people, and the efforts in the hills of Uttar Pradesh to evolve a new path for development through the protection of the environment.[7]

While each visit to a new village was always a unique experience, in the course of time, on the journey a pattern began to emerge. Sunderlal explained to me that they would often reach the new village at about dusk.

Typically, children would be playing in the common areas of the village, while their mothers would be preparing the evening meal. The visitors would ask the children to go and bring them one *chapati*. That would usually be sufficient to draw their parents' attention to their advent. In a short time a group of people would gather around to hear the purpose of their visit. Taped recordings of greetings from such well-known figures as Indira Gandhi quickly established their authority. Sometimes a person from one village where the visitors had been speaking would go forward to prepare the next village for their arrival. Presently they would unfurl their banner with chipko slogans, and presently the villagers would be making arrangements for a meeting with the community for the evening or for the following day. If there was a school in the village the teacher or headmaster would be involved. The school was the usual venue for a community meeting. Often Sunderlal would address the children in the school. Before nightfall they would be offered a meal with a family and a place to sleep. The next morning there would be meetings with the community or with the children in the school. Often they would make observations about the environment of the village explaining the causes of ecological damage and the measures needed to address it. After more conversations and the distribution of pamphlets often written by Sunderlal himself, the *padyatris* would bid the village a fond farewell and make their way to the next venue, taking note of environmental conditions as they went.

Crossing the Padri Pass at an elevation of four thousand feet, the marchers left Kashmir for the catchment of the Ravi River in the state of Himachal Pradesh. Here, says Sunderlal, a powerful lobby of private forest contractors was controlling the policies of the state. Because of overgrazing and the felling of trees on private lands, the Chamba Valley was fast losing its glory. On the pretext of private forests, thousands of hectares of forests had been clear felled, and the theft of timber had become a common practice in the region. The first phase of their journey came to an end after 384 kilometers of experiences like this. On June 27, 1981, at the onset of the monsoon, they reached the town of Chamba in Himachal Pradesh.

Before he began the second phase of the journey the following September, Sunderlal was busy with many activities. For one thing he made another visit to Jammu and Kashmir, where new activist groups were beginning to emerge. He also delivered a report to the chief minister and the governor of the state concerning their observations of ecological

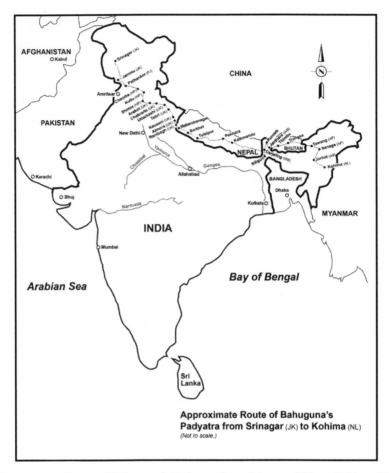

Approximate Route of Bahuguna's *Padyatra* from Srinagar (JK) to Kohima (NL)

conditions in the mountains of Kashmir. He pointed out that in the least accessible areas, there remained virgin stands of fir, deodar, kail, and other species, but that in the lowland areas a desert was gradually spreading. He observed that the common practice of rolling and dragging logs down the steep slopes had resulted in several major landslides and that the construction of roads required the felling of thousands of trees and much injury to as many not felled. He also observed significant damage to forests of chir pines from the excessive extraction of resin and noticed the location of sawmills in the most remote regions. While such exploitation had led to the increase in forest income, fiftyfold over thirty-five years, the devastation of forests from the movement of boulders and debris in landslides and the erosion of soil had resulted in the loss of tree cover from which no recovery would be possible. Upon receipt of this report the government of Jammu and Kashmir imposed a ban on the felling of green trees until the dead trees had been disposed of and imposed restrictions that cut resin tapping in these forests by 25 percent.[8]

During this break between the first and second phases of the *padyatra*, Sunderlal was given the opportunity to attend and address a United Nations conference on new and renewable energy sources to be held in Nairobi, Kenya. When he arrived to give his message about his march through the Himalayas, he did so with a bundle of firewood on his back to dramatize the loss of the world's forest cover. The visit abroad also afforded Sunderlal the opportunity to visit several countries in Europe. There he met with foresters and ecologists from England, Switzerland, and Austria and made a visit to Vienna to visit the ninety-year-old inspiration for his work in the hills, the Gandhian matriarch, Mira Behn. It was on this occasion that she gave him her jacket, which he kept as *prashad*.[9]

The second phase of the journey began at the end of the monsoon on September 12, 1981. Dhoom Singh Negi, who had played a critical role in the chipko activities in the Hemvalgathi region and who had been walking and spreading the chipko message in the region of Kumaon, now joined Sunderlal as they walked through the state of Himachal Pradesh. There a young social worker, Kul Bhusan Upamanya, with three of his colleagues and O. P. Thakur, a colleague from Jammu and Kashmir, joined the march. By then news of the march was gaining popular attention. The autumn weather was beautiful, and the villages and townspeople received them with affection. They walked for a total of fifty days in Himachal Pradesh, visiting remote villages in the districts of Chamba, Kangra, Kullu, Mani, and Shimla, far away from the reach of motor roads. They addressed children in schools, and in some villages they held meetings that continued into the early hours of the morning. Sometimes small groups would accompany the marchers for a day or for a week before returning to their own villages. In some cases they accompanied the marchers to the border of the state.

The marchers had made plans to be in Kullu, in Himachal Pradesh, for the annual festival of Dussehra. The festival of Dussehra is the celebration of the epic battle told in the Ramayana between Rama, the incarnation of Lord Vishnu, and his adversary, Ravana the ten-headed demon, who had abducted Rama's wife, Sita, during their exile in the forest. The festival that celebrates the defeat of Ravana and the recovery of Sita drew thousands of villagers from all over the Kullu Valley, as well as pilgrims from all over India. In all perhaps fifty thousand people would attend the festival. Because it commemorates a critical event in the life of the forest, it proved to be one of the best opportunities to spread the chipko message. Jayanta Bandyopadhyay joined the group before it reached Kullu and remained with it until it departed. In the account of his days with the marchers, he points out that they divided themselves in groups of two and with handmade posters and banners organized meetings at street corners, where they distributed chipko publications to townsfolk and villagers. In addition to the street corner meetings, Sunderlal often spoke under the chipko banner to groups of fifty or more using a handheld loudspeaker, which he used not only to tell the chipko story but also to teach the slogans of the chipko movement: "[T]he Himalayas have awakened today; the cruel axe will be chased away!" On their way to the capital of Himachal Pradesh at Shimla, they avoided the straight route that would have made for an easier journey and took the less traveled path to meet the hill people who would not otherwise be met. On average they organized three or four meetings every day. In some cases Sunderlal spoke to groups of fifty, in others to crowds of thousands. But he was hardly attracted to the attention of the crowds. Often he would stop to discuss the problems of the hill people when just a few individuals gathered by the roadside.[10]

Sunderlal points out that, like most of the states in the Himalayas, Himachal Pradesh was once covered by thick forests. He spoke to elderly people who could recall when forests near the villages were so thick they remained in darkness even in the light of the day. He states that with the advent of so-called scientific forest management the Ravi, Beas, and Sutlej river valleys were the first prey to clear felling as logs for railway ties or sleepers could easily be floated away. The development of motor roads then facilitated further clearing of forests for commercial purposes. The forests quickly became the highest source of income to the state. In his report to the state government, Sunderlal pointed out that although clear felling on private lands had formally ended in 1977, political pressure had led to the easing of restrictions. He states also that a new class of business people with links to government profited enormously from the sale of illicit timber. Because the sale of timber on private land had ended in 1977, the prevailing tactic to avoid the force of the law was for timber merchants to keep stock of stamped papers backdated to before the restrictions were imposed. Thus the timber profit that had almost doubled from 1977 to 1981 was devastating forest wealth. Sunderlal observed that the government reforestation program had developed plantations of chir pine that acidify the soil and dry up water sources. Pine forests have little capacity to check the erosion of soil. Moreover, the deep cuts for tapping the resin was weakening and killing many of these trees. While Sunderlal and his colleagues had seen problems of this nature in other places, they found that Himachal Pradesh revealed a strange irony. Despite the evident ecological threats, the state had enjoyed a significant measure of prosperity from the production of apples. Himachal Pradesh was known as the apple state, producing 2.4 million tons of apples a year, more than one-third of the total for the country. The irony was that the transport of the apple crop entailed the production of wooden cases, and this required the felling of 100,000 trees each year. As Sunderlal put it, the apples that brought prosperity were eating up the forests of the state.[11] According to Sunderlal, the consequences of the devastation of the forests of Himachal Pradesh included the drying up of the tributaries of the rivers, the silting of reservoirs downstream, and a scarcity of water for power generation.[12]

Having passed through the watersheds of the Ravi, Beas, Sutlej, and Tons rivers, the *padyatris* crossed into the Dehra Dun district of what was then Uttar Pradesh, and walking through the famous deodar forests of Deoban, they reached Chakrata. In their own home state the mission of the marchers was well known, and local people were already engaged in efforts to address forest issues at the grass roots. Support for the *padyatris* was overwhelming. In Uttarkashi hundreds of women formed a procession demanding the preservation of natural mixed forests. In several villages of the Jakkur Valley, the villagers framed rules and working plans for the preservation of forests and appointed their own forest guards. School children were taking care of tree nurseries for the reforestation plans of their villages. All showed great enthusiasm for the *padyatris*. These efforts stood in stark contrast to the damage to the state forests that had resulted from decades of abuse and mismanagement. Soil erosion and landslides were common. As in other states, they observed massive destruction of chir pines from the excessive tapping of resin. Sunderlal observed that the state forest corporation was reaping high profits from the sale of innumerable diseased, dead, and dying trees.[13] Official reforestation plans appeared ineffective. They observed that in the village of Kemara in the district of Tehri-Garhwal after two successive efforts at planting of chir pines, the services of the forest guard were no longer needed because there were no longer any trees left to guard![14]

Bahuguna observed that the state was raising new plantations of trees but that most of them were of conifers, with the thick oak forests that are better able to conserve water being clear felled, ironically for the raising of nurseries. He observed that in Gauraghati the people were facing severe shortages of water following the destruction of their oak forests. There, other than rain, the only sources of water for drinking and irrigation had fallen by 75 percent. In his report to the government of Uttar Pradesh, Sunderlal stated that at the beginning of the twentieth century the forests of the Uttar Pradesh hills were managed for the requirements of the local people. Settlements were few, and the area was covered with mixed forests, with ground cover of light doob grass. "Then forests began to be exploited to meet the demands for railway sleepers and fuel for the railway engines." After independence, the forests that had been managed for local needs for fodder and timber became commercial forests with the demand for species of industrial importance, especially eucalyptus for the production of paper. He notes that with the intervention of Indira Gandhi, a temporary ban had been imposed on the felling of trees at an altitude above one thousand meters but that vested interests were working hard to overturn that provision. For Sunderlal the most hopeful sign in Uttar Pradesh was the high level of consciousness among and village women about the value of the forest as the support for their survival.[15]

Having entered the UP hills in the district of Dehra Dun the marchers visited Chakrata, Barkot, Srinagar, Gauchar, Karnaprayag, Kausani, Almora, Nainital and Ranibagh where they suspended their march for the winter on December 15, 1981, the end of the second phase of their journey. After attending a number of conferences and seminars throughout the country Sunderlal returned to begin the third phase of the journey from Ranibagh in Uttar Pradesh to Siliguri in West Bengal. Before leaving Ranibagh they met with the now very elderly Sarala Behn. She was then residing in Ranibagh and was not in good health. Still strong in spirit, she mustered the strength to meet with Sunderlal, Dhoom Singh Negi, and their colleagues and conferred her blessing upon them all before they departed on February 25, 1982, for the next phase of the journey.

For one week they walked through the Terai region of Nainital, where the clearing of dense forests had begun in the 1950s. Here Sunderlal observed that the plantations of eucalyptus had radically changed the ecological conditions of the region. In his report to the government of Uttar Pradesh, he noted the research of Dhun Kalapesi, an environmentalist from Bombay, who pointed out that owing largely to deforestation, the once damp climate of Terai, which had effectively absorbed the heat of the plains, had recently turned dry, and the rise in temperature that could be noticed in Nainital could also be seen in the receding of the

Pindari Glacier in the mountains. He noted that in areas of eucalyptus plantations, the water level had dropped dramatically. He observed that hand pumps were without water, and many streams had dried up. He pointed out that eucalyptus plantations provide no cover for the wildlife that had disappeared from the region and that over the last ten years the bee population of the area had diminished by more than 50 percent.[16] The *padyatris* crossed the river Sharda at Banbasa and entered Nepal at Mahendranagar. They walked through the last remaining forest in the Terai region of Nepal between Dhangaddi and Mahendranagar, which was being clear felled to settle about ten thousand families from the hills. Population pressure in the hill regions of Nepal had forced people from the hills to the Terai where the government had started a massive program of colonization. But the new settlers to the region who were once concerned about the threat of tigers and hyenas were now more concerned with the scarcity of fuel wood. Sunderlal and others tell of a conversation with a local man near Mahendranagar. When asked how he addressed the fuel needs of his family, he replied that there was a time when fuel was readily available because there were sufficient branches and twigs to burn. He stated that with the proliferation of the sawmills in the Terai, they had access to the refuse from the mills. When the refuse was no longer available, they began to cut the stumps left over from the felling of the trees. When the last of the stumps were used, they began to dig into the ground for the roots of the stumps. When asked where he will turn for fuel if the supply of roots was exhausted, he was without a reply.[17] The reply that might have been given was suggested in the cow-dung cakes on the village walls. Dried cow dung was the main cooking fuel in the region, depriving the soil of much needed natural fertilizer.

From that region they climbed the mountain range of Mahabharat and reached Kathmandu after passing through Surkhet, Tulsipur, Peuthan, Tansen, Syangja, and Pokhara. On the way they talked to students and administrators, all of whom expressed support for the Chipko Movement and expressed the view that a similar movement was needed in Nepal. On the road to Kathmandu they saw cultivated slopes that could only accelerate soil erosion in areas already damaged by erosion. They saw villagers walking fifty kilometers to sell birds in the markets of Kathmandu and women walking for five or six days to bring household goods on their backs from markets in the Terai. Sunderlal notes that the eastern Terai of Nepal was mostly clear felled long ago but that the few remaining stands of forest were being felled to earn money and to make way for plantations of fast-growing commercial varieties of trees. He states that in Nepal a common saying has it that "green forests are the wealth of Nepal." The saying originally meant that the agricultural prosperity of Nepal depended upon the forests that provided fertile soil, fodder for the cattle, and water for agricultural productivity. But the saying had been exploited by the protagonists of commercial forestry for whom the forests could be turned to cash. While in Nepal, Sunderlal tried to revive the meaning of the saying in its original intention by giving it a new form: "[g]reen forests are the wealth of Nepal: Save, Save, Save!" Fortunately, he says, the younger generation was taking his admonitions seriously. Two young activists joined them for this phase of the journey, and along the way they hugged the trees as a symbol of welcome to the chipko message.[18] Sunderlal suggests that despite the many discouraging signs, the people of Nepal had begun a modest effort to conserve the forests. He notes that more than one village had appointed guards to protect them from illegal exploitation. He states that "alternative sources of energy and efficient methods of using fuel, together with a prudent pattern of tree plantation with preference to food trees, could be the beginning of the end to Nepal's downhill ecological slide." He states that the government is conscious of the threat to the country's ecological balance and has appointed a national committee for Man and Biosphere. This third phase of the Kashmir Kohima *Padyatra* ended at the onset of the monsoon on May 19, 1982.

In the interim, with the authority of a person who had seen the condition of the Himalayas at close range, Sunderlal was invited to London in June 1982, to the United Nations Environmental Program's Open Hearing on the State of the World's Environment. During his visit he gave talks at universities and environmental groups both in England and on the continent, addressing the new green parties in seven nations. In July he made a final visit to Mira Behn at her village just outside Vienna. She died only weeks after his visit.

On October 19, 1982, after receiving a taped message from Indira Gandhi, in which she expressed her support for the chipko *padyatra*, the marchers began the fourth and final phase of the journey. This began with their ascent to Darjeeling. Sunderlal and Dhoom Singh Negi were now joined by three more participants: Sri Harsh Joshi and Dinesh Kunjwal from Uttar Pradesh and Sri Neelkanth Phutane from Maharashtra. Sunderlal states that at the beginning of the twentieth century, when the British made Darjeeling their summer resort, the region was covered by thick natural forests. Over the following century much of these forests were replaced with tea plantations or by trees imported for their ornamental value. Among them was the *Criptomaria japonica* an exotic species from Japan, which he says is now a source of raw material for the paper industry. Sunderlal states that the West Bengal government had recently commercialized the hill forests and handed over their management to the State Forest Corporation. To generate revenue, the corporation had begun the clear felling of broad-leafed forests, at an altitude between 4,500 feet (1371 meters) and 7,500 feet (2285 meters), the elevation of the sources of mountain streams. This decisively changed the flow of water and accelerated soil erosion. Already one of the tea estates was complaining of water shortage. A ray of hope to which the *padyathris* gave their support was the five-year-old campaign of a local conservation group to save the remaining natural forests of the region. In Darjeeling they called upon the state governor to submit suggestions for improving the forests of the state.[19] From West Bengal they entered Sikkim, where they saw healthier forests less devastated by commercial felling. But in the northern region of the state the construction of new roads and a sudden increase in the population had lead to such destruction of virgin forests that in some areas landslides had become a regular occurrence. At the famous Rumtek monastery they shared with the monks the Buddhist admonition, which E. F. Schumacher brings out in his famous book, to plant five trees in the course of one's life. Before they departed for Bhutan, the Rumtek monks blessed them for the success of their mission.

On November 7, 1982, the royal government of Bhutan welcomed the marchers with a mass meeting as they entered the kingdom near Jaldhaka in West Bengal. The director of forests instructed his officials to provide whatever help the *padyatris* might need.[20] Bhutan declared the *padyatra* an official program of the royal government and assigned forest officers to walk with the *yatris* through the breadth of the country. It was in Bhutan that Sunderlal was joined by Ramakrishna, a man from Bangalore, and by Pandurang Hegde, who had worked with Sunderlal as part of his field work for his graduate degree in social work at the University of Delhi. Ramakrishna informed me that he had been a trekking enthusiast from his youth and had heard about Sunderlal's travels through the Himalayas in the news. He decided to join him. In December 1982 he set out from Bangalore, in Karnataka, for Siliguri by train, where he got a bus to Phunsiling (Phuentsholing), a town on the border with Bhutan. At the Indian embassy in Phunsiling he negotiated a travel permit to accompany Sunderlal in Bhutan. The Indian embassy sent him by jeep, a journey of four hours, to a forest guest house up in the mountains, far from any village. He stayed there overnight, the watchman at the guest house being the only other person present. The next day Bahuguna arrived at the guest house, accompanied by a forest guide from the Bhutan Forest Department. Ramakrishna then walked with Sunderlal to Tongsa (Trongsa), a trek of three hundred kilometers. The journey, he said, took between two and three weeks. He states that the Bhutanese government was fully involved in Sunderlal's program and provided him with a forest guide. When he was approaching a village, the forest guide would inform the village in advance and would be in communication with other people of the region by telephone. The first settlement they encountered was a labor camp at a paper and plywood factory under construction, a settlement for the workers. There Ramakrishna met a laborer from Karnataka, whom he recognized from the language he spoke to his son. This surprised the laborer. Bahuguna explained to him that forest destruction requires the work of laborers who come from far away, laborers who do not have a close relation with the forests they are required to destroy. They stayed in the labor camp and presented the chipko message to the people. Their second stop was the Chuka hydroelectric project, then under construction. There they visited the school for the children of the construction workers. This government school had arranged a program with Sunderlal to speak to the children and the teaching staff about the importance of the planting of new trees. He explained that when people set out to plant the seed for a new tree, they need to remember that it is the following generation and not the present generation that will reap the benefit. Thus to plant trees one must be motivated by the love of humanity as such, and not simply of one's own generation.

At the request of the royal Bhutanese government, the Indian government was building border roads through Bhutan as a defense against the possible threat of another Chinese invasion. For the technical staff and the labors of this enterprise, the government had constructed settlements. For the next two days Sunderlal and Ramakrishna stayed in a guest house of the one of these settlements. The roads were being constructed largely by Bengali laborers from Bangladesh. Sunderlal observed that conditions in the labor camps were less than satisfactory and that the education for the children of the laborers was largely neglected. He met with the management of these labor camps and argued for a more humanitarian outlook for the children of these laborers. He argued that for every twenty labor families, there should be one teacher for the children. Ramakrishna states that for most of this journey they stayed in the guest houses of other border road settlements. He would journey to the villages to speak to the villagers during the day and return to a border road settlement to sleep.

In this routine of speaking in villages and staying in border road settlements, they arrived finally at the Bhutanese capital of Thimpu. Here the royal Bhutanese government had made arrangements for their stay in a luxurious hotel. Sunderlal objected to this arrangement and pointed out that he had been walking with the chipko message and staying with the local people. "I've come," he said, "to share in the suffering of the people and not to be a guest of the government." He said he would not stay in a hotel even as a guest of the state. If he could be accommodated in a monastery, he said, he would be pleased to stay there. Finally government officials made arrangements to accommodate him and Ramakrishna in the home of a Forest Department employee. The government then held a function in honor of Sunderlal and his mission. At the capital of Bhutan, the Indian ambassador walked for a day with the marchers, while the first secretary of the Indian embassy and his wife accompanied them for two days to the town of Nobding. They then took a shortcut through a bridal path in the forest and visited a remote forest village. It was a pristine wildlife habitat. Here the royal government had arranged accommodation back along the path that they had taken. But, as in a pilgrimage, Sunderlal explained that he had taken a vow not to go back on the same path. He would make a lateral move to visit another village, but he would not go back on the same path he had taken. Finally government officials arranged for them to stay at the home of local people in the next village. Sunderlal and Ramakrishna accepted the plan. Ramakrishna points out that as they moved east from Thimbu the population became less and less. From there to Thongsa (Trongsa), he told me, they saw no more than two or three villages. It was about two or three days before they reached Thongsa (Trongsa) that they again encountered their colleague Dhoom Singh Negi. Negi had made enquiries with the Border Roads Organization. The Border Roads Organization officers had located Sunderlal in the forest and had instructed Dhoom Singh Negi where he could go to join them.[21]

Pandurang Hegde had also tried to reach the group and had spent several days trekking through the forest to find it. He had also begun in the border town of Phunsiling, but the group had moved on before he arrived. After many inquiries, much effort, and a hike of four days through the forest, he finally caught up with them in Thongsa (Trongsa) and walked with them for the following ten days. Pandurang spoke about the routine of walking through the day and meeting the villagers in the evening, when the work of their day would actually begin. He also comments on the extraordinary hospitality of the villagers. Pandurang was not long on the journey when he became concerned with the protein needs of his colleagues. One day while walking, he suggested to Sunderlal that, considering the level of their exertion and the difficulty of the terrain, they might supplement their diet with some eggs or meat. Thus it was a great surprise to all of them, that evening, during their meeting with the villagers, when the villagers brought the *padyatris* a gift of more than twenty boiled eggs. He states that with Sunderlal's communication skills, the village meetings were a great deal of fun. The villagers received them with kindness and listened intently to their stories.

Because the villages of the region were often far apart, the *padyatris* appreciated the hospitality of the Border Roads Organization. During their six weeks in Bhutan, the *padyatris* sometimes journeyed some 30 to 40 kilometers a day. On one occasion they arrived at about 5:00 p.m. at a village called Ura about 240 kilometers east of Thimpu and at an altitude of 10,000 feet. The village women were returning from the forests and fields when they encountered these unfamiliar faces. When the marchers identified themselves they were invited to the home of Cheema Wangchuk, the local member of the national assembly. After he welcomed the *padyatris* he took up his megaphone to call the village together. As the people streamed together, the *padyatris* played taped messages from Indian dignitaries, showed their slides, and told the story of how the women of Garhwal had taken the initiative to protect their forests. Soon it was a mass meeting involving both the visitors and the participation of the local community. Here the *padyatris* commented to the local people on the excellent condition of the forests of Bhutan as compared with other parts of the Himalayas and the need to continue to protect them. As Sunderlal put it to them, "The Himalaya is dead in Nepal, dying in India and is only alive in Bhutan the land of eternal happiness." As in other places the meeting went on to late in the evening.[22]

During their time in Bhutan the *yatris* addressed forest officers, border road officers, and public meetings. They observed that as compared with India and Nepal, the kingdom of Bhutan had succeeded at that time in conserving its natural forests and its wildlife. By that time it had established a number of wildlife sanctuaries and national parks wherein the beauty of nature was effectively preserved. Outside these protected areas, the natural forests of Bhutan provided rich fodder for the cows and yaks. They produced an abundance of butter and cheese that reminded Sunderlal of his visit to the Swiss Alps. They saw that the kingdom was rich in water resources that had not yet been disturbed by massive deforestation. Because there was little fluctuation in the flow of the rivers, Sunderlal thought that power projects would likely be more successful than those on rivers in other regions of the Himalayas. But they also noted that on the Indian border, forests had been destroyed by the smuggling of timber and firewood. In these regions the government had imposed a ban on all felling of trees. Bhutan had strict laws governing the conservation of nature. The penalty for hunting the musk deer, for instance, was a life sentence. In spite of these measures the marchers noticed that commercial exploitation of the forests had begun. Conifers were being exploited for timber, hardwood forests had begun to feed a new state-owned plywood factory, and in the eastern region of the country the extraction of resin had begun. They also noticed immense loss of forests from clear felling to meet requirements of the growing townships and the colossal wooden monasteries called dzongs. The most distressing sight was the evidence of dolomite quarrying in the foothills near Pagali that had created a desert of four square kilometers and was evidently spreading to the south. The *padyatris* walked west to east for 700 kilometers (435 miles) through the breadth of Bhutan. Their travel was mostly over the higher altitudes from Thimpu to Blanting, crossing some passes with altitudes between 11,000 and 13,000 feet. Both Ramakrishna and Pandurang Hegde departed from the *padyatra* on the border with Arunachal Pradesh. From Blanting, Sunderlal and Doom Singh Negi passed back into India into the state of Arunachal Pradesh and proceeded through the Tawang pass through which many years before the Dalai Lama had escaped from Tibet.

In two days they reached the town of Tawang, in the Indian state of Arunachal Pradesh, at an altitude of 11,000 feet. Here, the *padyatris* witnessed again the tragic sight of people digging the roots of stumps for firewood. The increasing population and the expansion of townships were fast taking their toll on the forests. As they proceeded over the Se la Pass at an altitude of 13,713 feet they walked for 15 kilometers (9.3 miles) through snow to where they saw the distressing sight of stumps where forests had been clear felled and where, owing to climatic conditions, the forest would never likely recover. In regions far from the motor roads, they did see areas of dense natural forests. Here, because the population was relatively low and the cycle of shifting cultivation called Jhum was relatively long, the practice of shifting cultivation had not endangered forest health. Between Seppa and Segali, areas where even officers seldom travel, the *yatris* visited village communities that claim ownership of the local forests. They told the visitors that they maintain these forests for game, for building material, and for edible roots. They indicated that they opposed government control over the forests and were known for their warning to outsiders that if they are connected to the forest department they would not be permitted to work. Nevertheless, where motor roads were present, the felling of trees for firewood and for timber had begun. In the southern and eastern regions of Arunachal Pradesh, a number of sawmills, plywood factories, and veneer factories were fast coming up, and young school dropouts were becoming the suppliers of timber to those industries. There the forests were disappearing fast and could be gone, according to one government minister, in as little as ten years. They entered the state of Assam at Lakhimpur and crossed the Brahmaputra River near Jorhat. From conversations with local people, it appeared that in Assam the forests were understood simply as a subject of stories of the past. They were no longer a living reality. Destruction of the forests in this region had begun with the British with the establishment of tea plantations. The *yatris* observed, however, that in the past three decades the destruction of forests had continued partly from agricultural expansion and partly to feed the plywood industry. As in Himachal Pradesh where the *padyatris* had witnessed the irony of forests being eaten up by the apples, there the forests were being consumed in plywood factories for the packaging of tea. Entering Nagaland from Mariani the *padyatris* walked sixteen kilometers through territory disputed by Nagaland and Assam to the Dessa Valley. There they observed two sawmills and a veneer factory. Taking advantage of the border dispute, workers were busy night and day felling trees for the factories and the mills. The *padyatris* found that as in Arunachal Pradesh, the forest communities of Nagaland held ownership of the forests. They noticed that in some cases villages were effectively protecting their forests and were raising new plantations of trees. But they observed that in most areas the pace of destruction was very high. Here the forests were being exploited to provide firewood for local townships and exported to nearby cities.[23]

When the *yatris* reached the Raj Bhavan, the state capital building, in Kohima they had traveled 4,870 kilometers (3,020 miles) over the course of three hundred days. They had traveled without knowing what the next day would bring and without knowing where they would receive their next meal. In an interview conducted while Sunderlal was trekking through Bhutan, he was asked about the sponsor of the journey. He said, "Our sponsors are the people, the common people of the hill villages." He went on to state that it was they who had provided their food and shelter. The villagers, he said, had looked after them as they would have treated their own relatives. Such generous hospitality, he says, reduced all our worries: "We are self reliant depending on local resources and support, we are volunteers working for the cause of the environment and our needs are meager. We have no funding from large agencies nor have we asked for any."[24] They arrived in Kohima without any sign of exhaustion or pain. Their journey had been strenuous and sometimes treacherous but they had received the support, warmth, appreciation, and hospitality of the people to whom they had gone. In their travels they had seen barren hill slopes and valleys that resembled deserts, receding glaciers, the drying up of water sources, and people bereft of the sources of life that had once been the gifts of the forests. Sunderlal states that in most of the areas women had to walk long distances to collect fuel and fodder. They saw children eight to ten years of age walking long distances to collect firewood instead of going to school. Except for the Kashmir Valley, Bhutan, and some parts of Arunachal, the travelers saw widespread problems of water scarcity. Their conclusion was that the glory of this magnificent range of mountains was fading fast, and the single most critical cause was deforestation from the commercialization of the forests. They reached Kohima on the February 1, 1983, where the governor of the state declared that the *padyatra* had been a historical event. He said that "it has special significance for Nagaland where the destruction of forests is inconceivable." He advised the chief minister and other ministers of the state to bring about legislation for the protection of the forests and admonished others to do something practical to materialize the message of the chipko march. The last thing they did in Kohima was to pay respects to Rani Gaidinliu the elderly freedom fighter about whom Sunderlal had heard from Sri Dev Suman, and who like him had participated in the freedom movement from her early teenage years.[25]

While the focus of his conversations and discourses on this *padyatra* was the people and especially the women of Garhwal and of the Chipko Movement, Sunderlal's message was about saving the Himalayas. Among his stated purposes in undertaking the journey was to widen the base of the movement to other regions of the Himalayas. With the support of others working in other regions of the Himalayas, local activists would be able to take up issues of concern to their own area. In the course of their travels three such activist groups began to take shape, one in Jammu and Kashmir, one in Himachal Pradesh, and another in Nepal. Sunderlal points out that these groups had succeeded in mobilizing support for such issues as the rights of villagers to forest produce. He remained in touch with these groups during the course of his journey and indicates that the result was a well-coordinated movement on ecological issues in the Himalayas. Bahuguna sometimes describes his efforts in the Himalayas as one of sewing seeds in the desert. He suggests that we can only really judge the success of the effort in the long run. Yet he also acknowledges that the emergence of activist groups in the Himalayas has given a great boost to the morale of the Chipko Movement itself. Their emergence suggests that the ideas of Chipko are relevant and that its methods are effective. He states that along the journey they tried always to involve young people as much as possible. Whatever success they have enjoyed, he says, is the result of the active response and participation of the youth and especially of women of the hills.

An interview with Sunderlal in Bhutan raised one of the most familiar and poignant questions concerning the objectives of his environmentalism in the Himalayas. "It is widely understood," the interviewer said, "that ecological demands like those of the Chipko Andolan are obstacles to the economic growth of the country." In his reply Sunderlal acknowledged the widespread impression that conservation stands opposed to economy and that the agenda of the conservationists would put economic development ages behind. He states, however, that his own experience and that of other chipko workers convinced him that this supposed dichotomy was mistaken. He states that there was a time when he also supported forest-based industries as a means to address the economic conditions of the people of the hills. Before the Chipko Movement received its name, he had believed that the people should be able to utilize forest wealth for limited commercial purposes. To that end he, Dhoom Singh Negi, and others worked intensively among forest laborers to better their condition. But it was during this period that their belief in such an approach was shattered. Says Bahuguna: "We were able to observe how even careful felling disturbs eco-systems, how the conifers dominate over broad leaf trees. We saw how such trees allow topsoil to wash away during monsoon. We saw perennial springs in the villages and forests drying up and leading to scarcity of drinking water. And during that period Garhwal Hills experienced massive land slides killing and burying hundreds of people and livestock. Villages were wiped out and the debris covered fertile fields."[26] He points out that these tragic events led to great losses in the agricultural economy. From these experiences he concluded that the short-term manipulation of nature for immediate economic benefit stands against the long-term economic benefit of the people. It was for this reason that he and other activists moved from an economic approach to an approach to conservation for a stable and permanent economy. It is the meaning of the slogan that Sunderlal and others had repeated through the *padyathra*: Ecology Is Permanent Economy. If even the controlled felling of trees could lead to economic loss, it is not difficult to imagine the long-term economic results of the kind of clear felling that Sunderlal and his colleagues witnessed throughout the Himalayan range. The results of that policy were already evident in the lives of the mountain people they encountered from Srinagar to Kohima.

To the question of whether an ecological approach would lead to a decrease in the demand for forest labor, Sunderlal states that he has practical data to show that if the existing lands and forests were managed for the long-term interest of society, then the existing labor force could be absorbed into the work of caring for the forests, especially for reforestation programs. Sunderlal states that the only alterative to shifting cultivation and the cultivation of cereals on steep slopes is raising crops from trees. He recommends the planting of trees for food, especially nuts, edible seeds, oil seeds, honey, and seasonable fruit as well as trees for fodder, fiber, fertilizer, and fuel. These, he argues, would provide the means to achieve the kind of village self-sufficiency in water, air, food, clothing, and shelter that Gandhi endorsed and promoted. He draws attention to the great wealth of trees of this nature that have been successfully cultivated in the hills. He points out that research in the field of tree crops has not received appropriate attention because forest research has always been oriented to timber for industrial production rather than for the needs of the people. Further study needs to be undertaken of species found in the forests, especially those that have sustained the lives of the tribal people.[27] The immediate need, he says is to preserve whatever forests remain, but the long-term strategy must be to adopt a new conception of development in which human beings and nature can coexist in harmony. Such changes in land use will require the will of the government and of the people.

For Sunderlal himself this great foot march was an exercise in self-education. Because the venture was the effort of independent social activists not connected with any organization or establishment, they had to depend on the people. He states that they enjoyed liberal support, both moral and financial, from all sectors of the people. For this reason the experience strengthened his faith in the goodwill and the wisdom of the common people of the hills. As we suggested earlier, he does not consider the crisis in the Himalayas to be an isolated event. It has its roots in a materialistic civilization that promotes an ever-spiraling demand on the ecosystem, a demand that is never satisfied. The result is that the nonrenewable resources of the earth are decreasing. Moreover, because of ever-increasing exploitation, what we have called renewable resources have become nonrenewable as well. The prosperity that materialistic civilization has provided is temporary. Sunderlal's purpose is not the return to a preindustrial economy but a move forward toward viable village economies that appropriate the wisdom of the past and combine it with the best insights of ecology for sound forest management: "Alternative sources of fuel and energy and efficient ways of using them are known. There is also no lack of expertise in proper forest management. But there is little identity of interest as between the people and those who control forests and other resources. The only way to redeem forests from the combination of corrupting contractors, corrupt politicians and corruptible officials is to vest their control openly with the community, with government in an over seeing role." Under these conditions it would be possible to protect and utilize the forests in a socially acceptable manner and to summon the blessings of science in the service of the people.[28]

Chapter 12

Protesting the Tehri Dam

The movement to save the forests of the Himalayas was underway. Fledgling environmental movements had begun to emerge in various regions of the hills. With heightened prestige from his direct experience of environmental conditions in the Himalayas, the man once maligned as the enemy of science and development was speaking with authority about the results of a long-standing forest policy that undermined the domestic economy and endangered the future economic prospects of the country. He was being invited to speak to environmental groups in India and abroad about the hazards of an understanding of nature that turns forest wealth into cash for the few while it impoverishes the many and the future of all. In the midst of these developments another crisis was emerging in the region of Bahuguna's own ancestral home. There the state government was planning a hydroelectric power project on the Bhagirathi River, the northern most tributary of the Ganges. The project would entail the construction of an earth-and-rock-filled dam 260.5 meters in height, the highest in Asia and one of the highest in the world. It was to be located just downstream from the confluence of the Bhagirathi and the Bhilangana rivers, less than a kilometer downstream from Tehri. It would flood 45 kilometers (28 miles) of the Bhagirathi Valley and 35 kilometers (22 miles) of the Bhilangana Valley, impounding 3.22 million cubic meters of water spread over 42.5 square kilometers (16.4 square miles). Among the benefits expected from the project was 2,400 megawatts (MW) of electric power, to be supplied to industry in such lowland cities as Allahabad and Kanpur, irrigation to 270,000 hectares of land mostly for sugar cane cultivation in the western districts of Uttar Pradesh, and 500 cubic feet per second of drinking water to Delhi.

Bahuguna points out that in the region upstream from the proposed dam site is a picturesque and peaceful valley with distinctive white houses generations old, their lintels meticulously carved with ancient mythological themes. The dam would submerge this valley, the entire town of Tehri, and twenty-three villages in the vicinity, and partly inundate an additional seventy-two villages. It would engulf fifty-two hundred hectares of fertile land, which the hard-working people of the area had been farming for many generations. It would also cover important religious sites and places of historical importance. The region of Tehri, on the pilgrimage route to Gangotri, is sacred, as one journalist put it, because of its association with the Bhagirathi.[1] It was the cradle of an ancient culture. It had given birth to eminent poets, scholars, and artists. There, the Vedantic saint Swami Ram Tirtha had taken the vow of *sannyasi* or renunciation. In the glow of his influence Tehri was renowned as a place of spiritual meaning. Tehri was also the site of the martyrdom of the freedom fighter Sri Dev Suman, Sunderlal's first guru. Freedom lovers had been inspired by the sacrifice of his life in the Tehri jail.[2] If the dam were built, the town of Tehri would be submerged, its population of twenty-five thousand uprooted. Estimates of the number people to be displaced by the dam varied from seventy thousand to more than one hundred thousand.[3]

Opposition to this project had already come from geologists, seismologists, and ecologists. In a variety of professional journals, they pointed out that the movement of the earth's continental plates renders the Himalayan region seismically active. The Himalayan range itself is the result of the movement of these plates. Over the past century, nine earthquakes above 7.5 on the Richter scale had occurred in the area. The project was to be located only 9.3 miles (15 kilometers) from the juncture of the Indian and the Eurasian plates. Because no earthquakes had occurred in recent times in the Tehri region, some seismologists suggested that the project might be close to a seismic gap, where earthquakes of a magnitude above 8 could occur within the one-hundred-year projected life of the dam. Evidence of past major landslides had also been observed along the Bhagirathi River. If a landslide into the reservoir should breach the dam, a wall of water would quickly reach the pilgrimage cities of Rishikesh and Haridwar. The disaster would be measured in tens of thousands of lives. Some experts suggested that the silt accumulation characteristic of Himalayan rivers could limit the life of the reservoir to as little as thirty to forty years.

For Bahuguna, the erection of the Tehri Dam presented an ecological, social, and religious challenge. He argues that when the Ganges flows in its natural course it benefits all, irrespective of caste, creed, color, or economic circumstances. When it is dammed, it becomes the possession of the privileged and powerful who dispense its blessings on a partisan basis.[4] The plan to build a dam on this site and public indignation against the plan had a long history, in which Sunderlal was involved. In an extended cost-benefit appraisal of the proposal published in 1988, Vijay Paranjpye pointed out that in 1949 the Geological Survey of India first identified the Bhagirathi Gorge at Tehri as a possible dam site provided subsurface investigations did not reveal contravening hazards. In 1965 the then union minister for irrigation and power, K. L. Rao, visited the area and met with representatives of the local people who opposed the project.[5] In an interview published in 1990 Sunderlal stated that his opposition to the proposed dam began in 1969. At the time those opposed to the dam had the support of their member of parliament, Rajmata Kamlendumati Shah. He states that because the project was widely viewed as vital for national development, there were few in government or industry who sided with her. He states that around this time he had many conversations with K. L. Rao and discussed several alternatives to the plan. The Uttar Pradesh government and the engineers dismissed his suggestions.[6] At this time, the Uttar Pradesh Irrigation Department was undertaking a detailed project report that, in 1969, it submitted to its planning commission. That report, envisaging a project with a generating capacity of six hundred megawatts, was approved in 1972. After that, the *gaon sabha* (village council) of thirty-five villages in the Tehri district passed a joint resolution expressing its opposition, and the *zilla parishad* (district council) called upon the government to drop the project. The government of Uttar Pradesh decided, nevertheless, to move forward with the project. In response, the people formed a committee known as the Tehri Bandh Virodhi Sangharsh Samiti, (TBVSS), Anti-Tehri Dam Struggle Committee. Sunderlal explained that this committee was composed of people of all political leanings, but in choosing a leader they were faced with the problem that if a person from a particular political party became the president, then those belonging to other political parties would likely not support such a person, and the work of the committee would suffer. Virendra Dutt Saklani, whom Sunderlal had known from his days in the Tehri Praja Mandal, was now a veteran freedom fighter and a distinguished lawyer. Sunderlal suggested that Saklani could be an effective leader of the committee because he belonged to no political party. Acknowledging his distinguished record of public service as a member of the Legislative Assembly the committee chose him as president. Sunderlal states that

Saklani made a thorough study of every aspect of the project and invited acknowledged experts from relevant disciplines to visit the project and offer their opinions of the promises and hazards it entailed. He gathered voluminous documents and mobilized the people, educating them to the risks and dangers of the project. From the beginning, and even while occupied with other issues, Sunderlal gave his support to Saklani and the work of this committee.

In 1972, the planning commission approved the Detailed Project Report of the Uttar Pradesh Irrigation Department, and in 1976 the government of Utttar Pradesh gave administrative approval to the project. In January 1978, the TBVSS unanimously passed its first resolution unequivocally opposing construction of the dam.[7] In March of the same year the government of Uttar Pradesh awarded contracts for the construction of diversion tunnels in the first phase of the construction of the dam. For them and for the Tehri Hydro Development Corporation, the construction of the dam was a symbol of progress and the promise of prosperity. But the local people saw it otherwise. Bahuguna states that on June 1, 1978, when the builders came to begin work on the diversion tunnels, the people blocked the roads. The slogans they painted on the rocks and walls expressed their views: "Tehri Dam is the symbol of total destruction." "Give up the construction of the Tehri Dam in the interests of the country and for the protection of the environment." Local opposition was massive. Here dam officials encountered thousands of men, women, and children who blocked their way and shouted: "You love electricity, we love our soil.[8] In the course of this protest 150–200 protesters, including Virendra Dutt Saklani, were arrested.[9] After collecting ten thousand signatures on a petition against the dam, committee members suspended their agitation, and their colleagues were released. The TBVSS now filed its petition against the dam with the Petitions Committee of Parliament, and a government committee was sent to assess the project. But the Lok Sabha (the lower house of parliament) dissolved in September 1979 before the petition was heard, and the TBVSS petition lapsed. Recognizing the distress of the local people, the then prime minister, Charan Singh, requested that the Department of Science and Technology assess the environmental impact of the dam.[10] Sunderlal states that when Indira Gandhi came to power in January 1980, the Anti-Tehri Dam Struggle Committee communicated with her. She assured them that the government had authorized an environmental study that would consider their concerns. Bahuguna states that when the environmental study committee came to Tehri, he and other opponents of the dam argued that construction work should be suspended until the committee completed its work. But construction work continued.

In November 1985, as construction continued, the Anti-Tehri Dam Struggle Committee decided to file a writ petition with the Supreme Court of India.[11] Among other things, the petition stated that the proposed dam was to be located in a seismically active area and that the risk of failure would endanger the lives and property of people in locations downstream, that because of sedimentation and erosion, habitations like Uttarkashi situated upstream of the inlet of the reservoir would be damaged and that the dam would create a feeling of insecurity among people at various locations on the reservoir rim slopes, jeopardizing the right to life guaranteed to citizens under the Indian Constitution.[12] It would not be until 2003 that a final determination on the part of the Supreme Court concerning the Tehri Dam would be heard. After the filing of this petition the Anti-Tehri Dam Struggle Committee suffered a crisis. Virendra Saklani, now in his seventies, fell ill and suffered paralysis. While he remained president of the TBVSS, he appealed to Sunderlal to take up the cause of the peoples' struggle against the dam. Sunderlal responded that he had neither Saklani's legal background nor his administrative skill. Nevertheless, he gave his word to Saklani that he would do his best to support the people in their struggle against the dam.

Turning his promise into action, on November 24, 1989, Bahuguna departed from the Parvatiya Navjeevan Ashram, which with his wife, Vimla, he had founded in 1956, to devote himself to the protest against the Tehri Dam. At that time he took a pledge that he would not return to the ashram in Silyara until the Tehri Dam issue was settled. Sunderlal and Vimla Bahuguna then proceeded to build a small *kuti* (hut) adjacent to a small temple just one hundred meters from the site of the project where the water of the Bhagirathi River was being diverted from its natural course during the construction of the dam. Here Sunderlal Bahuguna resolved to remain in *satyagraha* or nonviolent protest against the construction of the Tehri Dam, until the demands of the people were resolved. If, against the advice of eminent scientists and the needs of the local people, the dam should nevertheless be built, then this *kuti* would be the first human dwelling to be submerged in the rising waters behind the dam. In the time to follow, the Bahuguna's *kuti* became the rallying point for many dramatic activities of protest against the Tehri Dam that drew enormous public support and much media attention. In the course of time, Sunderlal's involvement with the protest against the Tehri Dam became a large parenthesis within the larger concern for the condition of the Himalayas. But it was a parenthesis that so typified the distinction between the traditional culture of the forest and the imperatives of centralized industrialized economics that it made high demands on his

Bahuguna's *Kuti* at Tehri Where for over Ten Years He Remained in Satyagraha

energy and attention. It would involve his leadership in the organization of massive nonviolent demonstrations, arrests, mistreatment by police, periods in jail, and periods of severe fasting.

Sunderlal states that his first fast in connection with the Tehri Dam began on Christmas Day of 1989. It proceeded for a total of sixteen days, during which construction work on the dam came to a halt. At the time Maneka Gandhi was the union minister of state for environment. From her, Sunderlal and his supporters expected much support.[13] She invited Sunderlal and his supporters for negotiations in Delhi. Their conversation centered on a study in progress by the Environment Ministries Appraisal Committee that found the dam to be hazardous on many grounds. Their meeting resulted in the agreement that blasting for the construction of the dam would be suspended until the study of the committee was completed and its report was received. Sunderlal states: "We agreed to call off the movement in the hope that the government would take a decision on the basis of the Environment Ministry's Appraisal Committee consisting of scientists of different disciplines and chaired by the eminent soil-scientist Prof. D. R. Bhumbla. The committee unanimously recommended that the high dam project be replaced by a small run-of-the-river scheme."[14] He explained that without disturbing the entire ecology of the river, the run-of-the-river technology can take a channel from a swift flowing river in the mountains, and after several kilometers engineer a fall to generate electricity. Such technology obviates need for a large dam with a reservoir that traps precious soil and displaces many villages. But with interest in the contribution of the Soviet Union to the project, this report was shelved, and the government constituted a new committee headed by the director of the Geological Survey of India. Within a week of their agreement, blasting for the prevailing plan resumed.[15] Government enthusiasm for the high dam project was quickly outpacing local opposition. As one observer put it, "The Tehri Dam was now a gold mine for contractors, engineers and politicians."[16]

Bahuguna's objections to the dam included environmental, cultural, and economic concerns. For him these issues were ethical in nature, and his ethical concerns were not dissimilar from those that motivated the Chipko Movement. Just as ash trees were allotted to outside contractors to generate income on the plains, through the manufacture of sporting goods for a distant market, the government was endorsing a project to provide water and hydroelectric power to distant Delhi and irrigation to the western districts of Uttar Pradesh. Just as the forest department had denied forest resources for the needs of the hills, the government was endorsing a project that denied water to the local people. There was an acute shortage of water in the hills, and the proposal for the dam had already preempted a project to address this problem. A water scheme sanctioned for fifty villages around Pratapnagar was rejected because it would cause a scarcity of water for the Tehri Dam! At the same time the dam was expected to increase the per capita supply of water to Delhi from 246 to 350 liters per day, where five-star hotels consume 1,000 kiloliters, and the homes of government ministers consume 550 kiloliters per day.[17] While serving the needs of cities and industry, it was imposing a disproportionate burden on the people of the hills. It is hardly surprising that the local people saw the project as the work of corrupt and greedy politicians, bureaucrats, and contractors. It is not difficult to interpret the opposition to the Tehri dam in terms of the demand for economic and environmental justice. For Bahuguna and other opponents of the dam, the protest was a matter of survival. It reflected his commitment to Gandhi's philosophy of village independence, as opposed to the centralized hegemony of bureaucrats and politicians, to considerations of ecological science as opposed to power politics, and to the religious and spiritual traditions of the forest as opposed to what he calls the religion of economics.

For Bahuguna, what was needed was more public awareness of the project, its hazards, and its significance for the Ganges, for the people, and for the nation.

As with the Chipko Movement, he felt the best strategy was to bring the message to the people. Sunderlal initiated a rally among young people and spoke to many groups. These young people eventually organized a cycle *yatra*, a bicycle journey, to carry the message. Their plan was to begin at the mouth of the Ganges River, at Ganga Sagar in West Bengal, and proceed on bicycles all the way to Gangotri, at the source of the Bhagirathi River, in what was then Uttar Pradesh. Their purpose was to raise consciousness among the local people about what was happening to the Ganga. In a sense this small group represented a new generation of activists in the cause of the environment. Among them were children and friends of children of *sarvodaya* workers from Bahuguna's earlier days. It was an enthusiastic group. For seventy-five days they traveled along the country roads of West Bengal, Bihar, and Uttar Pradesh, bearing signs that read: "The Ganga Is Dying," "Save the Ganga," and "Let the Ganga Flow." As they traveled the initial group began to grow. Young people from one hamlet would meet the *yatris* as they entered their town and accompany them through the visit. Others who had joined the group would accompany the group to the next destination or beyond. Thus the size of the group ranged from as little as twelve to more than forty. In describing the appeal of the cycle *yatra*, Sunderlal told me that young people love adventure. This was not only an adventure in travel but an adventure with a moral purpose with which the young people could identify. Ironically, having been raised in the hills, Sunderlal had never acquired the skill of riding a bicycle and was carried on the bar of a bicycle by one or another of the enthusiastic participants. As he had done with his many *padyatras*, he presented his case to the people at every village and town where they stopped in the course of their journey. His purpose was to educate the people along the length of the Ganges about the significance for their lives of the Tehri project and to raise awareness about their capacity to oppose it through nonviolent means.

After a journey of seventy-five days, the *yatris* received disturbing news that interrupted their adventure. A devastating earthquake had occurred in the region of Uttarkashi. It had occurred in the early hours of the morning on October 20, 1991. Measuring 6.6 on the Richter scale, the earthquake was felt as far as 350 kilometers away, from Keylong in the north, to Delhi in the south, and beyond Chandigarh in the west. The earthquake took the lives of 770 people and caused severe injuries to as many others. It destroyed more than twenty thousand homes and wreaked heavy damage to more than two hundred thousand more.[18] While most of the damage and loss of life occurred in area close to Uttarkashi, the earthquake had also caused damage to the buildings of the Parvatiya Navjeevan Ashram in Silyara and the death of two persons in that region. With this news Sunderlal suspended the bicycle *yatra* at Rishikesh and took a bus to Uttarkashi to undertake relief work and address the needs of the earthquake victims.

Devastation from the Uttarkashi earthquake soon drew media attention to the question of the safety of the Tehri project and to the hazard it posed to persons living downstream from the proposed site. Touring the quake-hit area the then prime minister, Narasimha Rao, publicly expressed doubt about constructing a dam in such a seismically active region.[19] Sunderlal's concern for the safely issue had already been expressed in a message inscribed on the wall of his *kuti* near the dam site. "If the Tehri dam bursts, a 260 meter high column of water would wash away Rishikesh in just 63 minutes; 17 minutes later the waters would reach Haridwar."[20] The earthquake also confirmed the apprehension of scientists about the possibility of an earthquake of high magnitude in the Tehri region. It drew attention to the question of the safety of the project not only from the public but from the contractors as well. Blasting for the construction of the dam ceased. But as the union power minister ruled out any review of the project in light of this disaster, blasting for the project and work on the construction on the dam resumed on December 3, 1991.[21]

Sunderlal states that for six years (from the time of the TBVSS petition), the dam site had been under guard by armed police. Now, with the disruption of the earthquake, Sunderlal and his supporters set up a camp with tents at the dam site where they began a *dharna*, a session of nonviolent sitting protest. A critical event occurred on December 14, after a rally that had the participation of more than five thousand people. On that day, Sunderlal took the decisive step of sitting on the tracks of one the bulldozers, preventing it from moving. Other protesters followed. Sunderlal states that they occupied the dam site and brought work on the dam to an end for seventy-five days. The response of the contractors and the police to these actions made this a tortuous period. The contractors responded to the actions of Sunderlal and his colleagues by supporting—some have said creating—the pro-dam organization *Bandh Bachao Samiti* (BBS) (Save the Dam Committee). This group heckled and abused Bahuguna and his supporters. While Bahuguna's supporters refused to be provoked by these opponents, the government found in their involvement the pretext to impose what is known as Section 144 (Section 144 of the Indian Constitution) upon the area. This provision meant a ban on all public assembly, even assembly for the purpose of peaceful protest. Then on the night of February 27, 1992, the police raided and broke up the camp and arrested fifteen people, mostly women, as well as Sunderlal,

Vimla, and their colleague Diksha Bisht.[22] One of the leaders of the TBVSS observed Sunderlal's arrest and his treatment at the hands of the police: "He was dragged from the camp site, abused and dumped into a cell like a sack of potatoes. The policemen seemed to have no idea of the stature of the man they were dealing with."[23]

Sunderlal states that with their arrest the three began an indefinite fast. He states that after three or four days they were shifted to a jail in Roorkee and then to Meerut Medical College where they continued their fast. Following this, the Indian National Trust for Art and Cultural History (INTACH) and the People's Union for Civil Liberties (PUCL), India's largest human rights organization, filed a writ petition with the appropriate court against their arrest. With this they were released without condition, and on March 7, 1992, the tenth day of their fast, returned to Tehri. Having been evicted from their original camp, they pitched their tents on the road leading to the dam site. Swami Chidananda, to whom Sunderlal refers as his spiritual guide, advised Sunderlal's colleagues to suspend their fast so that they could better take care of Sunderlal, while his fast continued. At this time Sunderlal added a small amount of honey and lemon to his daily intake of water. Sunderlal states that their camp was on a dusty road where monstrous earth-moving equipment and heavy trucks would torture them with their noise and dust. Officers of the Provincial Armed Constabulary (PAC), the state police, were posted all around their camp. Sunderlal states, "I can never forget the words and deeds of the PAC jawans, who would hit me in my bed with their gun butts saying, 'Here is the dacoit, sleeping like a respectable man.'"[24] News of Sunderlal's arrest and fast eventually reached the parliament in Delhi. George Fernandes, a prominent member of parliament, came to the protest site with a message from the speaker of the Lok Sabha, the lower house of parliament, reflecting the unanimous appeal of the house of parliament that he should break his fast and that the matter would be looked into. Sunderlal was not about to give in. He states that because the people remained firm in their resolve to stop work on the dam and continued to demonstrate, he resolved to continue his fast. On March 10, after a rally with the participation of more than fifteen hundred protestors mostly from the submergence zone, demonstrators broke through the police barricades, deliberately violating provisions of Section 144, and sat on the machines at the dam site for a symbolic half-hour.[25]

By this time the protest had massive public support. Often from remote regions, thousands of protestors were coming to the dam site in support of Sunderlal's fast, and the cause of putting an end to the Tehri

Dam. On March 20, 1992, a group of people who had come by bus from areas east of Tehri, around Silyara and Ghansyali, were on their way back when a critical incident occurred. On one of the sharp curves in the mountains, the bus ran off the road and tumbled down the precipice killing sixteen antidam protesters and causing severe injuries to almost all of the others. The incident was a shock to Sunderlal and to the movement. Initial explorations revealed that the bus driver was not the one who had come with the group, that he was not a regular employee of the transport company, and that he had leapt safely from the driver's door of the bus just before the fall. The people repeatedly requested that the authorities conduct a thorough investigation into the circumstances of the incident, to find out whether it was in fact an accident or sabotage. No such investigation was ever conducted. Many of the local people to this day regard the incident as the result of a conspiracy on the part of a group in favor of the construction of the dam.[26] In an interview in 2000 Sunderlal expressed his own opinion that the incident was planned.[27] Bahuguna was grief stricken at this colossal loss of life and the suffering of those who had sustained debilitating injuries. He visited those who were being treated in hospitals and grieved with the families and loved ones of those who were killed. Finally on April 12, 1992, Sunderlal received word that the government had issued the order to stop all work on the dam and had given assurance of a complete review of the project. With this assurance, Sunderlal finally ended his fast. The end of his fast and the circumstances surrounding it were covered the next day on the front page of the Hindustan Times and other leading national newspapers. From that date the government ordered a stop to work on the dam. At that point, construction on the dam was suspended and remained suspended for two and a half years.[28]

Among the conditions for the ending of Sunderlal's fast was the promise on the part of the prime minister, Narasimha Rao, that the Tehri Dam opponents would have an opportunity to express their concerns. To that end, on May 7, 1992, Sunderlal handed over to the prime minister a detailed memorandum. A year passed, and there was no response. Then to their surprise, on March 15, 1994, they heard that the cabinet of the central government had cleared the controversial project, and by October of that year, a little known company owned by politicians from Andhra Pradesh was in Tehri to begin construction of the coffer dam. Because this action by the government violated all their previous agreements, Sunderlal and his supporters decided to undertake a peaceful but perilous protest. They blocked the road to the dam site and stopped the movement of vehicles. The government did not address their breach in trust. Instead, on the twenty-fifth day of this demonstration, on May 9, 1995, Bahuguna and his supporters were arrested and taken to Saharanpur jail. Sunderlal states that since all other means of peaceful protest were denied, he announced that he would undertake an indefinite fast. By this time the government had seen the results of his fasts. On a very hot day that May, Sunderlal was taken by car to Sanjay Gandhi Institute of Medical Science 450 kilometers from the protest site. Later, on the intervention of the Allahabad high court, he was released and returned to Tehri, where he continued his fast in his famous *kuti*. By now, he says, the movement was again gaining ground. Demonstrators were coming from all over the country to participate in this very public protest. Then at three a.m. on June 9 their little camp was surrounded by two hundred policemen. Two policemen holding his hands and legs dragged Sunderlal from his *kuti* wearing only his undergarment and put him into an ambulance. Without the benefit of drinking water, the ambulance took him to the Jolly Grant air-strip in Dehra Dun, where he was put on a helicopter to the All India Institute of Medical Sciences in Delhi. There the doctors inquired about the ailment that brought him to the hospital. He replied that he knew of no reason why he should be there, but they should ask the policemen and the doctor from Tehri who had brought him there. Those persons had left him in the custody of the Delhi police, and there was no one to answer their question. Meanwhile, the Peoples Union for Civil Liberties (PUCL) filed a writ of habeas corpus with the Allahabad high court. The court then ordered that he be brought before them on June 13. Thus on the thirty-sixth day of his fast, Sunderlal was presented before the court where representatives of the Uttar Pradesh government stated that he had been taken to Delhi because the condition of his health was alarming and force feeding seemed necessary to save his life. The court immediately arranged for a medical examination in the next room, and the results were presented to the court and placed on record. Here the chief medical officer indicated that from all the tests performed it was his opinion that the patient was normal. Having received this report the high court declared that Sunderlal Bahuguna was not under detention and directed the authorities who brought him there to return him to Tehri. The order read: "He and his companions shall be provided 1st class A.C. accommodation in Prayag Raj Express from Allahabad to Delhi and shall be flown to Jolly Grant Airport, Dehradun, tomorrow by the State plane and shall be put in comfortable car to reach Tehri without delay." Says Sunderlal: "Thus I was able to get back to Tehri, on the banks of the sacred Bhagirathi, to continue my prayerful fast."[29] His fast continued until June 27,

1995, the forty-ninth day of his fast, when the governor of the state of Uttar Pradesh arrived with a message of assurance from Prime Minister Narasimha Rao that he would thoroughly review all aspects of the project and take whatever steps were necessary to see that Sunderlal's concerns were addressed. With this assurance Sunderlal broke his fast. Again the conclusion of his fast was front-page news in the Hindustan *Times* and other national newspapers.

Bahuguna states that they waited about a year to see the fulfillment of the prime minister's promise. He states that when it did not materialize, he began to feel guilty for being a party to such a false agreement.[30] On March 19, 1996, he wrote a detailed letter to the prime minister reminding him of their agreement and of his promise. But to this there was no reply. Sunderlal then expressed his intention to undertake a *prayaschit vrata* (fast of repentance) for letting down those village people who were looking to his long fast as the act that would finally bring them justice and safety. This fast would be different from others he had undertaken because it was not intended to move the hearts of the authorities but to express his repentance for his being taken in.[31] In an assertion that reminds us of similar actions of Gandhi, he states: "Even though the main responsibility of this sin falls upon those who had made the promise, yet, I regard myself as a party to this because my [earlier] prayerful fast had awakened the hope—that an independent review will bring to the surface the lies surrounding the Tehri project."[32] This fast would also be different from others in that it would not entail the complete abstention from all food and fluids. Under the supervision of Dr. Chandra Shekhar Sharma, of the Parmarth Nature Cure Centre in Rishikesh, he would take small medicinal portions of lemon, honey, and bael, the fruit of the wood apple tree. His spartan intake of food would be supported by other natural remedies, including hot fomentations to the abdomen, mud packs, cold water enemas, massages, and baths in the sacred Bhagirathi River. Thus on April 13, 1996, on the auspicious Vaisakhi Day—the day celebrating the enlightenment of the Buddha, and the day recognized in various part of India as the first day of the New Year—and with the support of his spiritual advisor Swami Chidananda, Sunderlal began a fast of repentance that would shine the spotlight of national attention upon the movement opposing the dam. Sunderlal states that the regimen that Dr. Sharma prescribed kept him fit. His condition was also observed by Dr. Inderjit Kaur of the All India Pingalwara Charitable Society in Amritsar. Sunderlal resolved to observe silence for twenty-three hours per day during this fast. He states that after morning prayers he would sit for four hours overlooking the river in silent meditation. He states that the open sky and the music of the living river infused him with energy. But his time was far from empty. He states that he kept busy answering letters, writing articles, and keeping a diary. He acknowledges that in the course of the *vrata*, these activities became increasingly difficult to manage. He recalls that on June 23, on the seventieth day of his fast, his blood pressure was 120/80 and that he had lost eight kilograms of weight. But he found strength in what he frequently calls the three D's, the three features of discipline that he said were necessary for any serious undertaking. The first was devotion. From his parents he had inherited a deep and profound devotion to the Ganges as a river of life. The second was determination. He had learned determination from the sacrifice of his Guru, Shri Dev Suman. The third was dedication. He had learned dedication from the two English disciples of Gandhi, Mira Behn and Sarala Behn that were so influential in his life and in that of his wife Vimla, a dedication that had been reinforced by the examples of Thakkar Bapa and Vinoba Bhave.[33]

Finally on June 18, 1996, he received the government's response. The prime minister, Deve Gowda, issued a statement that his government was "willing to have the ecological aspects, including its impact on the people of the area and resettlement of the displaced persons examined by a fresh group of experts" including those whom Bahuguna had recommended. His letter to Bahuguna stated that the government "will give the highest considerations to the recommendations of the expert group."[34] Thus on June 25, the seventy-third day of his fast, Sunderlal made his way by ambulance from Tehri to Haridwar and by train from Haridwar to Delhi, where, at the Raj Ghat, the site of the cremation of Mahatma Gandhi, and in the presence of Prime Minister Deve Gowda and other government dignitaries and officials, he broke his fast. The conclusion was again a national media event, and the coverage included a lengthy interview with Bahuguna. At the age of sixty-nine he took the opportunity to place the anti-Tehri Dam struggle within the larger context of other social concerns for which he had been known. He explained fully that for him the Tehri Dam itself is not the main issue. The main issue, he said, is the government's policy concerning the Himalayas. The Tehri Dam he explained is the symbol of an understanding of development that will kill both the Himalayas and the Ganga, and uproot the hill people from their homes.

In this interview he recalls that it was his wife, Vimla, who pulled him out of party politics when they were married in 1956. He explains that they then resolved to settle in a village to fulfill the last wish of Gandhi that every freedom fighter should settle down in a village. He states that they would have remained there and quite unknown were it not for the challenge of Vinoba Bhave in 1960 to bring Mahatma Gandhi's message of *gram swarajya* (self-reliant village republics) to the remote villages in the border regions of the Himalayas. Working in these remote villages they found that the menace of liquor had turned lives of the hill women to misery, and they launched the antiliquor movement. He points out, however, that it was the participation and support of the village women that led to its success. In the course of time, when it became clear that deforestation was the cause of local floods, they became involved in the Chipko Movement to save the Himalayan forests. He points out that in the nineteenth century the Garhwal Himalaya was a prosperous region. It exported musk, honey, ghee, herbs, cattle, and even food grains to Tibet. It had imported only jaggery, cotton, and salt. When the British began management of the forests for commercial purposes, the mixed forests began to disappear. With this, the soil and water they needed for their survival began to be stressed as well. He states that for him the last blow against the Tehri Dam was the claim that water would not be given to the hill villages above from the dam. He recalls that when he was a boy of five or six, his mother had to work so hard to gather fire wood, fodder, and water for the household that she sometimes said with a sigh, "Oh God! Give me death." He says he could never forget these words and notes that the hill women today are still known to ask for death from the gods. He states, "My last wish is to end this misery so that no woman is forced to repeat the words of my mother."[35]

Chapter 13

Social Ecology, Religion, and the Tehri Protest

The news of the end of Sunderlal's fast and the government's agreement was hailed as a victory for *satyagraha* and the cause of justice for the people of the hills. Bahuguna's many fasts were now national news. Ironically, for this most selfless service, he was accorded almost celebrity status. The publicity meant little to Sunderlal except to the extent that it brought public attention to the issues behind the dam: the displacement of thousands of people from their homes, loss of the way of life they had lived for generations, the danger of destruction to the life and property downstream from the dam, and the destruction of the Himalayan environment whose wealth for centuries had sustained the communities of the hills. Sunderlal also acknowledged that this victory had been won at a great cost to others, in particular the lives of sixteen protesters who had died in the bus incident four years before. In another interview in 2000 he stated that after 1995 he and his supporters no longer organized major demonstrations because he didn't want any more sacrifices of innocent lives.[1] It is perhaps for that reason that in the later days of the movement, he resorted to the fast rather than the action of mass protests.

From before Sunderlal's monumental fast, many groups and individuals were drawing attention to the safety issue of the dam and to the record of the government in providing for resettlement and compensation for those evicted from their homes. The dam was a public issue. Nevertheless, while it appointed a new committee under the direction of Hanumantha Rao to investigate all aspects of the project, the government again made no explicit provision that work on the dam should be suspended while the committee was undertaking its work. Thus while voices even in international journals and other publications were drawing attention to its hazards, work on the dam continued. In 1991 Fred Pearce, an internationally recognized environmental journalist based in the U.K., had published an article in *The Ecologist* raising serious questions about viability of the dam from the standpoint of the seismic activity of the region and the threat to populations downstream of the dam site. He described the project as monumental folly.[2] Over time, the Centre for Science and Environment in Delhi had published articles in several issues concerning the proposed dam, and about Bahuguna's activities, in its fortnightly publication *Down to Earth*.[3] In addition to the committee under the direction of Hanumantha Rao, the government also appointed a group of experts specifically to study the safely of the dam in light of the seismic activity in the area. When the group of experts finally submitted its report in February 1999, it concluded that, with changes that had been implemented in the plans for the project, "the present design of the dam is expected to be structurally safe to withstand the maximum credible earthquake (MCE) during the economic performance life of the dam-reservoir system."[4] But with another earthquake of 6.8 on the Richter scale in the area of Chamoli on March 29, 1999, and another in Bhuj in Gujarat with a magnitude of 7.9 on the Richter scale on January 26, 2001, this claim by the group of experts did little to alleviate public apprehension. The Chamoli earthquake was slightly higher in magnitude than the one felt in Uttarkashi in 1991. It was felt in the hill districts of Chamoli, Rudraprayag, and Tehri, where it claimed about 100 lives, left hundreds injured, and caused damage to about 6,000 houses. It also brought about landslides that isolated portions of the Mandakini and Mandal valleys and cut several major roads.[5] The earthquake centering in Bhuj was the second most deadly to strike India, on record. A month after the earthquake, figures from India's government place the death toll at 19,727 and the number of injured at 166,000. More than 600,000 were left homeless, with 348,000 houses destroyed and an additional 844,000 damaged. Government estimates placed economic losses at $1.3 billion.[6]

The Dam and the Hindu Right

An earthquake in the region of the dam, however, was not the only security threat that could be envisioned. After the terrorist attacks on the World Trade Towers in New York and the Pentagon in Washington D.C. of September 11, 2001, Professor Shivaji Rao, the director of the Centre for Environmental Studies, GITAM College of Engineering in Visakhapatnam, visualized another threat to the Tehri Dam and to the population below it. As a member of the Environmental Appraisal Committee of the Union Ministry of Environment in 1989 and 1990, he had studied the design of the dam and the plans for disaster management. He had also studied the geological, seismic, and economic aspects of the project. After its deliberations, this committee, headed by D. R. Bhumbla, had rejected the proposed dam, but the government had shelved its report. In 1992 he had published a book entitled *Tehri Dam Is a Time Bomb*. After the events of September 11, 2001, he published an abstract of this book in which he pointed out that the Tehri Dam would be an easy target for terrorists and that such an attack should be anticipated because it would be an inexpensive bid for them to destroy the life and culture of India, which he refers to both as Aryavarta and as "this holy land of Buddha, Mahavir, and Mahatma Gandhi." Because the dam was being made of earth, sand, and gravel, a bomb by terrorists or agents of enemy countries could easily cause its collapse, killing millions of Indians and destroying temples, sacred towns, and cities.[7]

The thought of an attack by enemies of India infused an element of nationalism in the discourse concerning the viability of the dam. It also gave support to those concerned with the Ganges for its religious significance. Among the groups for whom the religious significance of the Ganges was especially pronounced were members of what has been called the Hindu Right known together as the Sangh Parivar or "family of organizations." British scholar Emma Mawdsley explains that the principal constituents of this family include the political Bharatiya Janata Party (BJP) which, with its leader Prime Minister Atal Behari Vajpayee, was until 2004 the main party of the central government of India; the Rashtriya Swayamsevak Sangh (RSS), a cultural organization founded in 1925 that among other things promotes paramilitary and martial arts training; and the Vishva Hindu Parishad (VHP), or World Hindu Council set up in 1964 to bring together the diverse elements of Hindu belief and practice. She adds that the youth wing of the VHP, called the Bajrang Dal, is largely made up of disaffected Hindu youth "who can be called upon to intimidate and threaten opponents." She states that while the BJP tends to speak in moderate and accommodating terms, it often takes political advantage of the politics of hate espoused by the RSS, the VHP, and others. She explains that the core ideology of the Sangh is "Hindu-tva" (Hindu-ness), but she indicates that it has come to refer to the more narrow agenda of Hindu nationalism. "Essentially, Hindutva represents a 'blood and soil' vision of the sacred land of Hindustan for the Hindus."[8]

Members of the Sangh Parivar, the VHP in particular, were occupied with the sanctity of the Ganges River, which they saw as being desecrated by the dam. For them the Ganges in not simply a sacred river, but a river that is sacred to the Hindus, and a symbol of Hindu identity. The thought of a threat to the land of the Hindus combined with their concern for the safety of the dam and the sacredness of the Ganges. These issues together presented a strong case against continuing with the dam construction, a view that presented a challenge to its ally, the BJP, which had supported construction of the dam. After visiting areas in Gujarat devastated by the earthquake of January 2001, Ashok Singal, the president of the VHP, pointed out that an earthquake in the area of the Tehri Dam would cause colossal loss. He also pointed out that the damming of the Bhagirathi would result in the loss of the purity of the Ganges. "It is the water of the Bhagirathi which gives the Ganges its purity, and not streams like the Alakananda. And if the Bhagirathi flow is stopped, Ganges will no longer be what it is."[9] Public apprehension concerning the dam now seemed to have support in some of the concerns of the VHP.

For Sunderlal, the Tehri Dam was not only an ecological issue, but a social, cultural, and religious issue as well. He recognized the support of those concerned with the religious significance of the river as an appropriate religious concern. In January 2001, in a speech at the Kumbh Mela, a Hindu festival in Allahabad at the confluence of the Yamuna and the Ganges rivers, an event that attracts the largest gathering of human beings on the planet, Bahuguna pointed out that rituals are not performed in stagnant water. He thus stated that the damming of the Bhagirathi River will mean that "the original waters, descending from Gomukh, will no longer reach Allahabad and other centres of pilgrimage." He states here, "Once you damn (sic) the Ganga and contain its waters in the proposed 42.5 km lake, the river will lose its sanctity, and the consequences of that on the psyche of the people cannot be calculated." In an interview at the same Kumbh Mela, when he was told that the VHP had passed a resolution that condemned the proposed Tehri Dam, Sunderlal stated that he was glad of the support. He also pointed out that he had read that Swami Chinmayananda, another leader of the VHP, who was also a member of parliament, had spoken against the dam, and he commented that it is good that other persons are opposing the project. He also points out that he had never met Swami Chinmayananda and had not exchanged any ideas with him.[10]

On March 26 of that year Ashok Singhal announced to the press that he would undertake an indefinite fast "in defense of the Ganges," to begin at the end of the month, to protest the construction of the Tehri Dam.

Others in the VHP stated that when he did so, he would not be alone in his fast, that many *sadhus* (Hindu holy men) and *sants* (Hindu priests) were prepared to join him. But the interest of the VHP in a protest against the Tehri Dam provoked little notice among the people of Tehri, who as one journalist put it were nonplussed by the entry of Singhal and his supporters. Angry shop owners in the market area were dismayed that Singhal had not spoken a word about their demand, if the dam should be completed, for fair compensation and an adequate plan for resettlement.[11] Before the threatened fast took place, the Prime Minister Atal Behari Vajpayee assured Singal that a new committee of experts as well as religious figures would be constituted to reconsider the question of the safety of the dam and the impact of the dam on the sanctity of the river. Journalists suggested that the critical issues concerning the project were being co-opted by the VHP to further its nationalist agenda. Journalists and academics seized upon Bahuguna's approval of VHP opposition to the dam and began to interpret his concern for the religious aspects of the Ganges as an alliance with the political objectives of the VHP. Some drew particular attention to the similarity of Sunderlal's concern for the religious significance of the Ganges with the political rhetoric of the VHP. Mukul Sharma, a Delhi-based writer, points out that those opposed to the dam spoke the language of ecological politics but also invoked certain metaphors to engage with religious practices and mythical beliefs. He states: "In their use of these metaphors and myths, the environmentalists often come close to the beliefs of conservative Hindu forces and their chosen communal path."[12] He states that especially in the later part of the movement antidam politics was persistently "constructed through a conservative Hindu imagery, often in partnership with Hindutva politics. Ganga becomes holier and holiest. The ecological reasoning is blurred and goes beyond logic, eliciting Hindu support, patriotism and xenophobia"[13] Writing about the hazard of the involvement of the VHP with the protest against the Tehri Dam, Emma Mawdsley states that while Bahuguna had fought all his life for the wider goals of social and environmental justice for people of the hills, to many secular and Gandhian activists he was by this time "disturbingly compromised by his ties with the VHP."[14] Mawdsley fails here to demonstrate any ties at all between Bahuguna and the organization of the VHP, its personnel, or its nationalist objectives. It is evident, nevertheless, that in a context of increasing sectarian rhetoric the religious imagery that had been persuasive and meaningful in the context of the Chipko movement tended to undermine the credibility of the anti-Tehri Dam movement.

When I inquired with Sunderlal about the concern of the VHP for the preservation and promotion of Hindu traditions and its opposition to the Tehri Dam, he pointed out that there is a critical difference between spirituality and sectarian religion. "They [the VHP] had made it a political thing in order to get support of the people, in order to arouse their emotions [in favor of Hindu nationalism]." Commenting on the absence of ethical content in the rhetoric of the VHP, he stated: "You know in (the) practical, if one follows Hindu traditions then there should be austerity. They should use less and less things. And austerity should be practiced not only in private life but in the public life also, and again with respect for nature. The modern civilization converts nature into cash. This is the trouble with the present day society." When I asked him whether he considered Ashok Singhal and his followers to be a part of the anti-Tehri Dam movement, he replied emphatically that Singhal was not a part of the movement, that "Singhal has a movement of his own."[15]

Bahuguna's commitment to Gandhi's principle of truth through nonviolence has obvious implications concerning the elevation of one religious tradition over others. In one of our discussions at the Gandhi memorial complex at Sannidhi in Delhi, when we were discussing the significance of religion as a support for environmental concerns, he drew my attention to a statue of Kaka Kalelkar, Gandhi's close associate who worked to demonstrate the oneness of humankind by showing the coherence of the fundamental values embodied in the diverse religious traditions of India. Like Kalelkar, Bahuguna's attitude toward religion was very much shaped by the thought of Gandhi. The recognition of the equality of religions is one of the eleven critical vows or observances that Gandhi promoted as the rule of life in all his ashrams. This goes beyond mere tolerance. The word tolerance suggests that I may find the religion of my neighbor to be wrong, even to be an abomination, but in the interest of peace I choose to tolerate it, to let it be. "Tolerance," said Gandhi, "may imply a gratuitous assumption of the inferiority of other faiths to one's own, whereas ahimsa teaches us to entertain the same respect for the religious faith of others as one accords to one's own, thus admitting the imperfection of the later."[16] To recognize the equality of religions is to go beyond the practice of toleration. For Gandhi: "The principal faiths of the world constitute a revelation of Truth, but as they have all been outlined by man, they have been affected by imperfections and alloyed with untruth. One must therefore entertain the same respect for the religious faith of others as one accords to one's own. Where such tolerance becomes the law of life, conflict between different faiths becomes impossible, and so does all effort to convert other people to one's own faith. One can only pray that the defects in the various faiths may be overcome, and that they may advance, side by side, towards perfection."[17] He points out that we have yet to realize religion in its perfection, just as we have yet to realize God: "Religion of our conception, being thus imperfect, is always subject to a process of evolution and re-interpretation. Progress towards truth, towards God, is possible only because of such evolution. And if all faiths outlined by men are imperfect the question of comparative merit does not arise. All faiths constitute a revelation of truth, but all are imperfect and liable to error." He states that reverence for other faiths need not blind us to their faults. He argues that "we must be keenly alive to the defects of our own faith also, yet not leave it on that account, but try to overcome those defects." Moreover, looking at all religions with equal regard, we should not hesitate, he says, "to blend into our faith every acceptable feature of other faiths."[18] Bahuguna finds the same injunction toward austerity in the use of the earth's resources in all the great religions. The difficulty is that religion today is used to divide human beings rather than unite them. He states: "Unfortunately, religion today has been reduced to the level of certain rituals and this great unifying force has become a weapon in the hands of sectarian vested interests who use it to create enmity between man and man."[19] Sunderlal explained that in following this vow of Gandhi, in their personal religious life, both he and his wife say prayers every day from all the great religions of the world.[20]

The Rising Tide and the Judgment of the Supreme Court

As issues surrounding the Tehri Dam were gaining increasing public attention, Bahuguna was increasingly occupied with concerns that were conspicuously absent from the rhetoric of the VHP. By now many of the residents of Tehri had taken the compensation that the THDC had offered and began making plans to move their lives and families elsewhere. But the compensation and resettlement plans that were offered were rumored to be less than fair and equitable and not equal to the cost of resettlement. In my own conversations among the residents of Tehri, I spoke to persons who told me about cases in which authorities had offered compensation based upon the value of their homes after it was depreciated according to the length of time the family had lived there. I heard about one resident who could not specify the age of his home because his family had lived there for uncounted generations and was fearful that he would not receive compensation sufficient to resettle. I was told about another case in which the authorities assessed the depreciation for the age of the home in such way that the value of the dwelling was reduced to a mere fifty rupees. Some officials told me that, if true, such cases were deviations from accepted practice and could be subject to appeal. But many of the residents were not familiar with procedures for such appeals and felt that their needs were not adequately represented. As stories about such cases were heard, a strong perception of widespread injustice prevailed among those who remained.

With these and other concerns in mind, Bahuguna and his supporters set up a new camp at Maldeol, where his supporters again blocked the road to the dam site, preventing the transport of supplies. There Sunderlal was joined by a former member of the Legislative Assembly, Mantri Prasad Naithani who was also seeking a proper rehabilitation package for those displaced by the project. On March 31, 2001, their efforts again brought work on the dam to a halt.[21] But this time, three weeks into the protest, the Tehri Hydro Development Corporation complained to the Nainital High Court, and argued that the corporation had suffered colossal financial loss because of the agitation. Sunderlal testified to the court that the explosives employed at the dam site were creating environmental hazards and that issues of compensation and resettlement had not been adequately addressed. In its decision on April 20 the high court instructed the corporation not to undertake disturbing activities around the dam site and stated that the government must address the concerns of those displaced. But it also ordered the government to resume work on the dam. Taking shelter behind the high court decision, the district magistrate then threatened to use force against the protesters if they failed to leave the area and permit construction work to resume. They chose not to leave. Thus in a predawn assault on their camp on April 22, police took more than fifty persons into custody, and work on the dam resumed. According to one report, the arrest of their colleagues seemed to have a demoralizing effect upon the agitators who had tried to regroup and revive the movement. Two days later Bahuguna was himself arrested, along with seventy-four others, and with his arrest he again began an indefinite fast.[22] Yet even after Sunderlal's release, the release of the other protesters, and the end of his fast on May 4, there seemed to settle in the area a sense of inevitability about the construction of the dam. Enthusiasm for the movement began to wane. From 1996 to 2000 some fifty to sixty persons took part in the *prabhat pheri* (early morning circuit), daily demonstration marches, at Tehri. In 1998, on my first visit to Bahuguna in his *kuti*, he was conducting daily services of worship to the Ganges at a temple adjacent to his *kuti* on the banks of the Bhagirathi River. But, according to observers, after

2000 the movement seemed to lose momentum.[23] Bahuguna believes this was due to greed and fear, what he calls the two weapons of government. Many of the people were attracted by the offer of compensation money, and many were threatened by the fate of the protesters who died in the bus incident in 1992. He states that the movement was hardly able to make itself heard over the demand of vested interests around Delhi, the main consumer of water from the Tehri Dam. Jayanta Bandyopadhyay points out that because the Chipko Movement originated in the conflict over forest resources, it tended to unite the people of different regions of the Garhwal Himalaya. There the motivating issue was the sustainability of a forest culture and the agricultural and pastoral economy of the area. He states that the agitation against the Tehri Dam did not so unite the rural people. One hears, he says, of a pro-dam faction even in the submergence area of the dam. "It appears that this group is comprised of those who have managed to obtain disproportionately high compensations and have no remaining interest in their homeland." Many of these were shopkeepers who had come from outside the region from interest in business. Those who remained to oppose the dam were bereft of the mass support that the Chipko Movement enjoyed. "The unfortunate households in the submergence area were singled out while the rest of Garhwal was hardly involved."[24] In my own conversations with Bahuguna, he pointed out another critical factor that led to the decline of the movement. Sunderlal reminded me that the objective of *satyagraha* is never to intimidate, embarrass, or manipulate the person against whom the protest is directed. The appeal of *satyagraha*, is not to the behavior of a person but to the heart. In the case of the Chipko Movement there were government officials, contractors, and workers whose hearts could be moved. In the protest against the Tehri Dam, the struggle was not against persons but against a corporation. By its nature the corporation is not a person but an amorphous entity whose judgments are so defused among its members that there is no single individual who takes moral responsibility for decisions. A corporation is not a person with a heart that could be moved. As he put it to me, "The corporation has no heart!"

While constructing the Tehri project, the Tehri Hydro Development Corporation was also occupied with the construction of a new city on the slopes of one of the mountains adjacent to the dam. New Tehri would be a modern city with terraced streets, planned neighborhoods, and a city center that would replace the historic town of Tehri. By the year 2000 work on the planed city was nearing completion, and many of the businesses of Tehri had begun to move. By 2001 the administrative offices of

Tehri were transferred to the new town. Most schools, banks, and shops had moved, and many of the residents of the old town were moving there as well.[25] Yet, as news outlets reported, five thousand people remained in the town, angry and hurt over the loss of hearth and home and the apathy of authorities in their failure to finalize plans for their relocation. Until those issues were resolved, they had no intention of leaving. On December 2, 2001, the THDC closed two of the diversion tunnels, and the water behind the dam began to enter the old town of Tehri. A week later the press reported that angry residents were engaged in protests and rallies. Some had been fasting in protest at the town's ancient temple.[26] One resident explained that without providing adequate compensation, the authorities were pressuring the residents to vacate the town, but they were determined not to leave.[27] The iron bridge at the entrance to the town, the bridge at which in 1947 Sunderlal undertook his first exercise in *satyagraha*, was closed. As expected, the *kuti* in which Sunderlal and Vimla Bahuguna had been residing in *satyagraha* since 1989 was now accorded the distinction of the first human dwelling to be submerged beneath the rising waters of the Bhagirathi River behind the Tehri Dam. "The government has willed this to be Tehri's last winter," said Bahuguna, "but we are determined to fight to the finish before they drown us out."[28] For Sunderlal the rising waters meant more than the loss of his dwelling. It symbolized his loss of mother Ganga. As a devout son would do to express his grief at the death of his mother, Sunderlal shaved his beard and hair. From a hill overlooking the rising waters under which the iron bridge and his *kuti* was now submerged, he said, "I have shaven off my beard and head as I have lost my mother."[29] His concern now was for the rights of those evicted and the question of their relocation and compensation. One of the departing families of Tehri offered Sunderlal and Vimla Bahuguna another dwelling called Purana Dubar at the top of one of the higher reaches of the town. Here they pledged to remain to continue their fight for those displaced until the last of the inhabitants of Tehri had been evicted. Now all hope to stop the construction of the dam rested with the impending decision of the Supreme Court.

The writ petition by the TBVSS challenging the viability of the dam had been filed with the Supreme Court on November 20, 1985. As I stated earlier, that petition asserted: (1) that the dam, to be located in a seismically active region, had a high probability of failure and would endanger the lives and property of people living in settlements such as Rishikesh and Haridwar located downstream, (2) that habitations such as Uttarkashi located upstream from the inlet of the reservoir would be threatened, and

(3) that the project would create a feeling of insecurity among people residing at various locations on the rim slopes of the reservoir, jeopardizing the right to life guaranteed to citizens under the constitution.[30] Some sources have indicated that in November 1990 the Supreme Court turned down this petition. Shekhar Singh, then of the Indian Institute of Public Administration (IIPA), explained to me that the petition was withdrawn by the petitioners on the recognition that the case as stated could not be won. That, he said, is like losing the case, but it permits the petitioner to submit a revised petition.[31] The court had indicated that it was not competent to judge the earthquake risk or the probability of dam failure and thus whether the government had taken the right decision.[32] In October of 1992, N. D. Jayal, then of the Indian National Trust for Art and Cultural Heritage (INTACH) and Shekhar Singh of the IIPA filed a new public interest litigation petition with the Supreme Court raising questions as to whether the government had conformed to the conditions given with the clearance of the project. This case focused on environmental issues, issues of the safety of the dam, and issues of resettlement and rehabilitation of those evicted from their land.

The Supreme Court began to hear arguments in this case in January 2002. Sunderlal Bahuguna was among those called to offer testimony before the court. There, among other things, he drew the court's attention to the long struggle of the local people against a project that would bring no benefit to them but would be constructed at the cost of their homes, habitat, and heritage. He pointed out that in 1949 when Tehri Garhwal joined the state of Uttar Pradesh (then United Provinces) it was the poorest district in the country. The then chief minister promised that with their assimilation into the United Provinces their economic problems would be addressed. He argued that the decision to construct the Tehri Dam would inundate the most fertile land of the Bhagirathi and Bhilangana valleys. He drew attention to the opposition of the local people from 1972 to 1978, and pointed out that work on the dam was begun over the objections of these local people and under police guard that converted the town of Tehri into a police cantonment. He drew attention to the bus incident that killed sixteen protesters and left others as invalids, an event that was never investigated, and he recalled his prayerful fast in 1995 that resulted in the government appointment of a committee whose work was reviewed by the petitioners of the present brief.

The local people, he said, were fighting for their survival. As with the Chipko Movement, in which the local women set out to put an end to contract felling that deprived them of trees they needed for food, fuel, and fodder, to provide resources for a distant market, the movement against the Tehri Dam was a fight for water, the last of the resources available to the people of the hills. The plan for a dam that would provide irrigation to agriculture on the plains of Uttar Pradesh and drinking water to Delhi would provide no irrigation or drinking water to the water-scarce villages on the rim of the reservoir. In addition, while the river had provided fertile soil for local agricultural needs, this soil would now be trapped behind the dam. He suggested that diverting the water of the Bhagirathi to the plains of Uttar Pradesh and to the city of Delhi, where the Yamuna River was already polluted, would eventually create a feeling of humiliation among the people of the hills who had always regarded the river as Lok Mata, the mother of the people. He argued that instead of a dam that would provide water for a distant market, depriving the local people of soil and water, the whole Himalayan region should be converted into a permanent dam. Instead of felling the trees for timber, the forests should be preserved to conserve soil and water. The planting of trees providing food, fodder, fuel, fertilizer, and fiber could also provide a living for local people.[33]

Having begun to hear the arguments of the petitioners and the counterarguments of the respondents in January 2002, the Supreme Court deliberated for over a year before giving its final verdict on September 1, 2003. With a looming crisis of increasing drinking water scarcity in Delhi, the newspapers published with a sense of relief the decision of the Supreme Court in favor of the Tehri Dam. On that day the *Hindustan Times* announced "Tehri dam complied with environmental norms: SC" (Supreme Court). *The Hindu* put its announcement in similar terms. A day later the *Times of India* declared "Tehri Dam gets legal thumbs up." It stated, "The Supreme Court on Monday cleared all the hurdles in the completion of the over Rs 8,500-crore Tehri hydel dam project in Uttaranchal and held there was no material to say that environmental conditions had not been complied with in its construction."

In the view of some, this decision meant that the struggle against the Tehri Dam was finally over, that the case was lost, and that the movement had failed. This view invites examination. Was the movement against the Tehri Dam a failure? Was the effort a waste? Was the struggle worth the effort? What did the movement and the nonviolent efforts of Bahuguna accomplish?

Long before the ruling of the Supreme Court, Jayanta Bandyopadhyay had pointed out what he considered two positive achievements of the antidam movement. He states that in the course of the Chipko Movement the state accepted the demands of the people to end the private contract system of tree felling. By doing so it gained a kind of green credibility. However, the state consistently opposed the anti-Tehri Dam movement. He states that the movement against the Tehri Dam "was able to push the state to shed whatever 'green cover' it had, and to stand openly against environmental considerations." Thus the first achievement of the antidam movement, an ironical one, was a more realistic appraisal of the commitment of the state government to the environment. He states that the second achievement of the movement was to raise fundamental questions concerning the very nature of development. "The controversy over the Tehri Dam," he says, "threw light on the need to rethink the direction of development." It raised the critical question of what development to sustain and for whom?[34] These achievements, it would seem, would not have been diminished even by the complete defeat of a petition to the Supreme Court against the Tehri Dam. Japanese scholar Shinya Ishizaka states that while with the decision of the Supreme Court the movement had lost almost all the legal battles against the construction of the dam, it would nevertheless be hasty to assert that there is no possibility of reviving the movement.[35]

In fact, the details of the Supreme Court decision concerning the petition against the Tehri Dam reveal a more complex judgment than the headlines announced. (I have included more of the details of the arguments of the petitioners and the response of the Supreme Court in appendix 2. I here include only the more striking points.) For instance, while the court acknowledged that lapses had occurred in the progress of the studies concerning such issues as catchment area treatment, rehabilitation, command area development, water quality maintenance, and disaster management, studies and plans that were required to be completed in a time-bound manner, these studies were nevertheless in progress. The verdict of the court states: "The petitioners have disputed that the respondents have complied with the conditions of clearance. But a careful analysis of their pleadings will indicate the dispute is to the extent of compliance only and not that there is no compliance at all." They concluded that petitioners had not established nor is there material to conclude that no effort had been made to conform to those conditions. Second, the court rejected the claim of the petitioners that the land to be given in compensation must be comparable to the land given to those evicted in another case, the case of the Sardar Sarovar project. It also rejected the contention of the petitioners that it should treat as separate families the sons and unmarried daughters among those evicted of age eighteen rather than twenty-one.

The petitioners had argued that because the voting age is eighteen, those evicted at the age of eighteen should be treated as separate family units. The court submitted in reply that voting age has no bearing on the case. But the court also acknowledged the importance of plans for resettlement and rehabilitation of the people displaced by the dam. It stipulated that the project authorities must ensure that resettlement and rehabilitation plans are completed before the two remaining diversion tunnels are closed to impound the water in the reservoir of the dam. It stated, moreover, "To ensure that all the conditions for environmental clearance are fulfilled and for proper monitoring, we transfer all these cases to the High Court of Uttaranchal to be dealt with by the Division Bench."[36] Violations of the conditions for clearance would amount in that case to contempt of court. Thus rather than a defeat of the struggle against the injustices entailed in the construction of the Tehri Dam, the Supreme Court's final action was a positive acknowledgment of its concerns and provided a venue for the redress of the grievances of the people.

It is also significant that the verdict of the bench was a 2:1 split decision. For this reason the dissenting opinion is significant. The dissenting judgment of Justice D. M. Dharmadhikari highlighted the decision of the government not to accept the recommendation of four of the five members of the group of experts to conduct a 3-D non-linear analysis and a simulated dam break analysis. The 3-D non-linear analysis and the simulated dam break analysis are state of the art strategies to test the stability of a dam against the force of the maximum credible earthquake. In the majority ruling, Justices S. Rajendra Babu and G. P. Mathur had stated that there was a difference of opinion between the four experts and the fifth on the need to undertake these two additional tests as a matter of abundant caution. They stated that if, on the opinion of the expert bodies, the government decided against these tests, then the court could not advise the government to undertake such tests "unless maladies, arbitrariness or irrationality is attributed to that decision." Because the government had given reasonable consideration to the question of the usefulness of these tests, it was not appropriate for the court to interfere.[37] In his dissenting judgment, Justice D. M. Dharmadhikari stated that "the government cannot be allowed to claim scientific uncertainty of the 3-D Non-Linear Analysis to avoid taking effective measures to prevent environmental degradation." This point in his judgment accords with the "precautionary principle" articulated in the Rio Declaration on Environment and Development of 1992 to which India is a signatory. He stated further that when the state exploits natural resources in a big way and for big projects, social conflicts arise. "When such social conflicts arise between the poor and the more needy on one side and the rich or affluent or less needy on the other, prior attention has to be paid to the former group which is financially and politically weak." He went on to state that to avoid past mistakes in the resettlement and rehabilitation of people ousted by similar projects, the construction of the Tehri Dam should not be allowed to proceed leaving the oustees high and dry. In light of this dissenting judgment, Rajeev Dhavan, one of the advocates for the petitioners stated accordingly: "The success in this case is the one-third moral success of the dissenting judgment. The other partial success is that the tunnels cannot be blocked until rehabilitation is done."[38]

The ruling of the Supreme Court in the case against the Tehri Dam, even if seen as a mitigated success, would nevertheless be a narrow basis for evaluating the achievements of the movement against the Tehri Dam or the role of Sunderlal Bahuguna in that movement. Sunderlal has often said that victories in nonviolent struggles are never won without exertion. It is appropriate to be reminded that the appointment in July of 1996 of the Hanumantha Rao Committee and the group of experts was the ful-fillment of a promise by the prime minister to Bahuguna after his fast of seventy-four days. That was a fast of repentance, as he put it, for being taken in by the promise of the previous prime minister a year before to look scrupulously into all aspects of the project. Though unfulfilled, that promise had been made at the end of Bahuguna's fast of forty-nine days. While the government did not accept or implement all the provisions of the Hanumantha Rao Committee, it did accept and implement some of them. Moreover, the recommendations of that committee articulated the conditions that became the basis for the provisional clearance, which the project received from the Ministry of Forests and Environment, and the basis for much of the case against the dam in the Supreme Court. Without the people's movement against the dam and without Bahuguna's *satyagraha*, it is doubtful whether environmental issues relating to the dam, issues concerning resettlement and rehabilitation, and issues concerning of the safety of the dam, would ever have been given the attention they finally received.

I stated earlier that the Tehri Dam issue was a large parenthesis in Bahuguna's struggle to save the Himalayas. It was a parenthesis that typi-fied the contrast between the needs of the traditional culture of the for-ests and the imperatives of centralized industrialized economics. As such the demands of this movement on Bahuguna's energy and attention were unremitting. Nevertheless, for Bahuguna the Tehri Dam was one issue in the larger agenda to address the ecology of the Himalayas. For Sunderlal this decision was neither a victory nor a defeat, but one episode in the protracted struggle to save the Himalayas for the ecological health of the region and the nation. Even a complete victory of the movement against construction of the dam would by no means have ended the struggle.

By July 2004 the THDC had closed one of the two remaining diversion tunnels of the Dam. With heavy rainfall that swelled the local rivers over the month of July the entire submergence area was inundated for the first time. In a story from Dehra Dun on July 30, *The Hindu* reported that the Tehri district administration had shifted the final thirty-two families marooned in the abandoned Old Tehri town. Bahuguna and nine others had refused to leave until all the residents of the old city were resettled. Bahuguna indicated that if he was forced to quit the town before all were compensated, then he, once again, would undertake a fast.[39] With the removal of the last remaining families, it was time for the Bahugunas to depart as well.[40] On July 31, 2004, along with his wife, Sunderlal Bahuguna was evacuated from Purana Dubar, their temporary home. *The Telegraph* reported that Vimla was the last to leave, and that as she did, she sat still, her eyes fixed on the vast expanse of water as the boat in which she was evacuated departed from the old city. In an interview a month later, Bahuguna was asked about his personal loss. He replied that he and his wife had owned land in two villages, their ancestral homes. What is more important, he said "is the fact that our history, geography, culture, and everything is drowning. Our memories of childhood, youth, the freedom struggle, everything is going under water forever."[41] The submergence of Tehri and the surrounding villages was perhaps symbolic of the distance of the present Indian consciousness from those local happenings that had been a part of the larger independence struggle of India. Sites that remind us all of the struggles of Shri Dev Suman, the work of Swami Ram Tirtha, the historical significance of Tehri as a religious site, and Sunderlal's own initiation into Gandhi's constructive program were being submerged beneath a man-made sea. All this was being covered by a project to support the demands for electric power and water for a city that had so abused the Yamuna River that it could no longer provide for the needs of such a city.

Bahuguna had refused monetary compensation for his ancestral home and that of his wife, Vimla. He argued that since the corporation had taken away his ancestral home, they should be provided a dwelling fit for him and his wife to live in. The THDC found such a dwelling in a two-storied abandoned house, almost a hundred years old, overlooking what is now a lake formed by the waters behind the Tehri Dam. The dwelling was in Koti, the colony that stored and maintained the machinery deployed in the construction of the dam. The THDC called it Vishvakarmapuram, the town of the architect of the universe! Humbly, Sunderlal and Vimla accepted the offer of that dwelling. From there Sunderlal continues his work in the interest of a great number of environmental issues, especially one supporting a viable government policy toward the Himalayas.

Chapter 14

Against the Tide

Bahuguna's Philosophy of Life, Religion, and Nature

In the course of his journey in *satyagraha* Bahuguna eventually became the recipient of a significant number of recognition awards. Among them, perhaps the best known of his career is the one he refused. The Padma Shree Award is one of India's highest civilian honors. It is awarded by the government of India in recognition of distinguished contributions in such areas as art, education, science, sports, medicine, and social service. In 1981 he refused the Padma Shree Award because, as he said, "the flesh and blood of India is still flowing to the sea." In 1984 he was the recipient of the Singhvi National Integration Award by the president of India for his work with the Chipko Movement as the best expression of India's culture. In 1985 he was given the Man of the Trees Award by Friends of Trees, Bombay, and in 1986 the Jamnalal Bajaj Award, for his contribution to Gandhian constructive work in the hills. In 1987 he traveled with Indu Tikekar to Stockholm, Sweden, to receive, on behalf of the Chipko Movement, the Right Livelihood Award, sometimes also called the Alternative Nobel Prize. In 1989 the Indian Institute of Technology at Roorkee awarded him the honorary degree of Doctor of Science. In 1992 he was recipient of the Rathindra Puraskar Award from Vishwa Bharati University in Shantiniketan for popularizing science, in 1995 the Shirdi Sai Baba Medal for social work and the Golden Jubilee Award of the FAO (Food and Agriculture Organization) for writing in Hindi on sustainable development. In 1996 it was the Justice V. R. Krishna Iyer National Award and the National Citizen's Award for launching an untiring fight for the cause of ecology, forests, and the environment involving people. The list goes on: the Bhasker Award, the Saraswati Samman Award, the Satpal

Mittal National Award by the Indian Association of Parliamentarians, the Gandhi Seva Award, and in 2003 the Swami Ram Memorial Award for Environmental Protection. In 2009 he was awarded the Padma Vibhushan award by the president of India, the second highest civilian honor given by the Republic of India. Yet conversations about these awards revealed what they really meant to him. He states that the awards that he has come most to treasure are the awards of ridicule, neglect, isolation, and insult. These, he says, are the awards of the person who would swim against the tide. These are the awards that a committed social worker should expect and should learn to prize as much as any others.

Our exploration of the activism of Sunderlal Bahuguna has spanned more than six decades. It has taken us from his childhood and the influence of his devoted mother to his encounter with Sri Dev Suman, his first arrest, his imprisonment, a year underground, his first experiment with *satyagraha*, his work in the Praja Mandal, the struggle against caste discrimination, and the establishing of the Thakkar Bapa Chattravas. We have observed how his marriage to Vimla Nautiyal and the establishment of the Parvatiya Navjeevan Ashram opened new avenues for activism and service. We have observed how the influence of Gandhi and his disciples Mira Behn and Sarala Behn resulted in a commitment to the welfare of the mountain villages through the organization of labor, opposition to the proliferation of liquor outlets, and support of the environment. In the course of these ventures we saw Bahuguna's rise to public visibility and influence in the Chipko Movement and in the movement against the Tehri Dam. Are there themes that would bring together all the diverse features of the activism for which Bahuguna is known? My first conversations with Sunderlal began to highlight three interconnected themes that seemed to express the motivating ideas behind all of these activities. In the first place was the philosophy of Gandhi. The encounter with the writings of Gandhi at a formative stage in Sunderlal's life clearly set the direction for his thought. The constructive work of Sri Dev Suman demonstrated how to put these ideas into action. Gandhi's thought concerning village development, which Mira Behn and Sarala Behn implemented in the hills, brought issues concerning the environment into focus, and the second theme of the modern science of ecology. Also, Sunderlal found the ethos for a consideration of such ecological and social issues in the spiritual traditions of India and especially in those of the people of the hills. When I had the opportunity to broach this subject with Bahuguna, he affirmed that these three pervading themes fairly express the motivation behind his activism. But he also pointed out that the three are really

Sunderlal Bahuguna at Eighty-five

one. Gandhi's thought, he said, is rooted in the spirituality he found in traditions of India that had been marginalized by colonialism. That spirituality, he said, was rooted in the insights of the sages of old who had lived in the forests and who understood that the divine reality is embodied in all aspects of nature. Bahuguna's activities represent not only a protest against environmental policies that are destructive to the people of the hills but also a philosophy of nature rooted in the spiritual traditions of India and informed by modern ecology. When taken as a whole his thought represents a critical, comprehensive, and coherent environmental philosophy. In concluding this book, it is appropriate to look more closely at these three themes.

Bahuguna and Gandhi

It was in my very first conversation with Bahuguna that he pointed out that both he and his wife are products of two English disciples of Gandhi, Mira Behn and Sarala Behn, respectively. Like Gandhi and those determined disciples, Sunderlal and Vimla believe that every village should be self-governing and self-sufficient in its basic needs: its need for clean air and water, for food, clothing, and shelter. This, he says, was Gandhi's idea of *swaraj*. While many tend to identify the term *swaraj* with political independence from foreign powers, Bahuguna points out that its more embracive meaning is self-rule at the individual level, the village level, and upward. One ought to be able to rule one's self. Each village should be able to rule itself and provide for itself. With the implementation of this idea of *swaraj*, the ambition of national self-rule could come about as a matter of course. He points out that at the end of Gandhi's life, the very day before his assassination, Gandhi had written that while political independence was a historical fact, the *swaraj* of his dreams had not yet materialized. He then challenged the leaders of Congress to implement measures to facilitate *swaraj* at the village level. He argued that the freedom fighters should settle in a village and there implement the ideals of village *swaraj*. His purpose and that of his wife, he said, has been to continue this work of Gandhi. This commitment is perhaps best expressed in the prayer that Gandhi composed at the request of Mira Behn, the lines of which Bahuguna has often quoted to me. I referred to it before in the context of Bahuguna's year underground in the remote Punjabi town of Sikhanwala, but offer it here in full.

Hail Thee, Ocean of Compassion (tenderness)!
Hail the dweller of the humble cottage of the poorest
    scavenger!
Help us search for you everywhere
In this enchanting country
Moistened by the waters of the Ganga, Yamuna, and
    Brahmaputra.
Give us receptivity and an open heart;
Give us Your own compassion (tenderness);
Give us the strength and longing to be one with the people
    of Hindustan.
Oh Lord! You come to our aid
Only when reducing ourselves to nothing,
We seek refuge in you.
Give us your grace so that we may not be separated from
    the people,
Whom we want to serve.
Make us the embodiment of sacrifice, devotion, and
    compassion,
So that, we may understand and love our motherland for
    evermore.[1]

In almost all my conversation with Bahuguna he also found the occasion to recite the famous eleven vows by which Gandhi lived and which he tried to inculcate among his disciples. They include: *satya* (truth), *ahimsa* (nonviolence), *asteya* (not stealing), *asangraha* (renunciation of possessions), *sharir shram* (bodily labor), *brahmacharya* (self-control), *asvada* (control of the palate), *abaya* (not being afraid of anybody and not making anybody afraid), *samanalok* (recognition of the equality of all religions), *swadeshi* (self-reliance), and *sparshabhavana* (renunciation of untouchability).

For Gandhi these vows were not just disciplinary commitments of the participants in his ashrams; they were principles of life, principles for the development and maintenance of nonviolent and sustainable communities. Bahuguna takes them seriously. To get the full picture of Bahuguna's commitment to Gandhi's thought, it is worth our while to look closely at some of these vows and the way they pertain especially to the activism of Bahuguna. In 1978, when at Gangotri he committed himself to the welfare of the Himalayas in all its aspects, he expressed his vow of *asvada* (control of the palate) with the pledge to no longer consume rice, a palatable but especially water-intensive crop. His courage in the face of police brutality and imprisonment is an expression of *abhaya*, the vow of fearlessness and the resolution not to instill fear in others.

Of these principles, *satya* (truth) and *ahimsa* (nonviolence) are perhaps the most readily identified with the thought of Gandhi. He was committed to truth and held that the person devoted to truth must never resort to untruth even for the sake of the perceived good of the country. Because he believed not only that God is truth, but also that truth is God, he drew the conclusion that any departure from truth is also a departure from the Divine Reality. Gandhi acknowledged that the commitment to truth might, and for him sometimes did, require disobedience to persons and organizations in power. He argued that one must never submit to untruth or accommodate himself to injustice. But he also argued that to oppose authorities in the cause of truth always requires nonviolent action. A person committed to truth must not give in to anger even against the perpetrator of the greatest imaginable wrong. He must always love the perpetrator and suffer patiently and courageously the results of his peaceful opposition.[2] These principles provided Sunderlal with direction and focus. The struggle against caste prejudice was a struggle for the truth of equality and the indwelling of divinity in all. The struggle against the proliferation of liquor outlets was a struggle for the truth of the hazards of alcohol to the mountain communities. The struggle against contract felling was a struggle for the truth of the dependence of the mountain communities on nontimber forest products and the dependence of the entire country on the forests for soil, water, and pure air. The protest against the Tehri Dam was a struggle for the truth of the hazards of the project and its colossal and disproportionate costs to the people of the hills. All of these struggles were undertaken by nonviolent means. In his peaceful *dharnas*, strenuous foot marches, arrests, fasts, and periods in jails, Bahuguna's activism has embodied his commitment to nonviolence and to truth.

When I visited with Bahuguna in 1998 I raised the question whether the methods of *satyagraha* as practiced by Gandhi were adequate to address contemporary issues such as the construction of the Tehri Dam. Recalling and augmenting the views of Vinoba Bhave, he replied that there are three methods available to address all such issues. One is the method of the establishment, through the machinery of law and order, especially through the legislature and the judiciary. Today, he says, this method is inadequate because the machinery of government is breaking down. Representatives of the people no longer represent them. The political bureaucracy fails to acknowledge the truth of the plight of the poor and disenfranchised who are most affected by its actions. The second method is the method of terrorism. This, he says, is ineffective and unacceptable because the power of protest by means of terrorism is no match for the collective terrorism of the state. This method claims innocent human lives and undermines human values. The only method that remains, he says, is the method of *satyagraha*, the method of standing firmly for the truth, through peaceful assembly, through foot marches, through civil disobedience, and from time to time, when everything else has failed, through fasting. In discussing the fasts he undertook, both in his involvement with the Chipko Movement and in the protest against the Tehri Dam, Bahuguna pointed out that in fasting the motive can never be that of anger or manipulation. As with Gandhi he affirms that the fast is an act of devotion to God.

During the independence struggle none of the famous eleven vows of Gandhi was more celebrated than that of *swadeshi* (self-reliance). At the time *swadeshi* was widely associated with the *khadi* movement, the production of homespun cotton cloth and the boycott of textiles manufactured in England. For Gandhi, *swadeshi* is related to the idea of village *swaraj* and the commitment to address local needs at the local level. For Gandhi this meant the support of local workers within India as well. He states that we depart from the principle of *swadeshi* when we depart from our neighbor to satisfy our wants from far away. Speaking at a meeting in Madras, Gandhi said, "If a man comes from Bombay here and offers you wares, you are not justified in supporting the Bombay merchant or trader so long as you have got a merchant at your very door, born and bred in Madras."[3] For Bahuguna, the effort to address such problems as water shortage in Delhi by exploiting resources at great distances, and at the cost of distant local economies, is a departure from the principle of *swadeshi*. Bahuguna has stated that communities should be able to meet their basic needs from their immediate surroundings without recourse to the unproductive activity of transport. Projects to address the needs of communities from great distances are a departure from the principle of *swadeshi* and do extraordinary injury to nature.

Gandhi's principle of *asteya* is expressed in the vow not to misappropriate what belongs to another. Gandhi explains that this vow precludes the misuse of anything one has received in trust. It is significant that among the expected benefits of the Tehri Dam is its capacity to deliver drinking water from the Bhagirathi River to Delhi. For Bahuguna this is a critical issue. To the rulers he has raised the critical question, "What have you done to the Yamuna?"

He answers, "You have polluted the Yamuna and now you want the Ganges to wash off your sins in Delhi!"[4] He points out that the five hundred cubic feet per second (cusecs) of drinking water that the Tehri project had promised, to supply swimming pools and to flush toilets in Delhi, will be bought at the cost of the homes, heritage, and habitat of the hard-working and productive people in the Garhwal hills. Bahuguna argues that this water is needed in Delhi because unregulated industry and its untreated sewage have so contaminated the sacred Yamuna River that health authorities have declared it unfit for human consumption. The present state of the Yamuna as it passes out of Delhi is testimony to human violence to nature.

Bahuguna, Gandhi, and Ecology

Bahuguna's commitment to the vows of Gandhi is supported by his appreciation for the modern science of ecology. Yet for him, the insights of ecology and the issues it raises are simply an extension of the concerns for which Gandhi was working. In my last visit with Bahuguna, in January 2010, he said, "if Gandhi were alive today he would be working for the protection of the environment." Gandhi is known for his claim that "[n]ature provides just enough, and no more, for our daily need."[5] This implies both an ethic of conservation and of respect for nature. Extrapolating from Gandhi's concern for village self-reliance and his recognition of the capacity of nature to support the human community, Bahuguna suggests that Gandhi would have supported the kind of policy for the Himalayas that he has tried to advance. While Bahuguna is conversant with a great many studies of the ecology of the Himalayas and of global environmental issues, he states that it was the thought of Mira Behn that first brought issues of ecology to his attention and that her insight into the ecology of the hills remains the foundation of his environmental knowledge. Mira Behn, he said, was the first to recognize that the most important product of the Himalayas was not timber but water, and the first to recognize the importance of the indigenous Himalayan oak (banj) and its role in the stabilizing of that source. The Himalayan oak had a root system that holds water, and its production of leaf litter contributes to the renewal of the soil.

Bahuguna states that before colonial encroachment into the Himalayas, the economy of the hills centered on animal husbandry with the support of light agricultural activity. The mixed forests of the region provided leaf fodder and grasses for the cattle. From the milk of the cows they produced *ghee* (clarified butter), which could be bartered with people from Tibet and from the plains for salt, rice, jaggery (raw sugar), and other commodities. The British, he said, discouraged animal husbandry and supported the extraction of timber and the development of agricultural activity on the slopes of the hills. "Why," I asked, "did they discourage animal husbandry?" "The Britishers," he said, "were commercially minded. They wanted species of trees that had commercial value. In their view, the Banj or Himalayan Oak had no value as timber but only as fodder for the local people." They supported the cultivation of commercially valuable species such as the chir pine, and other conifers to the neglect of the banj. In doing so they altered the system of land use in the hills. The difficulty is that conifers such as the chir pine acidify the soil. In a chir pine forest there is little or no undergrowth and therefore no fodder for the cattle and no holding power for the soil. Increasing agriculture on the slopes and the proliferation of revenue-producing species led to the erosion of soil. While the people worked hard to fertilize their fields, the heavy downpour of the monsoon washed away the manure with the topsoil. "In every rainy season," he said, "the rivers were flowing with the flesh and blood of the mountains." In effect, he says, "they were providing manure to the fertile plains of Uttar Pradesh." That, he said, is the secret of the poverty of the hills. During his famous foot march from Kashmir to Kohima, (1981–83)

Bahuguna found that in Bhutan where the development of commercial forestry had not yet developed, the difference between the lean and peak flows of rivers was a ratio of 1:7. In the Himalayan rivers in India the ratio on average was 1:70. Drought, flood, and poverty are the effects of an alteration of a land use policy that has been proceeding for most of the past one hundred years. It needs to change.

To address conditions of water shortage, the received policy of the government has been and continues to be the construction of dams. For Bahuguna these are but "a temporary solution to a permanent problem." In the first place dams in the Himalayas have a limited life. The sediment load of the rivers of the Himalayas exceeds that of the plains. In the course of time, the silt carried by streams entering the reservoir accumulates. The storage capacity of the dam is gradually diminished, eventually rendering it inoperative. The new fertile soil, the produce of the forest, is trapped behind the dam. Finally, dams displace enormous numbers of people, most often the poor, for whom resettlement even under the best circumstances is a challenge. Bahuguna explains that while Americans and Europeans often move their place of residence several times in the course of a life, the displacement of the hill people turns their life to misery. For the people of the hills, displacement is a tragedy. Bahuguna was impressed with E. F. Schumacher's claim that small is beautiful, but he also expresses the corollary. "Small is beautiful," he said laughing, "and big is horrible!" He argues that big dams address the problem of energy and water shortage in one area of the country by creating an environmental disaster in others. Big is horrible, according to Bahuguna, because it does injury to local communities and the environment upon which they depend.

Sunderlal points out that in a study of interstate and interdistrict income conducted in 1960 the Tehri Garhwal district was found to be the poorest district of India, with an average annual income of only eighty-four rupees per year. Bahuguna believes that since that time, nothing significant has been undertaken to address the problem. He states that in the interest of development the government has constructed a significant network of motor roads. But motor roads don't generate income. What they do is facilitate the movement of able-bodied men from the hills to the plains. With the attenuation of the local economy, men follow their soil to the plains. There they work, and from there they send money orders to meet the needs of their families at home. Today, he says, the economy of the hills is a "money order economy." It is an economy that fractures families and undermines community. It is the antithesis of village *swaraj*.

A permanent solution to the need for water, according to Bahuguna, would not be one that displaces people from land they have worked productively for generations, that devastates the heritage of a village culture that has celebrated the meaning of their lives, and that destroys local ecosystems. Bahuguna's solution to the problem of water shortage is to clothe the entire Himalayas from Afghanistan to Burma with trees. He states that such a strategy would address the problem of water shortage by making the entire Himalayan range a natural dam. The same strategy could address the problems of poverty and pollution as well. During his activities with the Chipko Movement, Bahuguna came to the conclusion that the long-term economic needs of the people of the hills would be met neither by employment with companies that extracted timber for the export market nor in the development of local forest industries. Trees, he said, must be available to meet the needs of local people. They could do so without being destroyed. His view is that the forests of the Himalayas should be restored. "I feel," he said, "that the future lies in tree farming because trees give you all your requirements from your surroundings. Trees give you oxygen, trees give you water, trees give you food. They give fodder for cattle, fiber, and timber." The cultivation and care of trees of the forest could be a viable source of income for the Himalayan people. Bahuguna's priorities for the trees that should be planted and cultivated could be inferred from many other things he has said. The first priority is for trees providing food. This includes trees producing nuts like walnuts, then trees producing edible seeds like the seed of the wild apricot. The next is flowering trees that can provide for honey, then trees producing oil seeds for cooking, and trees producing seasonal fruits. In addition Bahuguna's priorities would include trees producing fertilizer from leaf litter, trees that provide fodder for cattle, trees that provide fiber for clothing and other needs, and finally trees that provide timber and fuel. The care of such forest resources could provide employment for local people, addressing the problem that has led to the money-order economy. Such forests would retain and help conserve water, help purify water, and help stabilize the entire ecosystem of the Himalayas. Bahuguna's recommended strategy is threefold: Bring water to the hilltops, plant trees on the slopes, and generate electricity from every water source. It is a solution that would support the local economy and facilitate village self-reliance and the Gandhian hope of true *swaraj*.

For Bahuguna, the question of man's relationship to nature and to other species is really the test of our civilization. This relationship has not received the attention it deserves. Rivers like the Bhagirathi are not just sources of water but ecosystems that include marine and aquatic life.

Their integrity is part of the *wealth* of the nation. He notes that ecological studies of such river systems have shown that the tempestuous agitation of a mountain river as it courses through rocky terrain absorbs oxygen that energizes and purifies it. Because of the energy in a turbulent flowing stream, a fish swimming against the stream in the mountains is able to swim faster than the same fish in still water on the plains.[6] In his statement to the Supreme Court in the case against the Tehri Dam, Bahuguna pointed out that the Mahseer is a fish that migrates from Ganga Sagar to Gomukh and back in the course of the year. The Tehri Dam will block the movement of this species and its breeding capabilities. The forests and rivers of the Himalayas constitute an integrated ecosystem that supports a vast biotic community, stabilizes the soil, and mitigates the flow of water.

It is perhaps because Bahuguna has advocated a restoration of the Himalayas that he has sometimes been interpreted as advocating a return to a preindustrial economy. Yet it would be a great misreading of the thought of Sunderlal Bahuguna to suggest that he was hostile to the accomplishments of science and technology, or to the production of energy for the needs of the nation. The problem is not with science and technology but with the use to which it has been put and the failure to apply science and technology to the needs of the people at all levels of society. In support of his position, he cites one of the formulas for which Vinoba Bhave was known. Science plus spirituality, he said, equals *sarvodaya*, the good for all. He compares this with another famous formula of Vinoba Bhave: science plus politics equals the atom bomb, destruction. For Bahuguna science and technology possess great resources for the production of energy. But to use technology in the interest of society, the needs of all, the cost to all, and the uplift of all ought to be considered. For Bahuguna the production of energy should be developed not by one but by a variety of means. In fact, he suggests seven forms of energy that might effectively be developed without imposing a major burden upon nature or upon rural communities. The first is human energy. With the help of science and technology, devices that employ human effort can be improved to produce more output with less effort. He reminded me that in the 1920s in the Sabarmati Ashram Gandhi himself used to ride a bicycle. The second is animal power and its improvement by means of technology. Third is biogas from animal waste. Fourth is solar energy. Fifth is wind energy. Sixth is geothermal energy. And the seventh, where appropriate, is hydroelectric power generated from the technology known as run of the river. These, he says, should be our energy priorities in a nonviolent and permanent society.

Bahuguna and Indian Spirituality

The question of the relationship of religion, especially the religions of India, to the environment, has been of interest to scholars of religion for a considerable period of time. Throughout his career, Bahuguna has found much support for his activism and in the religious traditions of India. While he does not consider himself a religious scholar, he has high regard for the religious traditions and especially for the religious life of the villages of the Himalayas. For instance, he pointed out that during his long *padyatra* through the Himalayas that began in 1981, it was not necessary to inform the villagers about the sacred character of nature. In their daily religious life, he said, they acknowledged divinity in rivers, plants, animals, birds, forests, and mountains. His role was simply to remind them of these traditions and to draw out the conclusion that the very nature upon which their well-being depends merits their protection.

On several occasions I raised with Bahuguna the question of the role of Indian religion or spirituality in his environmental activism. I could see many features of his activism and his philosophy that had evident religious roots. The *padyatra* was a religious practice that had a long history in the Hindu religious tradition. His fasts in support of one or another moral issue had a religious and spiritual meaning that was long practiced in India and that went back to Sunderlal's childhood. The *Bhagavad Katha* was also clearly rooted in religion. When I raised such questions his answers sometimes came in unexpected ways. On one occasion, Bahuguna recalled an ancient story from the Bhagavata Purana (book 9) in which the ancient king Bhagiratha wanted the goddess Ganga to descend from the heavens to wash off the sins of his forefathers. After much prayer and penance on the part of the king, she agreed to do so. But she warned the king that when she came down to earth she would have to be contained. Otherwise she would not be the life-giving waters he wanted, but a raging torrent that would cause chaos and destruction on the earth. King Bhagiratha then sought out someone strong enough to restrain the tempestuous Ganga. He found that the only power sufficient for the task was the mighty Shiva. He then prayed fervently to Lord Shiva to enclose the Ganga as she descended to the earth. Shiva agreed, and Ganga descended into the matted locks of his hair, from which she comes forth as a life-giving stream to the northern plains of India. For Bahuguna the matted locks of Lord Shiva are the natural forests of the Himalayas, which contain the water in the soil and protect the land from floods. In these matted locks the waters of the Ganges are entangled every year, turning it into a river of life by regulating its flow. But now, he says, the sacred locks of Shiva have been cut, turning the Ganges into the destructive force against which the story warned. Like Indu Tikekar, he finds in these religious sources a deep and profound ecological wisdom.

In 1967 while Bahuguna was undertaking padyatras in the Himalayas in the interest of village self-reliance, an influential essay appeared in the journal *Science* entitled "The Historical Roots of Our Ecologic Crisis." In this work, the author Lynn White, Jr., made the point that the present world environmental crisis can be attributed in large measure to attitudes concerning the natural world that are rooted in the Western religious tradition.[7] He argued that in this tradition the world is seen as the work of a craftsmanlike god who created the human being as a unique entity, endowed with a soul, and placed him in charge of the created world to use it for his own benefit. This, he said, is the most anthropocentric, or human centered, religion the world has seen. By contrast, he found the religious traditions of Asia and of India in particular, to be more congenial to the natural world. This article provoked a flourish of scholarship concerning the relationship of both Western religion and non-Western religion to the environment. While some scholars attempted to construct an environmental ethic based on ancient Hindu texts, others argued that the use of such texts is selective and misleading, and sometimes argued that the insights in these texts are irrelevant or obstructive to environmental concerns. One of the more common arguments was that because the goal of the Indian religious quest is a salvation of the soul that lies beyond the material world, environmental degradation is simply part of the material reality that Hindu spirituality enjoins its adherents to transcend.[8] Against the possibility of an environmental ethic grounded in the Hindu religious traditions, some scholars claimed that for the Hindu tradition the present world is merely a provisional reality sometimes called the realm of illusion or Maya. For this reason Hinduism has sometimes been called a world-negating religion. In his *Earth Insights*, the American environmental philosopher J. Baird Callicott states that from the Hindu perspective, "the empirical world is both unimportant, because it is not ultimately real, and contemptible, because it seduces the soul into crediting appearances, pursuing false ends."[9]

In light of this discussion I recalled Bahuguna's statement that the affluence of materialistic civilization is *not real*: "It has come all of a sudden with the application of technology to exploit the accumulated wealth of nature."[10] The affluence of the present society is *unreal* because it depletes the *real* capital of nature. It is also unsustainable, because it is fed by the unrealistic desire for more and more material things. This kind of affluence has brought, and by its nature can only bring, temporary satisfaction, temporary peace, and temporary fulfillment.

Bahuguna's thought and activism are relevant to the debate about the relationship between religion and ecology because they represent an active environmental philosophy whose practice is informed by spiritual traditions. In the light of this debate I raised the question why, considering the importance of the soul in Hindu religion, should a person be concerned with environmental problems of the material world? "You know," he said, "this is the animal instinct of man in which he cares only for his body, but he doesn't think that everything in nature has life. There is life all around him and no life should be eliminated simply for self-interest. Seeing life in all things, this is the essence of the Gita. And wherever there is life, that life should be respected." He went on to say that this is also the way to live happily in the world, "having a relationship with all that is around you, a relationship with birds, plants, animals, with everything." For Bahuguna the soul is the essence of the person, the divine principle within. But that divine principle is also embodied in the natural world. On another occasion when I was inquiring about the role of religions in his activism, he replied with a quotation from the Bhagavad Gita (10:25, 31): "Of rivers I am the Ganga, of the steadfast I am the Himalaya." The speaker in this quotation is Lord Krishna, presented in the Bhagavad Gita as the Supreme Lord. I asked the question, "What does that passage mean to you?" "It means," he said, "that this divinity is there in that river, it is in the Himalaya." For Bahuguna, the objective of life is not to be alienated from that principle but to realize it, to experience it, to live in harmony with that divine reality. "Seeing God everywhere, in all beings, that elevates you. That is what makes a person a real religious man. That is the real religion."

Looking at the philosophy and activism of Bahuguna we can see a sense in which his understanding of reality could be called world negating. The question is what world does it negate? It certainly does not deny the reality of the natural world in which the divine is embodied. This is the reality that he like most of devotional Hinduism affirms. The world he denies is the false world of materialism and the idea of development that promises fulfillment while it undermines the actual basis of life. For Bahuguna, this is a value system, a world view, and a civilization that, to use Callicott's phrase, seduces the soul into crediting appearances and pursuing false ends. True development, he says, would be directed towards conditions in which communities are able to experience peace, happiness, and fulfillment on a permanent basis. This is afforded not in a system that turns nature into cash, but one that sees divinity in all beings, not only in human beings, but in birds, beasts, trees, mountains, and rivers. That, he says, is spirituality. For the materialistic world view, civilization is seen in the capacity to exploit nature, to acquire affluence, and to consume energy. This is the world that Bahuguna negates, the world of so-called scientific forestry and of politicians, technicians, and contractors within whose knowledge nature is reduced to a commodity in a system of economic exchange that leaves the people destitute and dispossessed, that discounts their material needs and marginalizes the religious life that supports them. The spirituality of Bahuguna is a renunciation of this world and its promises.

In his activism and commitment to Indian spirituality, Bahuguna demonstrates the relevance of his religious thought to his ecological concerns. A second question in this connection is whether, if it is relevant to the environment, the use of such sources represents a compromise with the religious Right. We raised this question in connection with the involvement of the Sangh Parivar with the protest against the Tehri Dam. But because Bahuguna has said much more than we observed in that connection, it is appropriate to close with a more thorough understanding of his spiritual and religious views. Bahuguna told me that a journalist once asked him where he received the inspiration for his work with the Chipko Movement. His inspiration, he replied, was in "our philosophy of life." By this he was clearly pointing to the philosophy of life that is imbedded in the Hindu religious tradition. But the fact that his inspiration came from this religious tradition by no means implies that he considers environmentalism to be the unique property of Hinduism or that Hinduism is in any other way superior to other religious traditions in its regard for nature. The real contrast is not between religions but between the environmental values embedded in the great religious traditions and the values of that civilization that has emerged with the technical control of nature. In the essay "The Crisis of Civilization and the Message of Culture in the Context of Environment," Bahuguna explains that the philosophy of life that informs the prevailing attitude toward nature came into prominence during the Industrial Revolution. This, he says, gave birth to a new kind of civilization and brought about a basic change in the outlook of man toward life and nature. The steam engine put unprecedented power in the hands of man. With the use of this power, his relationship with nature underwent a sudden change. Nature for him now remained only a resource, a commodity, and man became the sole master of this resource. In addition, man began to consider himself superior to other beings because no other animal possessed the power and means to control nature. With this he limited the definition of society to the society of human beings. These ideas became the basis for the development of human civilization from then on.[11]

Contemporary civilization, he states, regards affluence and the consumption of energy as the index of what it calls development. "To achieve affluence for development, man engaged himself in unlimited exploitation of the treasures of nature." Rich nations have generated wealth on the basis of industrial production, and their standard of development has also become the ideal for the poor countries of the world. He also points out that in order to maintain this economic system, the rich countries exercise control over the treasures of the earth. They do this largely, he says, through aid to the poorer countries and by the promise of defense against their enemies. The result is an astonishing increase in the defense expenditures of the countries where people are without adequate food, clothing, or shelter. Because the defense industry contributes to the economies of the rich countries, they maintain an atmosphere of apprehension among the poor countries and their neighbors. In the role of defenders, they supply these countries with arms. To adapt to the defense and development strategies of the rich, the poor countries require foreign exchange. For many, he says, foreign exchange has been more important than God. In order to earn it, they are willing to give up their forests and with them the soil they produce. The clear felling of these forests for agricultural expansion, dams, and other development projects has resulted in the extinction of many species. Much agriculture is now dependent on oil, which we, in a way, are now consuming as our food. Fields have become addicted to chemical fertilizers, and an ever-increasing need for irrigation has depleted the ground water.[12] Modern man, he says, is at war with nature. He has forgotten that he is the child of nature. He sees nature only as something for his consumption through technologies that can turn it to cash. For Bahuguna the result of this idea of development is that we are poorer than our ancestors, the so-called primitive people who lived in harmony with nature.

The desire to exploit nature to generate foreign exchange has engendered what Bahuguna has called a new religion. This is not at all like the great religions of the world. It is the religion of economics. The god of this religion, he says, is the dollar. The priests of this religion are the bureaucrats, technicians, engineers, and politicians who profit materially from the presence of this god. He suggests that throughout the Third World, political leaders are impatient to possess this god and are prepared to make the highest sacrifice to bring it into their respective countries. But in the process nature is destroyed, and with it the communities who depend upon it. Bahuguna states that in his years in the Chipko Movement, his purpose was to convince the people that their interests were in the preservation of the forests that provided soil, water, and pure air, rather than in destroying the forests for the sake of timber, resin, and foreign exchange. The rich countries, he says, are enticing the poor countries with the idea that the foreign exchange is their most important product. He states that his duty is to warn the people that the promises of this project and others like it are based on a false view of reality that equates progress with the affluence of the few.[13] Projects like the Tehri Dam, he says, are the temples of the new religion. He states that Jawaharlal Nehru regarded such dams as the new temples of India. Bahuguna argues, however, that Gandhi had a different view than Nehru, one in which each person in each village could be afforded the means for a decent life. For Bahuguna, the ultimate objectives of life are happiness, peace, and fulfillment. The materialist society offers a kind of development that provides for temporary happiness, temporary peace, and temporary fulfillment, all coming from without. Because it sees nature as a commodity to be turned into cash, it makes the human being the butcher of nature. He explains that this began with the exploitation of the Himalayan forests by the British in the nineteenth century. It continued in the policy of contract felling by the Indian Forest Departments, and it obtains in the exploitation of the water resources of the Himalayas today.

Bahuguna often describes himself as one who swims against the tide. The prevailing tide is the commercialization of nature, so-called scientific forestry, and the centralized system of production. Beneath all of these is a materialistic view of the world and a materialistic civilization that cannot be sustained. Bahuguna states that, against this self-destructive civilization, wise men of the world have raised their voices again and again. He states that in the nineteenth century this voice was heard in England in the writings of John Ruskin and in America in those of Henry David Thoreau. Thoreau argued that the human race had lost its way and that in order to find his way he needed to return to his roots. From the insights of these voices we might have proceeded toward a real civilization rather than an artificial life. Yet the voices of Ruskin and Thoreau fell largely on deaf ears. While their contemporaries succeeded in understanding many of the mysteries of the physical world, they "could not acquire the other power which since time immemorial has been influencing the human beings and whose impact has been so deep and permanent that the national boundaries and time factor could not eliminate it. That was the power of the heart."[14]

Bahuguna states that this power of the heart has been expressed in the thought and actions of a number of great personalities that have appeared in the course of human history. India, he says, has been fortunate in having been influenced by such personalities from Vedic times to the present. In ancient times the Buddha reminded his society that misery comes from desire. Later Zambhoji, the medieval saint of Rajasthan, saw that the severe droughts through which his people suffered were the result of human behavior. He was the founder of a sect that came to be known as the Bishnois, who lived by the twenty-nine rules he formulated that supported a sustainable relationship with nature. Among them was the injunction not to fell green trees or to kill the wild animals. In our discussion of the Chipko Movement we indicated that it was the Bishnois who in 1731, under the leadership of Amrita Devi, embraced their Khejri trees to protect them from the destructive designs of the maharajah of Jodhpur, a protest in which 363 Bishnois lost their lives. Another great personality was Nund Rishi, a Muslim teacher born in Kashmir in 1375, who learned from his observations of nature and journeyed from village to village with the message that the supply of food depends on the health of the forests. Bahuguna makes the point that neither the British system of education nor British rule was able to completely eliminate the influence of this power of the heart. English learning in India, in fact, motivated Indians to look to their own glorious past and inspired a new renaissance of Indian learning. Among them, Gandhi challenged the definition of progress of materialistic civilization and argued that the solution to the major problems of our time was in the decentralization of production.[15]

Bahuguna suggests that modern man has become so materialistic that he has little or no interest in the inner self. He has observed that the material wealth promised through the centralized system of material production does not make people happy. Instead it makes them greedy. It does so, he says, because it seeks to provide satisfaction through the accumulation of more and more material things. The tragedy is that modern man seeks satisfaction from without. Real satisfaction, he said, comes not from outside but from within. That is the difference between materialistic civilization and what he calls *aranya* culture, the culture of the forest. I stated above that for Gandhi nature provides just enough, and no more, for our daily need. Gandhi has made similar statements in different writings that have often been translated in differing ways. One such rendering, to which I have already referred, says, "The Earth provides enough to satisfy every man's needs, but not every man's greed."[16] Conscious of the ways in which this statement can be taken, Bahuguna points out that the appropriate rendering of this statement is the following: "The earth provides enough to satisfy every man's needs, but not enough for anybody's greed."[17] The statement is more about the nature of greed than about the nature of the earth. Materialistic civilization has continually to produce more and more material things because it is the nature of greed that it can never be satisfied, not even with the resources of the whole earth.

Against the greed of materialistic civilization, Bahuguna poses the ancient virtue of *santosh* or contentment. The curse of discontent all over the world, he says, arises from the fact that things never satisfy, they provide no contentment. They have no *santosh*. However, for the person who is inwardly content, the accumulation of more and more goods is without appeal. This is why Gandhi said that nature has enough to satisfy the need of all but nothing to satisfy the greed of one. Our culture, says Bahuguna, has shown the way to overcome the crisis to which a materialistic civilization has brought us. The distinction between the exterior and the interior of the person, according to Bahuguna, is a fundamental insight of this tradition. The heart of the Bhagavad Gita, says Bahuguna, is that you are not simply a body but an immortal soul. We observed that Bahuguna referred to the Bhagavad Gita when he cited the words of Lord Krishna, "Of rivers I am the Ganga." He went on to say that for him, as for Vinoba Bhave, the Bhagavad Gita is a book of practical knowledge that develops a clear picture of the ideal person. He stated that when Vinoba Bhave was jailed during the freedom struggle, his fellow freedom fighters who were jailed with him requested that he give them some talks on the Gita. He did so, covering all the chapters of the Gita in the course of a week. Bahuguna affirms that Vinoba's *Talks on the Gita* contain insights of great importance for the present world.[18] For Vinoba, he said, the Gita is not a book about the other world but a book of practical wisdom for this world. For the Gita, says Bahuguna, the ideal person is a person of knowledge and insight, firmly established in wisdom. Such a person remains undisturbed by success or failure, by honor or humiliation. He is stable minded in all adversities. The Bhagavad Gita articulates this ideal and points the way to achieving it. The Gita, he said, begins with the despondency of Arjuna. At the outset of the battle between the Pandavas and the Kauravas, Arjuna recognizes that the enemy he is expected to fight includes his respected relatives and teachers. He declares to Krishna that he cannot fight them. Then Krishna gives him the knowledge that the bodies arrayed for battle are perishable, that his body too is perishable, but the soul within is immortal. "Weapons cannot cleave if, fire does not burn it, water cannot wet it nor does the wind make it dry. It is immortal and eternal" (1: 23–34). Bodies are perishable, he said, but the soul will remain even when the body is gone. "All the great men who left an impression on humankind were men who knew their soul and who tried to enlighten the light within." The soul, said Bahuguna, is the spiritual element inside the body. "Until you begin to feed this soul," he said, "the person is just like an animal. The animal takes food, takes sleep, feels fear, and engages in sexual activity. But the divine quality is found in the refinement of the soul and mind." It is seen in the inquisitiveness of the person as to where he has come from and to where he has to go. Otherwise he is just an animal. I said, "It seems to me that this is the teaching not only of the Gita but of the Upanishads as well." He interrupted to say, "That *is* Indian philosophy. That is the soul of Indian thought. You are not a body alone, you are soul." He went on to say that you have to feed yourself with spiritual food every day. "Just as you need food for the body so for your soul you need spiritual food. That spiritual food is prayer."

In the midst of this discussion I began to understand why it was that Sunderlal could remain so cheerful in the midst of intimidating opposition and even in the midst of defeat. This is not to say that he did not grieve over those who lost their lives in the bus incident of 1992, or over the loss of home and hearth of those evicted for the Tehri Dam. Yet in victory and in disappointment his attitude seemed always to remain the same. While many were disappointed with the Supreme Court decision in favor of the Tehri Dam, and many deeply discouraged, Bahuguna remained positive. It is hard to imagine how a person who suffered so much during the course of this resistance could remain so affirmative unless we understand that he had undertaken the kind of discipline the Gita describes. For Bahuguna the spiritual food that supports the inner self is daily prayer and meditation. "Doing your daily prayer," he said, "you equip yourself for the whole day. You provide food for the soul. Man takes food for the body but the real man takes food for the soul. When you are giving nutrition to your body you are doing animal work. Like animals people need nutrition for their bodies. But you should think about nutrients of the soul. And that is prayer." I asked him whether in his daily prayers there was a particular divine form that was the focus of his attention. His answer was that Vinoba Bhave did a great service to all of us by composing a prayer that contains the names of God that appear in all the great religions.

I suggested to Bahuguna that one of the problems with religion today is that people identify with their religion and identify their religion with their own community. As a result they are often inclined to regard the adherent of another religion as their enemy. Bahuguna replied that the true essence of the great religions is really all the same. That essence is to see the divine reality everywhere. "That is why Gandhi used to say prayers which he received from all the great religions." He derived them from the Bhagavad Gita, from the Qur'an, from the Christian tradition, and from Judaism as well. Bahuguna suggested that different religions developed in different parts of the world. Because man was limited in his ability to travel, these religions developed an identity before they encountered one another. But now the world has become small, and people of different religions encounter one another everywhere. "The differences among the religions," he said, "were created by selfish people who created barriers between people." One of Gandhi's principal objectives, he said "was to bring equanimity to all religions." Bahuguna's appeal to the religious significance of nature does not lend support to any narrow or exclusive religious point of view. It is supported by a tradition that sees the earth as our mother and human beings as her children, who should live close to her and recognize their dependence upon her bounty. In doing so it recognizes the view to which Gandhi was also committed, *vasudhaiva kutumbakam,* This whole earth is my family.

Appendix 1

Some Critical Dates in the History of Modern India and the Activism of Sunderlal Bahuguna

1869   Birth of Mohandas Karamchand Gandhi in Porbandar, in Western India.

1889   Richard St. Barbe Baker is born in Hampshire, England.

1892   Mira Behn (Madeline Slade) is born in London.

1895   Birth of Vinoba Bhave in Gagode Maharashtra.

1901   Sarala Behn (Catherine Mary Heilemann) is born in London.

1916   Birth of Sri Dev Suman.

1920   Richard St. Barbe Baker's first assignment as forester in Kenya.

1921   Vinoba Bhave arrives in Wardha.

1922   Richard St. Barbe Baker establishes Men of Trees organization in Kenya.

1925   Mira Behn arrives in India.

1927   Birth of Sunderlal Bahuguna in Marora Village in Tehri Garhwal.

1930   Massacre of Forest Protesters at Tilari on May 30.

1932   Vimla Nautiyal is born in Malideval Village in Tehri Garhwal.

1932   Sarala Behn arrives in Udaipur, Rajasthan.

1935   Sarala Behn travels to Wardha and meets Gandhi.

1940   First meeting of Sunderlal Bahuguna with Sri Dev Suman.

1944   Martyrdom of Sri Dev Suman, Sunderlal Bahuguna jailed for
            five months in Narendranagar.

1945   Sunderlal Bahuguna goes underground and remains in Sikhan-
            wala for one year.

1947   India achieves national independence.

1947   Sunderlal Bahuguna returns to Garhwal from Sikhanwala,
            undertakes his first experiment in *satyagraha* at the entrance
            to the town of Tehri.

1948   Gandhi is assassinated at Birla house in New Delhi. Sunder-
            lal Bahuguna is elected general secretary of the Praja Mandal
            (citizen's forum) in Tehri. Sarala Behn opens Lakshmi Ashram
            in Kausani.

1949   Tehri Garhwal is assimilated into the new Indian state of Uttar
            Pradesh. Vimla Nautiyal is admitted as a student to Lakshmi
            Ashram in Kausani. Geological Survey of India identifies the
            Bhagirathi Gorge at Tehri as a possible dam site.

1950   Establishment of Thakkar Bapa Chattravas or Thakkar Bapa
            Hostel.

1951   Vinoba Bhave initiates Land Gift Movement (Bhoodan). At age
            twenty, on leave from the Lakshmi Ashram, Vimla Nautiyal
            participates in the movement.

1954   First meeting of Sunderlal Bahuguna and Vimla Nautiyal.

1956   Marriage of Sunderlal Bahuguna and Vimla Nautiyal and the
            establishment of the Parvatiya Navjeevan Ashram, the ashram
            for new life in the hills.

1964   Chandi Prasad Bhatt organizes Dashauli Gram Swarajya Sangh.

1968   Villagers around Tilari renew their pledge to protect their for-
            ests even at the cost of their lives. Indu Tikekar settles in Ujeli
            Ashram, on the banks of the Bhagirathi River in Uttarkashi.

1970   Devastating flood occurs in Alakananda Valley.

1972   Mass demonstration concerning discrimination against local
            forest industries in Uttarkashi and Gopeshwar. Planning com-
            mission approves of Tehri Dam.

1973   Conflict of chipko activists with Symonds Company. Chipko
            Movement receives media attention. Chipko protest takes place
            in Mandal forest. Publication of *Small Is Beautiful* by E. F.
            Schumacher.

1977   First meeting of Sunderlal Bahuguna with Richard St. Barbe
            Baker. Bahuguna undertakes fast at Narendranagar. Protest in
            Advani Forest: hundreds of women vow to protect the trees if
            necessary at the cost of their lives.

1978   At Gaumukh, where the Bhagirathi River has its source in the
            Gangotri Glacier, Sunderlal Bahuguna takes a pledge to devote
            himself to the protection of the Himalayan environment in all
            its aspects. Construction of Tehri Dam begins under police
            guard.

1979   Bahuguna undertakes fast at Badiyargad concerning tree felling.

1980   Environmental Appraisal Committee is appointed by Indian
            government.

1981   Sunderlal Bahuguna and Rattan Dehloo begin foot march from
            Srinagar in Kashmir to Kohima in Nagaland on May 30. Bahu-
            guna refuses Padma Shree Award. Moratorium on felling of
            green trees for commercial purposes in Uttar Pradesh above
            the elevation of one thousand meters.

1982   Death of Mira Behn, Vinoba Bhave, and Richard St. Barbe
            Baker.

1983   Sunderlal Bahuguna and others complete the journey from Sri-
            nagar in Kashmir to Kohima in Nagaland February 1.

1984   Bahuguna is recipient of the Singhvi National Integration
            Award for his work with the Chipko Movement as the best
            expression of India's culture.

1985   Bahuguna is given the Man of the Trees Award by Friends of
            Trees, Bombay.

1987   With Indu Tikekar, Bahuguna is recipient, on behalf of the
            Chipko Movement, of the Right Livelihood Award (also called
            the Alternative Nobel Prize).

1989   Bahuguna departs from the Silyara ashram to devote himself
            to the protest against the Tehri Dam, undertakes his first fast
            in connection with the Tehri Dam protest.

1990 Environmental Appraisal Committee, under D. R. Bhumbha, rejects plans for the Tehri Dam.

1991 Bahuguna participates in a bicycle *yatra* from Ganga Sagar to Gangotri, interrupted by an earthquake on October 20 that strikes the Uttarkashi region. It renews concerns over seismic safety of the Tehri Dam. December 14, Bahuguna sits on the tracks of one of the bulldozers, preventing it from moving.

1992 Police break up protest camp at the dam site and arrest fifteen people, including Sunderlal Bahuguna, his wife, and Diksha Bisht. Bahuguna undertakes a fast. Work on the dam is temporarily suspended. On March 20, a bus carrying antidam protesters runs off the road and tumbles down a precipice killing sixteen.

1994 Bahuguna and his supporters receive word that the central government had cleared the Tehri Dam project.

1995 Bahuguna undertakes fast of forty-five days against the construction of the Tehri Dam.

1996 Bahuguna is the recipient of the Justice V. R. Krishna Iyer National Award and the National Citizen's Award for launching an untiring fight for the cause of ecology, forests, and the environment involving people. Bahuguna undertakes a fast (*prayaschit vrata*, a discipline of self-purification) for letting down the people of the Bhagirathi Valley who had counted on his previous fast to address the threat of the Tehri Dam. Indian government sets up expert committee to study the safety aspects of the dam and an additional committee, under the direction of Hanumantha Rao to study issues concerning resettlement and rehabilitation.

1999 Earthquake on March 29 causes extensive damage in the Chamoli district. Committee of Secretaries of the Indian government clears the dam.

2000 Uttaranchal becomes the twenty-seventh state of the Republic of India.

2001 Earthquake occurs in January in a region of Bhuj. Administrative offices of the town of Tehri are transferred to New Tehri. Ashok Singal of the VHP expresses opposition to the dam. THDC closes two diversion tunnels. Water begins to inundate the town of Tehri. Bahuguna's *kuti* is submerged.

2002   The Supreme Court begins to hear arguments in a Public Interest Litigation (PIL) against the Tehri Dam.

2003   In a 3:2 verdict, and with provision for relocation issues, the Supreme Court rules in favor of the Tehri Dam.

2004   THDC closes one of the two remaining diversion tunnels of the Dam. Sunderlal and Vimla Bahuguna are evacuated from Purana Dubar, their temporary home in Old Tehri.

2007   Uttaranchal is renamed Uttarakhand.

2009   Bahuguna is awarded the Padma Vibhushan by the president of India, the second highest civilian honor given by the Republic of India.

Appendix 2

Arguments of the Petitioners in the Public Interest Litigation against the Tehri Dam

In July 1996 following Sunderlal's seventy-four-day *prayaschit vrata* (repentance fast), the central government had set up a five-member expert committee to study the safety aspects of the dam. In addition, it had set up a twelve-member committee, under the direction of C. H. Hanumantha Rao to study issues concerning the environment and issues of resettlement and rehabilitation. The government had accepted parts of the Hanumantha Rao committee recommendations and the principal recommendations of the expert committee, but it did not implement its recommended 3-D nonlinear analysis and a simulated dam-break analysis. Among other things, the petitioners in the new public interest litigation petition argued that the Tehri Project was not assessed for its environmental impact before environmental clearance was given, and that even after clearance was given, the studies and plans concerning such issues as catchment area treatment, rehabilitation, command area development, water quality maintenance, disaster management, were not completed in the stipulated time, and some remained incomplete even at the time of the petition. They further argued that the clearance for the project stipulated that in case the conditions of clearance were not met, the work on the project would be stopped. Even though the conditions of the clearance were not met, the statutory responsibility of stopping work on the project was not fulfilled. The Tehri Project was neither properly assessed in terms of its impact on the environment, nor were the conditions of its clearance complied with. They argued therefore that the environmental viability of the project was not established and that the project was being constructed in violation of the laws and constitution of India.

Concerning safety issues, the petitioners observed that unreasonable constraints had been placed on the availability of information to the expert committee. The expert committee members were not given full access to all of the data and documents they needed and were basing their assessment only on what had been shown or given to them. Members of that committee felt that a careful analysis of these documents required deeper study and requested that copies be made available to them for such study. This had not been permitted. They had therefore qualified their final recommendations indicating that their recommendations were based only on a review of those reports made available to the group. Consulting members of the expert group, the petitioners found that three of the four members who signed the main report could not consider the project safe without an assessment of the results of a 3-D nonlinear analysis. Thus the decision of the government against the use of a 3-D nonlinear analysis was not only at variance with the recommendations of the expert group but also raised a question about the safety of the dam. Considering the immensity of the threat to the lives and property of hundreds of thousands of people in case of a failure of the dam, the petitioners found the decision of the government against such an analysis unacceptable.

Concerning resettlement and rehabilitation, the petitioners pointed out that in the past a large proportion of people displaced by such projects have been impoverished and have even disappeared from official statistics. Concerning the present project, they observed that the Hanumantha Rao Committee found serious deficiencies in the rehabilitation package and in its implementation. They appealed to the Supreme Court to insure that those displaced by the project receive justice. They pointed out that in a country such as India, it is not sufficient to carry out an economic and financial cost-benefit analysis to ensure that the benefits over the costs justify the project. What is more important is a class-benefit analysis to determine which class of people pays the costs and which reaps the benefit. If the benefits of the project are twice the cost then justice requires that those who pay the primary cost, especially those who are displaced by the project, receive twice as much as they have lost. Among other things they argued that the offer of two acres of land to each displaced family is unfair, when two hectares of land have been promised to families displaced by another project, the Sardar Sarovar Project in Gujarat. Such discrimination, they argued, violates the constitutional right to be treated as equal under the law. The petitioners argued further that it is inappropriate for rehabilitation purposes to treat sons and unmarried daughters who are twenty-one as separate families.

Because the constitution of India accords voting rights to persons of eighteen, the age in question should be eighteen and not twenty-one. Therefore sons and unmarried daughters of eighteen should be treated as separate families. For the petitioners, the most critical issue concerning resettlement and rehabilitation remained the availability and acquisition of resettlement land. They argued that no further construction on the project should be permitted until adequate and appropriate land is identified in the Uttarakhand region so that villages and hamlets could be relocated together. Once this is done, construction work should be undertaken at an equal pace, with the acquisition of the land required, so that land is available for the relocation of families at least six months before their homes are submerged.[1]

Notes

Chapter 2

1. Ramachandra Guha, *The Unquiet Woods: Ecological Change and Peasant Resistance in the Himalaya* (New Delhi: Oxford University Press, 1991), 80.

2. Peter Kropotkin, *An Appeal to the Young* first appeared in French as "Aux Jeunes Gens," in Le Révolté, (June 25, July 10, August 7, 21, 1880). http://dwardmac.pitzer.edu/Anarchist_Archives/kropotkin/appealtoyoung.html.

3. Kropotkin, 1.

4. Ibid., 2–3.

5. Ibid., 3.

6. Ibid., 6–7.

7. M. K. Gandhi, *Hind Swaraj or Indian Home Rule* (1908) (Ahmedabad: Navajivan, 1938), 53.

8. *Hind Swaraj*, 56.

9. Ibid., 34.

10. Ibid., 57.

11. Ibid., 65–66, 69.

12. Ibid., 82.

13. Ibid., 90.

14. Vimala Thakar, "Dada Expounds Sarvodaya Philosophy," in *Philosophy of Sarvodya*, by Acharya Dada Dharmadhikari (Mumbai: Popular Prakashan, 2000), vii.

15. Bharat Dogra, *Living for Others: Vimla and Sunderlal Bahuguna* (New Delhi: Bharat Dogra, 1993), 23.

Chapter 3

1. In 1999 Bahuguna published a short pamphlet that gives a brief account of the year after his first arrest *The Making of a Social Worker: From Sunderlal to S. Maan* Singh. That pamphlet was the point of departure for the interviews in June of 2004 on which this chapter is based.

2. Ramachandra Guha, *The Unquiet Woods: Ecological Change and Peasant Resistance in the Himalaya* (New Delhi: Oxford University Press, 1991), 80.

Chapter 4

1. The narrative of this chapter is based on interviews I conducted with Sunderlal Bahuguna in Rishikesh on June 11 and in Old Tehri on June 14, 2004.

Chapter 5

1. Mirabehn, *The Spirit's Pilgrimage* (Arlington VA: Great Ocean Publishers, 1960), 20–21.

2. Ibid., 12.

3. Mira Behn, "Autobiographical Note," in Krishna Murthi Gupta, *Mira Behn, Gandhiji's Daughter Disciple: Birth Centenary Volume* (New Delhi: Himalaya Seva Sangh, 1992), 295.

4. Mirabehn, 58.

5. Krishna Murti Gupta, *Mira Behn, Gandhiji's Daughter Disciple: Birth Centenary Volume* (New Delhi: Himalaya Seva Sangh, 1992), 4–6. See also [http://www.mkgandhi.org/associates/Mirabehn.htm].

6. Mira Behn, "How Bapuji Trained his Followers." in Gupta, 285–86.

7. Mirabehn, 103, cited in Gupta, 9.

8. Mirabehn, 170.

9. Cited in ibid., 166.

10. Ibid., 171.

11. Ibid., 170–71.

12. Gupta, 14–15.

13. Ibid., 20–23.

14. Ibid., 24.

15. Mirabehn, *The Spirit's Pilgrimage* (Arlington VA: Great Ocean Publishers, 1960), 277 cited by Gupta, 24.

16. Mirabehn, 296, cited by Gupta, 32.

17. Mirabehn, 295, cited by Gupta, 33.

18. Gupta, 33.

19. Ibid., 34.

20. Mirabehn, 302.

21. Gupta, 34.

22. Mirabehn, 306.

23. Ibid., cited by Gupta, 36.

24. Gupta, 35–36.

25. J. P. Uniyal, "Memories of Mira Behn," in Gupta, 253–54.

26. Sunderlal Bahuguna "Fount of Motherly Love," in Gupta, 252.

27. Gupta, 62–63. Traditionally, one expresses respect in Hindi by adding the syllable *ji* to the name of the respected person. In the sentence above Mira Behn expresses respect for the Ganges River this way.

28. Gupta, 34, 100ff.

29. Ibid., 110.

30. Ibid.

31. Ibid., 141.

32. Ibid., 144–45.

33. Ibid., 141.

34. Ibid., 137.

35. "Something Wrong in the Himalayas," in Gupta, 145.

36. Ibid. 146.

37. Ibid, 146–47.

38. Sunderlal Bahuguna, "Fount of Motherly Love," in Gupta, 251.

39. Mirabehn, 307.

40. Ibid., 308.

41. Ibid., 312.

42. Sunderlal Bahuguna, "Fount of Motherly Love," in Gupta, 252.

Chapter 6

1. Bharat Dogra, *Living for Others: Vimla and Sunderlal Bahuguna* (New Delhi: Bharat Dogra, 1993), 27.

2. For the details of the life of Sarala Behn, I am very much indebted to Anupam Mishra of the Gandhi Peace Foundation, in New Delhi. He very kindly summarized each of the chapters of the Hindi edition of Sarala Behn's autobiography, *Practical Vedanta*, and provided me with much insight concerning her life and influence. Sarala Behn's autobiography has since been translated into English under the title *A Life in Two Worlds: Autobiography of Mahatma Gandhi's English Disciple*, translated by David Hopkins (Kausani Uttarakhand: Kasturba Mahila Utthan Mandal, 2010).

3. Mohandas K. Gandhi, *Constructive Program: Its Meaning and Place* (Ahmedabad: Navajivan, 1945), 14.

4. Ibid., 16.

5. Bharat Dogra, 11.

6. Ibid., 12–13.

7. Thomas Weber, *Gandhi as Disciple and Mentor* (Cambridge: Cambridge University Press, 2004), 151–52.

8. Glyn Richards, "Vinoba Bhave," in *A Source-Book of Modern Hinduism*, ed. Glyn Richards (London: Curzon, 1985), 198–199.

9. Madhav Gadgil and Ramachandra Guha, *Ecology and Equity: The Use and Abuse of Nature in Contemporary India* (New Delhi: Penguin, 1995), 64–65.

10. Vinoba Bhave, *Thoughts on Education* (Varanasi: Sarva Seva Sangh Prakashan, 1959), 72–78 cited in Richards, 202.

11. Cited in Vishwanath Tandon, *Acharya Vinoba Bhave* (Builders of Modern India), (New Delhi: Publications Division, Ministry of Information and Broadcasting, Government of India, 1992), 59.

12. Richards, 198.

13. Bharat Dogra, 14.

14. Acharya Dada Dharmadhikari, *Philosophy of Sarvodaya*, trans. S. S. Pandharipande (Mumbai: Popular Prakashan, 2000), 239.

15. Bharat Dogra, 16.

16. www.dlshq.org/saints/chida.htm.

Chapter 7

1. Ramachandra Guha, *The Unquiet Woods: Ecological Change and Peasant Resistance in the Himalaya* (New Delhi: Oxford University Press, 1991). Thomas Weber, *Hugging the Trees: The History of the Chipko Movement* (New Delhi: Viking, Penguin Books, 1988).

2. Guha, 15.

3. Ibid., 16.

4. Ibid., 20.

5. Ibid., 27.

6. Ibid., 22.

7. D. P. Joshi, "Logging History in India with Special Reference to U.P.," in *History of Forestry in India* ed. Ajay S. Rawat (New Delhi: Indus, 1991), 99.

8. Guha, 39–40.

9. Ibid., 42–43.

10. Ibid., 63–65.

11. Ibid., 67–69.

12. Ibid., 69.

13. Ibid., 66.

14. Ibid., 74.

15. Weber, 21; Guha, 76. Guha states that estimates of those killed vary from two to two hundred. Seventeen is the figure that is given in most of the sources. He also states that others frantically jumped into the Yamuna and drowned, while many villagers fled to the forest or into neighboring British ruled Jaunsar Bawar. While we cannot precisely determine the number of deaths, it is significant that deaths in such protests had not occurred before.

16. Krishna Murti Gupta, "The Chipko Movement: Its Genesis and Purpose," *Himalaya: Man and Nature* 2: 10 (March 1979), 15.

17. Weber, 39.

18. Anupam Mishra and Satyendra Tripathi, *Chipko Movement: Uttarakhand Women's Bid to Save Forest Wealth* (New Delhi: Gandhi Peace Foundation 1978), 3.

19. Weber, 36–8; Mishra and Tripathi, 3.

20. Weber, 37.

21. Guha, 156.

22. Mishra and Tripathi, 5.

23. Weber, 37–38.

24. Guha, 154.

25. Chandi Prasad Bhatt, "The Chipko Andolan: Forest Conservation Based on People's Power," in *The Fight for Survival*, ed. Anil Agarwal, Darryl D'Monte, and Ujwala Samarth (New Delhi: Centre for Science and Environment, 1987), 47–48; Weber, 61. Guha, 155–56.

26. Guha, 156.

27. Weber, 39.

28. Ibid., 40.

29. Guha, 157.

30. Weber, 40.

31. Ibid. In differing sources, the company in question is variously called Symonds and Simons. Cf. Bharat Dogra, *Forests and People: The Efforts in Western Himalayas to Re-establish a Long Lost Relationship* (Rishikesh: Himalaya Darshan Prakashan Samiti 1980), 47.

32. Mishra and Tripathi, 14.

33. Ibid.

34. Ibid.

35. Weber, 43.

36. Mishra and Tripathi, 27.

37. Ibid., 29–30.

38. Guha, 159.

39. J. C. Das and R. S. Negi, "Chipko Movement," in *Tribal Movements in India*, ed. K. S. Singh (New Delhi: Manohar, 1982), cited by Guha, 159.

40. Guha, 160.

41. Weber, 46–47.

42. Guha, 160.

Chapter 8

1. Guha, 172–73.

2. Weber, 46.

3. Ibid., 89.

4. Translated from the original Garhwali by Govind Raturi, in Bharat Dogra, *Living for Others: Vimla and Sunderlal Bahuguna* (New Delhi: Bharat Dogra, 1993), 54.

5. Translated Govind Raturi, in Bharat Dogra, 55.

6. Weber, 90.

7. Ibid., 89–90.

8. Sunderlal Bahuguna with Shree Padre, "The Forests Are Sacred," in *Chipko Message* (Silyara: Chipko Information Centre, 1981), 9–10.

9. Quoted in Ranchor Prime, *Hinduism and Ecology: Seeds of Truth* (London and New York: Cassell, 1992), 96.

10. Cf. Victor Turner, *Process, Performance and Pilgrimage: A Study in Comparative Symbolology* (New Delhi: Concept, 1979).

11. Vandana Shiva, *Staying Alive: Woman, Ecology, and Development* (New Delhi: Kali for Woman, 1989), 75. Jayanta Bandyopadhyay and Vandana Shiva, "Chipko: Rekindling India's Forest Culture," *The Ecologist* 17: 1 (1987), 30.

12. Guha, 162.

13. A. L. Basham, *The Wonder That Was India* (New York: Grove, 1959), 23–24; See also Steven G. Darian, *The Ganges in Myth and History* (Honolulu: University Press of Hawaii, 1978), 42–43.

14. Adapted from *The Concise Srimad Bhagavatam*, trans. and ed. Swami Venkatesananda (Albany: State University of New York Press, 1989), 251.

15. "A Humble Life: Indu Tikekar Linked Environmentalism and Spirituality," *Down to Earth* 15:15 (December 2006), 45.

16. Bidisha Kumar unpublished manuscript December 2006.

17. *Down to Earth* 15:15 (December 2006), 45.

18. Weber, 51.

19. Ibid.

20. Ibid., 51–52.

21. Ibid., 52–53.

22. Vandana Shiva, *Staying Alive: Woman, Ecology, and Development* (New Delhi: Kali for Woman, 1989), 77.

23. Kisan Mehta, "Barbe Baker, Crusader and World Citizen," in *Richard St. Barbe Baker: Man of the Trees, A Centenary Tribute,* ed. Indira Ramish and N. D. Jayal (New Delhi: INTACH).

24. Vandana Shiva, *Staying Alive,* 75–76; Jayanta Bandyopadhyay and Vandana Shiva, "Chipko: Rekindling India's Forest Culture," *The Ecologist* 17:1 (1987), 30; Weber, 53–56.

25. Guha, 166.

26. Weber, 55–56. The Chief Minister at the time was Ram Naresh Yadav, who left office the following month.

27. Mohandas K. Gandhi, *Gandhi's Autobiography: The Story of My Experiments with Truth,* trans. Mahadev Desai (Washington D.C: Public Affairs, 1948), 404.

28. Gandhi, *Autobiography,* 391.

29. Ibid., 418.

30. Ibid., 418–19.

31. Ibid., 419.

32. Mohandas K. Gandhi, *Young India,* March 24, 1920.

33. *Autobiography,* 420.

34. Ibid., 520–22.

35. Ibid., 526.

36. Ibid., 527.

37. Ibid., 527–28.

38. Gandhi, *Harijan,* December 21, 1947.

39. Ibid., *Collected Works,* 13: 295.

40. Ibid., cited by Bart Gruzalski in *On Gandhi* (Belmont CA: Wadsworth, 2001), 6–7.

41. Ibid., *Harijan*, July 26, 1942.

42. Ibid., *Collected Works*, 48: 189; 69: 69; 83: 317.

43. Ibid., *Harijan*, Sept. 9, 1933.

44. Ibid., December 21, 1947.

45. Weber, 69 citing *Hindustan Times*, January 1979.

46. Gandhi, *Harijan* December 21, 1947.

47. Interview with Bahuguna, Rishikesh, June 11, 2004.

48. Interview with Bahuguna, Chennai, January 13, 2006.

49. Interview with Bahuguna, Old Tehri, June 24, 1998.

Chapter 9

1. Weber, 47.

2. Ibid., 67.

3. Theodore Roszak, "Introduction," *Small Is Beautiful: Economics as if People Mattered* (New York: Harper and Row, 1973), 5–6.

4. E. F. Schumacher, *Small Is Beautiful: Economics as if People Mattered* (New York: Harper and Row, 1973), 51–53.

5. Ibid., 45–46.

6. Ibid., 48.

7. Ibid., 46 (Schumacher's emphasis).

8. Ibid., 54.

9. Ibid., 47.

10. Ibid., 313.

11. Ibid., 60.

12. Ibid., 61.

13. Ibid., 62.

14. Ibid., 63–64.

15. J. C. Kumarappa, *Economy of Permanence* (Varanasi: Sarva Seva Sangh Prakashan, 1997, first published 1945), 18–30.

16. Sunderlal Bahuguna, "The Man Who Dedicated His Life to Forests," in *Richard St. Barbe Baker: Man of the Trees, A Centenary Tribute*, ed. Indira Ramesh and N. D. Jayal (New Delhi: INTACH).

17. Interview with Bahuguna, June 14, 2004, Old Tehri.

18. Sunderlal Bahuguna, "A Tribute to St. Barbe, Man of the Trees," in *Richard St. Barbe Baker: Man of the Trees, a Centenary Tribute*, ed. Indira Ramesh and N. D. Jayal (New Delhi: INTACH). [http://gyanpedia.in/tft/Resources/books/saintbaker.pdf].

19. Richard St. Barbe Baker "Reverence for Life—Reverence for Trees," in *Richard St. Barbe Baker: Man of the Trees, a Centenary Tribute*, ed. (New Delhi: INTACH, 1981).

20. Interview with Bahuguna, June 14, 2004, Old Tehri.

21. Ibid.

22. Richard St. Barbe, *My Life My Trees* (Forres: Finhorn, 1979, first published London: Lutterworth, 1970), 10–11. Cf. Indira Ramesh and N. D. Jayal, "Preface," *Richard St. Barbe Baker: Man of the Trees, a Centenary Tribute* (New Delhi: INTACH, 1989).

23. Richard St. Barbe Baker, *My Life, My Trees*, 11, also in *Man of the Trees: Selected Writings of Richard St. Barbe Baker,* ed. Karen Gridley (Willits, CA: Ecology Action, 1989), 19–20.

24. Richard St. Barbe Baker, *My Life, My Trees*, 21. Cf. Karen Gridley, "Introduction: Richard St. Barbe Baker, the Man," in *Man of the Trees: Selected Writings of Richard St Barbe Baker*, ed. Karen Gridley (Willits, CA: Ecology Action), 8, 62.

25. Richard St. Barbe Baker, *My Life, My Trees*, 37.

26. Ibid., 50.

27. Ibid., 60–66.

28. Ibid., 67–79, 78.

29. Ibid., 94ff.

30. Kisan Mehta, "Barbe Baker, Crusader and World Citizen," in *Richard St. Barbe Baker: Man of the Trees, a Centenary Tribute,* ed. Indira Ramesh and N. D. Jayal (New Delhi: INTACH).

31. Richard St. Barbe Baker, "Reverence for Life—Reverence for Trees," in *Richard St. Barbe Baker: Man of the Trees, a Centenary Tribute,* ed. Indira Ramesh and N. D. Jayal (New Delhi: INTACH).

32. Ibid.

33. Ibid.

34. Richard St. Barbe Baker, *My Life, My Trees*, 55.

35. Interview with Bahuguna, June 14, 2004, Old Tehi.

36. Richard St. Barbe Baker, Speech delivered at a public reception in Bombay, August 20, 1980, in *Richard St. Barbe Baker: Man of the Trees, a Centenary Tribute*, ed. Indira Ramesh and N. D. Jayal (New Delhi: INTACH).

37. Sunderlal Bahuguna, "A Tribute to St. Barbe, Man of the Trees," in *Richard St. Barbe Baker: Man of the Trees, a Centenary Tribute*, ed. Indira Ramesh and N. D. Jayal (New Delhi: INTACH).

38. Indira Ramesh and N. D. Jayal, eds., *Richard St. Barbe Baker: Man of the Trees, a Centenary Tribute* (New Delhi: INTACH).

39 Richard St Barbe Baker, "Chipko-Hug to the Tree People," *Chipko Message* (Silyara: Chipko Information Centre, 1981), 5. Cf. Weber, 68.

40. Sunderlal Bahuguna, "A Tribute to St. Barbe, Man of the Trees."

41. Madhav Gadgil, "The Indian Heritage of a Conservation Ethic," in *Ethical Perspectives on Environmental Issues in India*, ed. George A. James (New Delhi: APH, 1989), 150.

42. Kisan Mehta, "Barbe Baker, Crusader and World Citizen," in *Richard St. Barbe Baker: Man of the Trees, a Centenary Tribute,* Indira Ramesh and N. D. Jayal (New Delhi: INTACH).

43. Ron Rabin, "St. Barbe and Sunderlal," in *Richard St. Barbe Baker: Man of the Trees, a Centenary Tribute,* ed. Indira Ramesh and N. D. Jayal (New Delhi: INTACH).

Chapter 10

1. David Landis Barnhill and Roger S. Gottlieb, eds., *Deep Ecology and World Religions: New Essays on Sacred Ground* (Albany: State University of New York Press, 2001), 4–8.

2. *Indian Express,* February 1, 1979, cited in Weber, 70.

3. Weber, 157 n7.

4. Ibid., 69.

5. *The Statesman,* April 16, 1979, cited in Weber, 70.

6. *Hindustan Times,* April 16, 1979, cited in Weber, 71.

7. Interview with Bahuguna, January 10, 2007, Amritsar.

8. Weber, 71.

9. Weber, 73. cf. Anil Agarwal and Sunita Narain, *The State of India's Environment 1982: A Citizen's Report* (New Delhi: Centre for Science and Environment, 1982), 42–43.

10. Anil Agarwal, *The State of India's Environment,* 43.

11. Jayanta Bandyopadhyay and Vandana Shiva, "Chipko: Rekindling India's Forest Culture," *The Ecologist* 17:1 (1987), 34.

12. Guha, 182–83.

13. Ibid., 179. Cf. Sunderlal Bahuguna, *Walking with the Chipko Message* (Silyara: Chipko Information Centre, 1983), 18.

14. Sunderlal Bahuguna, *Walking with the Chipko Message,* 19.

15. Ibid., 18–19.

16. Weber, 73.

17. J. Bandyopadhyay and V. Shiva, "Chipko," *Seminar* 330 (February 1987), 38.

18. Ibid., 39.

19. Ramachandra Guha, "Communications," *Seminar* 334 (June 1987), 45–46.

20. Ibid., 47.

21. J. Bandyopadhyay and V. Shiva, "Communication," *Seminar* 336 (August 1987), 42.

22. Ibid., 43.

23. Ibid., 44.

24. Ibid., 45.

25. Bandyopadhyay and Shiva, "Chipko," 36.

26. Ramachandra Guha, "Communications," *Seminar* 334 (June 1987), 46.

27. Bandyopadhyay and Shiva, "Communication," 45.

28. Richard St. Barbe Baker, *Chipko-Hug to the Tree People,* in *Chipko Message* (Silyara: Chipko Information Center, 1981), 4.

29. Richard St. Barbe Baker, "Reverence for Life—Reverence for Trees," in *Richard St. Barbe Baker: Man of the Trees, a Centenary Tribute*, ed. Indira Ramesh and N. D. Jayal (New Delhi: INTACH, 1981).

30. Weber, 157 n8.

31. Indira Gandhi, "Launching the World Conservation Strategy in India," Keynote address at New Delhi 6, March 1980," in *Indira Gandhi on Environment*, (New Delhi: Department of Environment, Government of India, 1984), 38 also in Weber Appendix (iv), 139.

32. Indira Gandhi, 34–35, in Weber, 137.

33. Indira Gandhi, "Conserving Our Forests." Speech to the eighteenth meeting of the Central Board of Forestry at New Delhi, 25 August, 1980, in *Indira Gandhi on Environment* (New Delhi: Department of Environment, Government of India, 1984), 49.

34. Weber, 77, 157, n8.

35. St. Barbe Baker, *Chipko-Hug to the Tree People*, 5.

Chapter 11

1. Sunderlal Bahuguna, *Walking with the Chipko Message* (Silyara: Chipko Information Centre, 1983), 1–2.

2. Pandurang Ummayya and J. Bandyopadhyay, "The Trans-Himalayan Chipko Footmarch," *The Ecologist* 13:5 (1983), 179.

3. Pandurang Ummayya, "An Interview with Chipko Bahuguna," *The Ecologist* 13:5 (1983), 183.

4. Bahuguna, *Walking with the Chipko Message*, 6.

5. Bharat Dogra, *Living for Others: Vimla and Sunderlal Bahuguna*, 34.

6. Bahuguna, *Walking with the Chipko Message*, 7.

7. Ummayya and Bandyopadhyay, "The Trans-Himalayan Chipko Footmarch," 180. Dogra, 36.

8. Weber, 105, Ummayya and Bandyopadhyay, 180.

9. Bahuguna, "Fount of Motherly Love," in Gupta, 252.

10. Ummayya and Bandyopadhyay, 180.

11. Bahuguna, *Walking with the Chipko Message*, 7.

12. Sunderlal Bahuguna, "What Man Does to Mountain, and to Man: A Healing Message for Violent Times," in *Fire in the Heart, Firewood on the Back*, ed. Tenzin Rigzin (Amritsar: All India Pingalwara Charitable Society, 2005), 82.

13. Ibid., 82.

14. Ummayya and Bandyopadhyay, 181.

15. Ibid., Bahuguna 83.

16. Ummayya and Bandyopadhyay, 182.

17. Ibid., Bahuguna, *Walking with the Chipko Message*, 9

18. Bahuguna, *Walking with the Chipko Message*, 10; Weber, 108.

19. Weber, 109; Bahuguna, *Walking with the Chipko Message*, 11. Ummayya and Bandyopadhyay, 182.

20. Ummayya and Bandyopadhyay, 182.

21. Interview with Ramakrishna, December 30, 2006.

22. Ummayya and Bandyopadhyay, 182.

23. Bahuguna, *Walking with the Chipko Message*, 13. Ummayya and Bandhyopadhyay, 183.

24. Pandurang Ummayya, "An Interview with Chipko Bahuguna," *The Ecologist* 13:5 (1983), 183.

25. Bahuguna, *Walking with the Chipko Message*, 14.

26. Pandurang Ummayya, "An Interview with Chipko Bahuguna," 183.

27. Bahuguna, *Walking with the Chipko Message*, 20–21.

28. Bahuguna, "What Man Does to Mountain, and to Man: A Healing Message for Violent Times," 87.

Chapter 12

1. Anuradha Dutt, "The Gentle Crusader," *The Illustrated Weekly of India*, January 21, 1990, reprinted in *Fire in the Heart, Firewood on the Back*, ed. Tenzin Rigzin (Amritsar: All India Pingalwara Charitable Society, 2005), 53.

2. Sunderlal Bahuguna, "Tehri Dam: Blueprint for Disaster," in *Fire in the Heart, Firewood on the Back*, ed. Tenzin Rigzin (Amritsar: All India Pingalwara Charitable Society, 2005), 95.

3. Sunderlal Bahuguna, "Development and Environment," in *Chipko Message: Development, Environment and Survival* (Tehri: Chipko Information Center, 1997), 13.

4. Sunderlal Bahuguna, "Make Silent Majority Vocal," in *Save Ganga*, ed. Inderjit Kaur (Amritsar: All India Pingalwara Society, 1997), 5.

5. Vijay Paranjpye, *Evaluating the Tehri Dam: An Extended Cost Benefit Appraisal*, Studies in Ecology and Sustainable Development 1 (New Delhi: Indian National Trust for Art and Cultural Heritage, 1988), 22–31.

6. Anuradha Dutt, "The Gentle Crusader," in *Fire in the Heart, Firewood on the Back*, ed. Tenzin Rigzin (Amritsar: All India Pingalwara Charitable Society, 2005), 54.

7. Paranjpye, 24.

8. Sunderlal Bahuguna, "Tehri Dam: A Blueprint for Disaster," *Fire in the Heart, Firewood on the Back*, edited by Tenzin Rigzin (Amritsar: All India Pingalwara Charitable Society, 2005), 90.

9. Dutt, "The Gentle Crusader," 55.

10. Paranjpye, 24.

11. Paranjpye, 26–27. According to Bahuguna this writ petition was filed in 1987 and signed by Virendra Dutt Saklani, Vidya Sagar secretary of the district, and Sunderlal. Sunderlal Bahuguna, "Tehri Dam: A Blueprint for Disaster," 90.

12. Paranjpye, 27; Sunderlal Bahuguna "Tehri Dam: A Blueprint for Disaster," 91.

13. Devashish Mukerji, "Moving Mountains," in *Fire in the Heart Firewood on the Back: Writings on and by Himalayan Crusader Sunderlal Bahuguna*, ed. Tenzin Rigzin (Amritsar: All India Pingalwara Charitable Society, 2005), 16.

14. Sunderlal Bahuguna, "The Trick Unveiled," in *Fire in the Heart Firewood on the Back: Writings on and by Himalayan Crusader Sunderlal Bahuguna*, ed. Tenzin Rigzin (Amritsar: All India Pingalwara Charitable Society, 2005), 165.

15. Devashish Mukerji, "Moving Mountains," *The Week*, May 3, 1992, in *Fire in the Heart Firewood on the Back: Writings on and by Himalayan Crusader Sunderlal Bahuguna*, ed. Tenzin Rigzin (All India Pingalwara Charitable Society, 2005), 16; "Sunderlal Bahuguna's Crusade" in *Fire in the Heart Firewood on the Back: Writings on and by Himalayan Crusader Sunderlal Bahuguna*, 64.

16. Sunderlal Bahuguna, "The Trick Unveiled," in Firewood on the Back: Writings on and by Himalayan Crusader Sunderlal Bahuguna, 165.

17. Anuradha Dutt, "If the Himalayas Die, this Country is Nowhere: An Interview with Sunderlal Bahuguna," Rediff on the Net http://uttarakhand.prayaga.org/bahuguna.html.

18. Surendar Kumar and A.K. Mahajan, "The Uttarkashi Earthquake of 20 October 1991: Field Observations," *Terra Nova* 6 (1) 1994, 95–99.

19. Ashish Kothari, "Memorable Fast," *Mainstream*, April 18, 1992, 3.

20. Ajit Bhattacharjea, "The Old Man and the Dam," *Outlook*, June 26, 1996, in *Fire in the Heart Firewood on the Back: Writings on and by Himalayan Crusader Sunderlal Bahuguna*, ed. Tenzin Rigzin (Amritsar: All India Pingalwara Charitable Society, 2005), 21–22.

21. Devashish Mukerji, "Moving Mountains," *The Week*, May 3, 1992, in *Fire in the Heart Firewood on the Back: Writings on and by Himalayan Crusader Sunderlal Bahuguna*, ed. Tenzin Rigzin (Amritsar: All India Pingalwara Charitable Society, 2005), 16.

22. Sunderlal Bahuguna "The Trick Unveiled," in *Fire in the Heart, Firewood on the Back: Writings on and by Himalayan Crusader Sunderlal Bahuguna*, ed. Tenzin Rigzin, (Amritsar: All India Pingalwara Charitable Society, 2005), 166.

23. Devashish Mukerji, "Moving Mountains," *The Week*, May 3, 1992, in *Fire in the Heart, Firewood on the Back: Writings on and by Himalayan Crusader Sunderlal Bahuguna*, ed. Tenzin Rigzin (Amritsar: All India Pingalwara Charitable Society, 2005), 17.

24. Bahuguna, "The Trick Unveiled," 166.

25. Ashish Kothari, "Memorable Fast," *Mainstream*, April 18, 1992, 3.

26. Shinya Ishizaka, "The Anti Tehri Dam Movement as New Social Movement and Gandhism," *Journal of the Japanese Association for South Asian Studies* 18 (2006), 80.

27. Sunderlal Bahuguna, "The Rulers Should Know That the Himalayas Are for Water and Not for Revenue." The Rediff Interview July 8, 2000. [www.rediff.com/news/2000/jul/08inter.htm].

28. Sunderlal Bahuguna, "The Trick Unveiled," 166; Shinya Ishizaka, 80.

29. Sunderlal Bahuguna, "The Trick Unveiled," 167–69.

30. Ibid., 169.

31. Ajit Bhattacharjea, "The Old Man and the Dam," *Outlook*, June 6, 1996. In *Fire in the Heart, Firewood on the Back: Writings on and by Himalayan Crusader Sunderlal Bahuguna*, ed. Tenzin Rigzin (Amritsar: All India Pingalwara Charitable Society, 2005), 21.

32. Madhu Kishwar, "A Victory for Satyagraha: Prime Minister Concedes a Review of Tehri Dam," *Manushi* 94 (1996), 18–19.

33. Sunderlal Bahuguna, "The Trick Unveiled," 170–71.

34. Kishwar, "A Victory for Satyagraha: Prime Minister Concedes a Review of Tehri Dam," 18–19.

35. Anuradha Dutt, "If the Himalayas Die, This Country Is Nowhere: An Interview with Sunderlal Bahuguna." Rediff on the Net http://uttarakhand. prayaga.org/bahuguna.html.

Chapter 13

1. Sunderlal Bahuguna, "The Rulers Should Know That the Himalayas Are for Water and Not for Revenue." [The Rediff Interview July 8, 2000. www.rediff. com/news/2000/jul/08inter.htm].

2. Fred Pearce. "Building a Disaster: The Monumental Folly of India's Tehri Dam." *The Ecologist* 21:3 (May/June 1991). "Himalayan Earthquake Confirms Worst Fears over Dam," *New Scientist* 1793 (November 2, 1991); Rob Butler, "The Dam That Should Not Be Built" *New Scientist* 1753 (January 26, 1991); Bob Holmes, "Big Crunch Looms for Northern India," *New Scientist* 1956 (December 17, 1994).

3. Anjani Khanna, "Tehri: Hanging over Troubled Waters," *Down to Earth* (May 31, 1992); "Tehri Report Delayed," *Down to Earth* (July 31, 1992); "Tehri Tirade" *Down to Earth* (June 30, 1995); "Shaky Revelations," *Down to Earth* (April 15, 1996); "Is the Tehri Dam Safe?" *Down to Earth* (June 15, 1998); "Development or Destruction," *Down to Earth* (March 31, 1999).

4. R. Ramachandran, "The Tehri Turnaround," *Frontline* 18:10 (May 12–25, 2001).

5. "29 March 1999 Chamoli Earthquake: A Preliminary Report on Earthquake-induced Landslides Using IRS-1C/1D data." [www.ias.ac.in/currsci. july 10/articles 10.htm].

6. "Indian Gujarat Earthquake, 26 January 2001," *Global Education*. www.globaleducation.edna.edu.au/globaled/go/pid/1248. "26 January 2001 Bhuj Earthquake, Gujarat, India." [http://cires.colorado.edu/~bilham/Gujarat2001.html].

7. Rao, Shivaji. *Tehri Dam Is a Time Bomb* (New Delhi: Vani Printers) 1992; "Tehri Dam a Boon or a Curse for India?" [www.gitam.edu/cos/env/tehri/ tehridam.html].

8. Emma Mawdsley, "The Abuse of Religion and Ecology: The Vishva Hindu Parishad and Tehri Dam," *Worldviews* 9:1 (2005), 7–8.

9. "Singal Threatens Fast against Tehri Dam," *The Hindu*, March 24, 2001.

10. Prem Panicker, "Bahuguna at Kumbh, Sounds Alarm over Damming Ganga," [www.rediff.com/news/2001/jan/20kumbh.htm].

11. T. K. Rajalakshmi, "A Saffron Twist: The Vishwa Hindu Parishad's Opposition to the Tehri Dam on Religious Grounds Sidesteps the Real Issues Involved in the Matter," *Frontline* 18:08 (April 14–27, 2001).

12. Mukul Sharma, "Saffronising Green," *Seminar* 516 (2002), 3 [www.indiaseminar.com/2002/516/516%20sharma.htm].

13. Mukul Sharma, "Saffronizing Green." 6.

14. Emma Mawdsley, "The Abuse of Religion and Ecology: The Vishva Hindu Parishad and Tehri Dam," *Worldviews* 9:1 (2005), 1–24.

15. Interview, June 14, 2002, Old Tehri.

16. Mohandas K. Gandhi, "From Yeravda Mandir: Essays on the Observations," in *Vows and Observations*, ed. John Strohmeier (Berkeley: Berkeley Hills Books), 141.

17. Mohandas K. Gandhi, "The Eleven Observances," in *Vows and Observances*, ed. John Strohmeier Berkeley: Berkeley Hills Books, 1999, 33.

18. Mohandas K. Gandhi, "From Yeravda Mandir: Essays on the Observances," in *Vows and Observances* ed. John Strohmeier (Berkeley: Berkeley Hills Books, 1999), 141–42.

19. Sunderlal Bahuguna, "Peoples Programme for Change," in *Fire in the Heart Firewood on the Back: Writings on and by Himalayan Crusader Sunderlal Bahuguna*, ed. Tenzin Rigzin (Amritsar: All India Pingalwara Charitable Society, 2005), 115–16.

20. Interview, August 11, 2005.

21. C. K. Chandramohan, "Tehri Dam Work at a Standstill," *The Hindu*, April 5, 2001.

22. J. P. Shukla, "Damming the Protests," *The Hindu*, April 29, 2001.

23. Shinya Ishizaka, "The Anti Tehri Dam Movement as New Social Movement and Gandhism," *Journal of the Japanese Association for South Asian Studies*, 18 (2006), 82.

24. Jayanta Bandyopadhyay, "From Environmental Conflicts to Sustainable Mountain Transformation: Ecological Action in the Garhwal Himalaya," in *Grassroots Environmental Action: Peoples Participation in Sustainable Development*, ed. D. Ghai and J. Vivian (London: Routledge 1992), 273, 276; cf. Jayanta Bandyopadhyay, "Sustainability and Survival in the Mountain Context," *Ambio: A Journal of Human Environment* 21:4 (June 1992), 301–02.

25. Shinya Ishizaka, "The Anti Tehri Dam Movement as New Social Movement and Gandhism," *Journal of the Japanese Association for South Asian Studies* 18 (2006), 82.

26. Soma Wadhwa, "Drown Town," *Outlook*, December 31, 2001.

27. S. M. A. Kazmi, "No Tears, Tehri Drones in Anger before Deluge," *The Indian Express*, December 10, 2001.

28. *Outlook*, December 31, 2001.

29. *Indian Express*, December 10, 2001.

30. Vijay Paranjpye, *Evaluating the Tehri Dam: an Extended Cost Benefit Appraisal*, Studies in Ecology and Sustainable Development 1 (New Delhi: Indian National Trust for Art and Cultural Heritage, 1988) 26–27.

31. Correspondence, August 29, September 1, 2001.

32. Fred Pearce and Rob Butler, "The Dam That Should Not Be Built: India Is Building the Largest Dam in Asia in a Valley Beset by Earthquakes and Landslips," *New Scientist*, January 26, 1991.

33. Sunderlal Bahuguna, "Tehri Dam: A Prayer for Hon. Supreme Court" (unpublished paper).

34. Jayanta Bandyopadhyay, "From Environmental Conflicts to Sustainable Mountain Transformation: Ecological Action in the Garhwal Himalaya," in *Grassroots Environmental Action: Peoples Participation in Sustainable Development*, ed. D. Ghai and J. Vivian (London: Routledge 1992), 276–77.

35. Shinya Ishizaka, "The Anti Tehri Dam Movement as New Social Movement and Gandhism," *Journal of the Japanese Association for South Asian Studies* 18 (2006), 82.

36. In the Supreme Court of India Civil Original Jurisdiction, Writ Petition No. 295 of 1992, N.D. Jayal and Anr. VS Union of India and Others, 53.

37. Ibid., 13–16.

38. Siddharth Narrain, "The Tehri Project: The Judicial Go-ahead." Frontline 20:20 (September 27–October 10, 2003). [www.hinduonnet.com/fline/fl2020/stories/20031010002810000.htm].

39. *The Hindu* July 31, 2004. [www.thehindu.com/2004/07/31/stories/200407/3104720500.htm].

40. *The Telegraph*, August 2, 2004.

41. "My Fight Is to Save the Himalayas," Interview with Sunderlal Bahuguna, *Frontline* 21:17 (August 14–27, 2004). [www.flonnet.com/fl2117/stories/20040827002803600.htm].

Chapter 14

1. Translated from the Hindi by Bidisha Kumar.

2. Gandhi, *Collected Works*, vol. 48, 107–108; Gandhi, *Vows and Observances*, ed. John Strohmeier (Berkeley: Berkeley Hills Books, 1999), 29–33.

3. Gandhi, *Collected Works*, vol. 15, 171.

4. "In Conversation: Sunderlal Bahuguna with George James," *Seminar* January 2004.

5. Gandhi, *Collected Works*, vol. 15, 109.

6. Olof Alexandersson, *Living Water: Viktor Schauberger and the Secrets of Natural Energy*, trans. Kit and Charles Zweigbergk (Dublin: Gateway, 1990), 19–23.

7. Lynn White, Jr. "The Historical Roots of Our Ecologic Crisis," *Science* 155 (1967), 1203–07.

8. Cf. Lance E. Nelson, "Reading the Bhagavadgita from an Ecological Perspective," in *Hinduism and Ecology: The Intersection of Earth, Sky, and Water* (Cambridge MA: Harvard University Press, 2000), 127–64. "The Dualism of Nondualism: Advaita Vedanta and the Irrelevance of Nature," in *Purifying the Earthly Body of God*, ed. Lance E. Nelson (Albany: State University of New York Press, 1998), 61–88; J. Baird Callicott, *Earth's Insights: A Multicultural Survey of Ecological Ethics from the Mediterranean Basin to the Australian Outback* (Berkeley: University of California Press, 1994).

9. Callicott, *Earth's Insights*, 48.

10. Sunderlal Bahuguna, "The Crisis of Civilisation and the Message of Culture in the Context of Environment," in *Fire in the Heart, Firewood on the Back*, ed. Tenzin Rigzin (Amritsar: All India Pingalwara Charitable Society, 2005), 126.

11. Bahuguna, "The Crisis of Civilisation," 125–26.

12. Ibid., 126, 128–32.

13. Sunderlal Bahuguna, "Development and Environment," in *Chipko Message: Development, Environment and Survival* (Tehri: Chipko Information Centre, 1997), 7.

14. Bahuguna, "The Crisis of Civilisation," 134.

15. Ibid., 134–38.

16. Cited by T. N. Khooshoo, *Mahatma Gandhi: An Apostle of Applied Human Ecology* (New Delhi: Tata Energy Research Institute, 1996), 69.

17. Bahuguna, "The Crisis of Civilisation," 139.

18. Vinoba Bhave, *Talks on the Gita* (Wardha: Paramdham Prakashan, 2007).

Appendix 2

1. Correspondence with Shekhar Singh, September 1, 2001.

Selected Bibliography

Agarwal, Anil. "Human-Nature Interactions in a Third-World Country." In *Ethical Perspectives on Environmental Issues in India,* edited by George A. James. New Delhi: A.P.H., 1999.

———, Darryl D'Monte, and Samarth Ujwala, eds. *The Fight for Survival: People's Action for Environment.* New Delhi: Centre for Science and Environment, 1987.

———, and Sunita Narain. *The State of India's Environment 1982: A Citizen's Report.* New Delhi: Centre for Science and Environment, 1982.

Alexandersson, Olof. *Living Water: Viktor Schauberger and the Secrets of Natural Energy.* Translated by Kit and Charles Zweigbergk. Dublin: Gateway, 1990.

Alveres, Claude. "The Gentle Crusader." In *Fire in the Heart, Firewood on the Back,* edited by Tenzin Rigzin. Amritsar: All India Pingalwara Charitable Society, 2005. Originally Published in *The Illustrated Weekly of India* June 23, 1985.

———. "Yes Prime Minister, Re-enacted All over Again." In *Fire in the Heart, Firewood on the Back,.* edited by Tenzin Rigzin. Amritsar: All India Pingalwara Charitable Society, 2005. Originally Published in *The Observer* April 8 1992.

Bahuguna, Sunderlal. "The Man Who Dedicated His Life to Forests." In *Richard St. Barbe Baker: Man of the Trees, a Centenary Tribute,* edited by Indira Ramesh and N. D. Jayal. New Delhi: INTACH, Date Unknown.

———. *Chipko Message.* Silyara: Chipko Information Centre, 1981.

———. *Walking with the Chipko Message.* Silyara: Chipko Information Centre, 1983.

———. "What Man Does to Mountain, and to Man: A Healing Message for Violent Times." In *Fire in the Heart, Firewood on the Back,* edited by Tenzin Rigzin. Amritsar: All India Pingalwara Charitable Society, 2005. Originally Published in *Manushi,* 1983.

———. *Chipko Message.* Tehri: Chipko Information Centre, 1984.

———. "Interview: The Forests Are Sacred." In *Fire in the Heart, Firewood on the Back,* edited by Tenzin Rigzin. Amritsar: All India Pingalwara Charitable Society, 2005. Originally Published in *The Sunday Herald* April 22 (1984).

———. *A Walk in the Woods.* Amritsar: Pingalwara, 1986.

———. *The Chipko Message.* Tehri: Chipko Information Centre, 1987.

————. "Tehri Dam: A Blueprint for Disaster." In *Fire in the Heart, Firewood on the Back*, edited by Tenzin Rigzin. Amritsar: All India Pingalwara Charitable Society, 2005. Originally Published in *Imprint* (1988).

————. "Interview: Sunderlal Bahuguna's Crusade." In *Fire in the Heart, Firewood on the Back*, edited by Tenzin Rigzin. Amritsar: All India Pingalwara Charitable Society, 2005. Originally Published in *Manushi* May–June (1992).

————. *Chipko Message 1994: Save Himalayas*. Tehri: Save Himalaya Movement, 1994.

————. *"Yes" to Life: "No" to Death*. Varanasi: Sarva Seva Sangh Prakashan, 1995.

————. *The Himalayan Threat*. Tehri: Ganga Himalaya Kuti, 1996.

————. Chipko *Message: Development, Environment and Survival*. Tehri: Chipko Information Centre, 1997.

————. "Development and Environment." in *Chipko Message: Development, Environment and Survival*, Tehri: Chipko Information Centre, 1997.

————. "Priorities of IX Plan—A Grassroot View." In *Chipko Message: Development, Environment and Survival*. Tehri: Chipko Information Centre, 1997.

————. "Save Himalaya—With Special Reference to Tourism." In *Chipko Message: Development, Environment and Survival*. Tehri: Chipko Information Centre, 1997.

————. "Make Silent Majority Vocal." In *Save Ganga*, edited by Inderjit Kaur. Amritsar: All India Pingalwara Society, 1997.

————. *The Making of a Social Worker: From Sunderlal to S. Maan Singh*. Tehri: Ganga Himalaya Kuti, 1999.

————. "Towards Basic Change in Land Use." In *Fire in the Heart, Firewood on the Back*, edited by Tenzin Rigzin. Amritsar: All India Pingalwara Charitable Society, 2005.

————. "The Crisis of Civilisation and the Message of Culture in the Context of Environment. In *Fire in the Heart, Firewood on the Back*, edited by Tenzin Rigzin. Amritsar: All India Pingalwara Charitable Society, 2005.

————. "Technical Education and the Environment." In *Fire in the Heart, Firewood on the Back*, edited by Tenzin Rigzin. Amritsar: All India Pingalwara Charitable Society, 2005.

————. "The Crisis of Democracy and the Way Out." In *Fire in the Heart, Firewood on the Back*, edited by Tenzin Rigzin. Amritsar: All India Pingalwara Charitable Society, 2005.

————. "The Voice of the Birds—A Tribute to Dr. Salim Ali." In *Fire in the Heart, Firewood on the Back*, edited by Tenzin Rigzin. Amritsar: All India Pingalwara Charitable Society, 2005.

————. "Saving the Bugyal and Gomukh Region." In *Fire in the Heart, Firewood on the Back*, edited by Tenzin Rigzin. Amritsar: All India Pingalwara Charitable Society, 2005.

————. "Peoples Programme for Change." In *Fire in the Heart, Firewood on the Back*, edited by Tenzin Rigzin. Amritsar: All India Pingalwara Charitable Society, 2005.

———. "The Trick Unveiled." In *Fire in the Heart, Firewood on the Back,* edited by Tenzin Rigzin. Amritsar: All India Pingalwara Charitable Society, 2005.

———. *The Road to Survival.* edited by P. K. Uthaman. Kozhikode Kerala: Mathrubhumi, 2009.

———, with Shree Padre. "The Forests Are Sacred." In *Chipko Message.* Silyara: Chipko Information Centre, 1981.

Bandyopadhyay, Jayanta. "From Environmental Conflicts to Sustainable Mountain Transformation: Ecological Action in the Garhwal Himalaya." In *Grassroots Environmental Action: Peoples Participation in Sustainable Development,* edited by D. Ghai and J. Vivian. London: Routledge 1992.

———, and Vandana Shiva. "Chipko: Rekindling India's Forest Culture," *The Ecologist,* 17: 1 (1987).

Bankoti, T. S. *Chipko Movement.* New Delhi: Global Vision, 2008.

Barnhill, David L., and Roger Gottlieb, eds. *Deep Ecology and World Religion: New Essays on Sacred Ground.* Albany: State University of New York Press, 2001.

Basham, A. L. *The Wonder That Was India.* New York: Grove, 1959.

Bhatt, Chandi Prasad. "The Chipko Andolan: Forest Conservation Based on People's Power." In *The Fight for Survival,* edited by Anil Agarwal, Darryl D'Monte, and Ujwala Samarth. New Delhi: Centre for Science & Environment, 1987.

Bhate, Shishir. "Bahuguna's Diary." In *Fire in the Heart, Firewood on the Back,* edited by Tenzin Rigzin. Amritsar: All India Pingalwara Charitable Society, 2005. Originally Published in *The Indian Express* June 16 (1995).

Bhave, Vinoba. *Thoughts on Education.* Varanasi: Sarva Seva Sangh Prakashan, 1959.

———. *Science and Self-Knowledge.* Varanasi: Sarva Seva Sangh Prakashan, 2000.

Bhattacharjea, Ajit. "The Old Man and the Dam." In *Fire in the Heart, Firewood on the Back,* edited by Tenzin Rigzin. Amritsar: All India Pingalwara Charitable Society, 2005. Originally Published in *Outlook* June 26 (1996).

Callicott, John Baird. *Earth's Insights: A Multicultural Survey of Ecological Ethics from the Mediterranean Basin to the Australian Outback.* Berkeley: University of California Press, 1994.

———. "Multicultural Environmental Ethics." *DAEDALUS* 130: 4 (2001).

Chaitanya, Krishna. "The Earth as Sacred Environs." In *Indigenous Vision: Peoples of India Attitudes to the Environment.* New Delhi: Sage, 1992.

Chowdry, Kamla. *Industrialisation, Survival and Environment: A Dialogue on Development.* New Delhi: INTACH, 1988.

Darian, Steven G. *The Ganges in Myth and History.* Honolulu: University Press of Hawaii, 1978.

Das, J. C., and R. S. Negi. "Chipko Movement." In *Tribal Movements in India,* edited by K. S. Singh. New Delhi, 1983.

Dharmadhikari, Acharya Dada. *Philosophy of Sarvodaya,* translated by S. S. Pandharipande. Mumbai: Popular Prakashan, 2000.

Dogra, Bharat. *Forests and People: The Efforts in Western Himalayas to Re-establish a Long Lost Relationship.* Rishikesh: Himalaya Darshan Prakashan Samiti 1980.

————. *The Debate on Large Dams.* New Delhi: Bharat Dogra, 1992.

————. *Forests, Dams and Survival in Tehri Garhwal.* New Delhi: Bharat Dogra, 1992.

————. *Living for Others: Vimla and Sunderlal Bahuguna.* New Delhi: Bharat Dogra, 1993.

Dutt, Anuradha. "The Gentle Crusader." In *Fire in the Heart, Firewood on the Back,* edited by Tenzin Rigzin. Amritsar: All India Pingalwara Charitable Society, 2005. Originally published in *The Illustrated Weekly of India,* January 21 (1990).

Dwivedi, O. P., and Tiwari, B. N. "Environmental Protection in the Hindu Religion." In *Ethical Perspectives on Environmental Issues in India,* edited by George A. James. New Delhi: A.P.H., 1999.

Gadgil, Madhav. "The Indian Heritage of a Conservation Ethic." In *Ethical Perspectives on Environmental Issues in India,* edited by George A. James. New Delhi: A.P.H., 1999.

————, and Chandran, M. D. Subash. "Sacred Groves." In *Indigenous Vision: Peoples of India Attitudes to the Environment.* New Delhi: Sage, 1992.

————, and Guha, Ramachandra. *This Fissured Land: An Ecological History of India.* Delhi: Oxford University Press, 1992.

————, and Guha, Ramachandra. *Ecology and Equity: The Use and Abuse of Nature in Contemporary India.* New Delhi: Penguin Books, 1995.

Gandhi, Indira. "Launching the World Conservation Strategy in India. Keynote address at New Delhi 6, March 1980." In *Indira Gandhi on Environment.* New Delhi: Department of Environment, Government of India, 1984.

Gandhi, M. K. *Hind Swaraj or Indian Home Rule.* Ahmedabad: Navajivan, 1938.

————. *Constructive Program: Its Meaning and Place.* Ahmedabad: Navajivan, 1945.

————. *Gandhi's Autobiography: The Story of My Experiments with Truth.* Translated by Mahadev Desai. Washington D.C: Public Affairs, 1948.

————. *Village Industries.* Ahmedabad: Navajivan, 1960.

————. *Village Swaraj.* Ahmedabad: Navajivan, 1962.

————. "From Yeravda Mandir: Essays on the Observations." In *Vows and Observations by M. K. Gandhi,* edited by John Strohmeier. Berkeley: Berkeley Hills Books, 1999.

Goldsmith, Edward. "Gaia Is the Source of All Benefits." In *Indigenous Vision: Peoples of India Attitudes to the Environment.* New Delhi: Sage, 1992.

Guha, Ramachandra. *The Unquiet Woods: Ecological Change and Peasant Resistance in the Himalaya.* New Delhi: Oxford University Press, 1991.

————. "Radical American Environmentalism and Wilderness Preservation: A Third World Critique." In *Ethical Perspectives on Environmental Issues in India,* edited by George A. James. New Delhi: A.P.H., 1999.

Gupta, Krishna Murthi. *Mira Behn, Gandhiji's Daughter Disciple: Birth Centenary Volume.* New Delhi: Himalaya Seva Sangh, 1992.

Haberman, David L. *River of Love in an Age of Pollution: The Yamuna River of Northern India.* Berkeley: University of California Press, 2006.

Ishizaka, Shinya. "The Anti Tehri Dam Movement as New Social Movement and Gandhism." *Journal of the Japanese Association for South Asian Studies* 18 (2006).

James, George A. *Interpreting Religion: The Phenomenological Approaches of Pierre Daniël Chantepie de la Saussaye, W. Brede Kristensen, and Gerardus van der Leeuw.* Washington, D.C.: Catholic University of America Press, 1995.

————. "The Construction of India in Some Recent Environmental Philosophy." *Worldviews: Environment, Culture, Religion* 2 (1998).

————. "The Significance of Indian Traditions for Environmental Ethics." In *Ethical Perspectives on Environmental Issues in India,* edited by George A. James. New Delhi: A.P.H., 1999.

————, ed. *Ethical Perspectives on Environmental Issues in India.* New Delhi: APH, 1999.

Jayal, N. D. *Alternative Strategies for Development.* New Delhi: INTACH, 1992.

Joshi, D. P. "Logging History in India with Special Reference to U.P." In *History of Forestry in India,* edited by Ajay S. Rawat. New Delhi: Indus, 1991.

Khoshoo, T. N. *Mahatma Gandhi: An Apostle of Human Ecology.* New Delhi: Tata Energy Research Institute, 1995.

————. "Gandhian Environmentalism." In *Ethical Perspectives on Environmental Issues in India,* edited by George A. James. New Delhi: A.P.H., 1999.

Kishwar, Madhu. "A Victory for Satyagraha: Prime Minister Concedes a Review of Tehri Dam." *Manushi* 94 (1996).

Kumar, Surendar, and A. K. Mahajan. "The Uttarkashi Earthquake of 20 October 1991: Field Observations." *Terra Nova* 6:1 (1994).

Kumarappa, J. C. *Economy of Permanence.* Varanasi: Sarva Seva Sangh Prakashan, 1997. First published 1945.

Mawdsley, Emma. "The Abuse of Religion and Ecology: The Vishva Hindu Parishad and Tehri Dam." *Worldviews* 9:1 (2005).

Mehta, Kisan. "Barbe Baker, Crusader and World Citizen." In *Richard St. Barbe Baker: Man of the Trees, a Centenary Tribute,* edited by Indira Ramish and N. D. Jayal. New Delhi: INTACH, 1989.

Mirabehn. *The Spirit's Pilgrimage.* Arlington VA: Great Ocean, 1960.

Mishra, Anupam, and Satyendra Tripathi. *Chipko Movement: Uttarakhand Women's Bid to Save Forest Wealth.* New Delhi: Gandhi Peace Foundation 1978.

Mukerji, Devashish. "Moving Mountains." In *Fire in the Heart Firewood on the Back: Writings on and by Himalayan Crusader Sunderlal Bahuguna,* edited by Tenzin Rigzin. Amritsar: All India Pingalwara Charitable Society, 2005.

Nair, Sathis Chandran, and N. D. Jayal. *Forest Policy: Population, Environmental Degradation and Survival Strategies.* New Delhi: INTACT, 1991.

Nandy, Pritish. "The Old Man and the River." In *Fire in the Heart, Firewood on the Back,* edited by Tenzin Rigzin. Amritsar: All India Pingalwara Charitable Society, 2005. Originally Published in *The Observer* April 12–18 (1992).

Narayanan, Vasudha. "Water, Wood, and Wisdom: Ecological Perspectives from the Hindu Traditions." *DAEDALUS* 130:4 (2001).

Patkar, Medha. "Interview: The Strength of a People's Movement." In *Indigenous Vision: Peoples of India Attitudes to the Environment*. New Delhi: Sage, 1992.

Paranjpye, Vijay. "Evaluating the Tehri Dam: An Extended Cost Benefit Appraisal." In *Studies in Ecology and Sustainable Development 1*. New Delhi: Indian National Trust for Art and Cultural Heritage, 1988.

Pearce, Fred, and Rob Butler. "The Dam That Should Not Be Built: India Is Building the Largest Dam in Asia in a Valley Beset by Earthquakes and Landslips." *New Scientist* (January 26, 1991).

Prasoon, Kunwar. "He Stakes His Life to Save the Hills." In *Fire in the Heart, Firewood on the Back*, edited by Tenzin Rigzin. Amritsar: All India Pingalwara Charitable Society, 2005. Originally Published in *Yug Vani* March (2005).

Prime, Ranchor. *Hinduism and Ecology: Seeds of Truth*. London and New York: Cassell, 1992.

Rajalakshmi, T. K. "A Saffron Twist: The Vishwa Hindu Parishad's Opposition to the Tehri Dam on Religious Grounds Sidesteps the Real Issues Involved in the Matter." *Frontline* 18:08 (April 14–27, 2001).

Ramesh, Indira, and Jayal N. D. "Preface." *Richard St. Barbe Baker: Man of the Trees, a Centenary Tribute*. New Delhi: INTACH, 1989.

Rangan, Haripriya. *Of Myths and Movements: Rewriting Chipko into Himalayan History*. New York: Verso, 2000.

Rao, Shivaji. *Tehri Dam Is a Time Bomb*. New Delhi: Vani, 1992.

Ray, Amit. "Rabindranath Tagore's Vision of Ecological Harmony." In *Ethical Perspectives on Environmental Issues in India*, edited by George A. James. New Delhi: A.P.H., 1999.

Richards, Glyn. "Vinoba Bhave." In *A Source-Book of Modern Hinduism*, edited by Glyn Richards. London: Curzon, 1985.

Rigzin, Tenzin, ed. *Fire in the Heart, Firewood on the Back*. Amritsar: All India Pingalwara Charitable Society, 2005.

Rolland, Romain. *Mahatma Gandhi: The Man Who Became One with the Universal Being*. New Delhi: Vishv Books, 1924.

Schumacher, E. F. *Small Is Beautiful: Economics as if People Mattered*. New York: Harper and Row, 1973.

Sen, Geeti, ed. *Indigenous Vision: Peoples of India Attitudes to the Environment*. New Delhi: Sage, 1992.

Shiva, Vandana. *Staying Alive: Woman, Ecology and Development*. New Delhi: Kali for Woman, 1989.

———. "Women's Indigenous Knowledge and Biodiversity Conservation." In *Indigenous Vision: Peoples of India Attitudes to the Environment*. New Delhi: Sage, 1992.

Singh, Shekhar. "Sovereignty, Equality, and the Global Environment." In *Ethical Perspectives on Environmental Issues in India*, edited by George A. James. New Delhi: A.P.H., 1999.

St. Barbe, Richard. *My Life My Trees*. Forres: Finhorn, 1979. Originally published London: Lutterworth, 1970.

St. Barbe Baker, Richard. "Chipko-Hug to the Tree People." In *Chipko Message*. Silyara: Chipko Information Center, 1981.

———. *Man of the Trees: Selected Writings of Richard St. Barbe Baker*, edited by Karen Gridley. Willits, California: Ecology Action, 1989.

Strong, Maurice F. "Only One Earth." In *Indigenous Vision: Peoples of India Attitudes to the Environment*. New Delhi: Sage, 1992.

Sudhir, T. S. "Fire in His Heart, Firewood on His Back." In *Fire in the Heart, Firewood on the Back*, edited by Tenzin Rigzin. Amritsar: All India Pingalwara Charitable Society, 2005. Originally Published in *The Economic Times* (Date unknown).

Tandon, Vishwanath. *Acharya Vinoba Bhave: Builders of Modern India*. New Delhi: Publications Division, Ministry of Information and Broadcasting, Government of India, 1992.

Thakar, Vimala. "Dada Expounds Sarvodaya Philosophy." In *Philosophy of Sarvodaya*, edited by Acharya Dada Dharmadhikari. Mumbai: Popular Prakashan, 2000.

Tikekar, Indu. *Revolution: A Leap beyond History*. Sarva Seva Sangh Prakashan, 1973.

Tucker, Mary E., and John A. Grim. "Introduction: The Emerging Alliance of World Religions and Ecology." *DAEDALUS* 130:4 (2001).

Ummayya, Pandurang, and J. Bandyopadhyay. "The Trans-Himalayan Chipko Footmarch." *The Ecologist* 13:5 (1983).

Vannucci, Marta. "Tradition and Change." In *Indigenous Vision: Peoples of India Attitudes to the Environment*. New Delhi: Sage, 1992.

Vatsyayan, Kapila. "Ecology and Indian Myth." In *Indigenous Vision: Peoples of India Attitudes to the Environment*. New Delhi: Sage, 1992.

Vohra, B. B. *The Greening of India*, edited by Karen Gridley. New Delhi, INTACH, 1985.

Weber, Thomas. *Gandhi as Disciple and Mentor*. Cambridge: Cambridge University Press, 2004.

———. *Hugging the Trees: The History of the Chipko Movement*. New Delhi: Viking, Penguin Books, 1988.

Index